Neil Diamond

The Biography

Neil Diamond
The Biography

Laura Jackson

PORTRAIT

Visit the Portrait website!

PORTRAIT Portrait publishes a wide range of non-fiction, including biography, history, science, music, popular culture and sport.

Visit our website to:
- read descriptions of our popular titles
- buy our books over the internet
- take advantage of our special offers
- enter our monthly competition
- learn more about your favourite Portrait authors

VISIT OUR WEBSITE AT: www.portraitbooks.com

First published in 2004 by **Portrait**
an imprint of
Piatkus Books Ltd
5 Windmill Street
London W1T 2JA
e-mail: info@piatkus.co.uk

ISBN 0 7499 5025 0

Edited by Jinny Johnson

This book has been printed on paper manufactured with respect for the environment using wood from managed sustainable resources

Typeset by Action Publishing Technology, Gloucester
Printed and bound in Great Britain by MPG Books, Bodmin, Cornwall

Dedicated to David
– the most precious husband in the world

PICTURE CREDITS

Contents

Acknowledgements

Grateful appreciation to those who helped with this book. My thanks for all contributions to: Sir Tim Rice; Dr Stephen Perrin; Fish; Malcolm McLaren; Peter Robertson.

Thanks also to: Dame Joan Plowright; Janet Macklam; Clive Whichelow; June Allen; The Diamond Connection; Elgin Library staff; *Evening Standard*; *Sun*; *The Story of Pop*; *Rolling Stone*; *Record Mirror*; *Titbits*; *Rave*; *Weekend News*; *Family Weekly*; *People's Weekly*; *Hot Press*; *Melody Maker*; *Record Collector*; *Los Angeles Times*; *Brewers*; *Billboard*; *Halliwell's Film Guide*; *Q Rock Stars*; *VH1*; *Daily Mirror*; *Q*; *NME*; *Daily Telegraph*; *The Hollywood Reporter*; *Time*; *Leonard Matlin's TV & Film Guide*; *Australian Post*; *New York Times*; *Daily Express*; *Vanity Fair*.

Special thanks to: David for his unstinting encouragement, and to Alice Davis and everyone at Piatkus not only for all their professional assistance but for the compassion extended to me throughout an extremely testing time.

CHAPTER 1

Where It Began

NEIL DIAMOND is one of the most dynamic live performers in popular music. Now in his fifth decade as a recording artiste, and having written some of the world's best-loved songs, he has notched up global album sales in the region of 120 million. A bona fide superstar, with legions of loyal fans, Diamond cuts a distinctive and enduring figure with fascinating depth and dimensions. Of the human voice, he once declared: 'It is more than just a sound. It is the soul itself.' And he is, indeed, long established as an interpretive vocalist. Still, throughout his life, Neil has been an intriguing blend of contradictions – an intensely private and deeply introverted man, whose songwriting has conversely been nakedly autobiographical, offering an acutely compelling window on his inner demons. Perhaps that has been the essential safety-valve for a man sometimes described as a brooding loner. Life has frequently been tough for the Brooklyn-born star.

His formative years were far from easy. Growing up amid the mean streets of New York City's largest borough, he tasted life on the fringes of Brooklyn's desperate gangland world until he survived being shot twice in the head at the age of 12. Years later Diamond revealed: 'After that, I took my chances on being alone.'

Meanwhile, his home life was a series of unsettling upheavals. Although Neil always knew he was assured of his Jewish parents' loving devotion, there were less stable aspects of his young life. Like so many others, the Diamond family struggled even to survive on the breadline. As shopkeepers, Neil's parents had to go wherever they could make enough money to keep body and soul together. This led to a fairly itinerant existence, not at all conducive to making long-term friends, and one that resulted in Neil attending nine schools by the time he was 16. It was a necessary way of life, and played a strong part in shaping Neil's internal, fiercely self-reliant personality, creating in him a pathological resistance to conformity of any kind.

Undoubtedly, being very much his own man has served Neil Diamond well. Defying musical swings and shifts throughout his career, he continues to reign as one of the top five most successful solo pop performers. Yet this status would have been hard to predict.

Neil's first obvious talent lay in the dexterous and elegant art of sword fencing, for which he discovered an inherent flair. Then, attending New York University, his career path looked like taking him towards medicine, but, as doubts set in, the prospect of becoming a doctor started to founder. He began to be, as he put it, 'bothered by the impersonal nature of medicine'. By then, anyway, music had come increasingly to dominate his world. Transparently driven by a need to articulate his soul-searching interpretation of life, he would face yet more years of debilitating struggle before his feet found their chosen path.

Characteristically, too, just as Neil sampled the first fruits of success, his first marriage ran onto the rocks. His second marriage also became a casualty. On reflection, Diamond has blamed his dedication to his craft for impacting significantly on his ability always to give the fullest emotional commitment possible to the women in his life. He admits openly that he has had to pay a heavy personal cost for his glittering, global success. Throughout the years of pain and pleasure, he has essentially trodden a solitary path. But it wasn't always so.

Neil Leslie Diamond was born on 24 January 1941 in the Coney Island district of Brooklyn, New York City, the first child of Rose and Akeeba (known as Kieve) Diamond. Kieve was a shopkeeper by trade. Neil's grandparents were Jewish immigrants. Abraham and Molly Rapaport had emigrated to the US from Russia, while Abram and Sadie Diamond hailed originally from Poland.

Lodged at the southwest end of Long Island, Brooklyn is home to around 100 separate ethnic groups, forming a patchwork of diverse cultures in a vivid and vibrant, if sometimes edgy, environment. Once a rich and powerful city in its own right, and the site of the historic Battle of Long Island, the first bloody conflict after the Declaration of Independence, Brooklyn was annexed to New York City towards the end of the 19th century. By that time, with the opening of the spectacular Brooklyn Bridge over the East River to Manhattan, the borough had begun to enjoy great economic prosperity.

That continuing boom was epitomised by the wealth and reckless extravagance abounding in Coney Island, with its glamorous casinos and elegant eateries, its world-famous amusement parks, the magnificent 80-foot-wide boardwalk and the piers which stretched along its three-mile promenade. On the Atlantic shoreline of Brooklyn, and boasting the only sea beach within New York, Coney Island had, however, had its heyday as a paradise playground by the time the Diamonds' first-born arrived.

When America finally entered the Second World War in 1941, altering the atmosphere for its suddenly appreciably sobered citizens, Coney Island's dizzy attractions gradually began to lose their lustre. Wintertime, when the pleasure seekers had gone to ground, brought particularly desperate times for those in commerce; striving to make ends meet was a continual way of life for Rose and Kieve. Their own parents had come to America because it was perceived to be the land of opportunity. Never one to stick, by early summer Kieve opened up a dry-goods store in nearby, heavily Italianate, Bensonhurst, optimistic of making this business pay.

A hallmark of Neil's parents was their remarkable resilience; the force of their individual personalities mainly masked the strains of their eternal struggle. Diamond has spoken of his mother as having had a more intense attitude to life than the one his father adopted, indicating that Kieve was more a go-with-the-flow sort. In any event, his parents were a happy and extremely attractive couple. Despite the perennial lack of money, Rose Diamond was a naturally beautiful, stylish woman. Likewise dark-haired, Kieve cut a dash as a dapper, scrupulously groomed gent who, for a while, sported a natty Clark Gable-style pencil moustache. One of Neil's earliest memories is of his parents' love of socialising. Years later he fondly recalled: 'They would do anything to go dancing, Saturday nights. They would crash a wedding, just to dance to the band.'

First and foremost, however, they doted on their baby son. With his head of generously thick, dark-brown hair and liquid hazel eyes, Neil was a contented, smiling infant, inquisitive about his surroundings, and showing no signs of the broody, introspective individual he would become. In due course, his reign as an only child ended just five days shy of Neil's second birthday, when Rose Diamond gave birth to another son, whom they named Harvey – completing the Diamond household.

Theirs was a close-knit family in which love and affection was openly, sometimes emotionally, displayed. Roots and religious traditions were also important, to the extent that Neil was raised in the strictly Orthodox Jewish faith. As he revealed: 'The first language I learned was Yiddish.' With a kid brother whom he could, as Neil later joked, beat up on whenever he was bored, life – captured on the odd reel of jerky, grainy, 8mm black and white film shot by Kieve – was pretty much a daily trial of endurance. 'Brooklyn is not the easiest place to grow up in,' Diamond would feelingly attest.

It was made even tougher by the perpetual need to move around in order to chase the available custom. Neil was destined never to be in any one neighbourhood long enough to establish lasting friendships with other boys. Every move was within the immense borough of Brooklyn, except when, in 1945, 27-year-old Kieve Diamond was obliged to enter the US Army. Lock, stock and barrel, the family duly headed to Cheyenne, Wyoming, north of Denver in the Midwest, where Kieve was stationed, and where, over the next two years, Neil was exposed to a vastly different pace and way of life. Despite his young age, Cheyenne made its mark on him.

Diamond has declared unreservedly: 'That was a great experience, very different from Brooklyn. Cheyenne was chock-full of cowboys and great stuff that you only see in films.' It was during these two years that Neil developed an abiding love of the Wild West. Some of that was a direct consequence of hunkering down in the cheap seats at the local cinema, enthralled by the surfeit of singing cowboy movies that were so popular at the time. He was also drawn to adverts in comic books that showed a Stetsoned cowboy in the saddle, toting an acoustic guitar. 'My eyes always went right to that guitar,' he recalled.

That said, Neil was still too young to feel any inclination towards music. Rather, he embraced the cowboy culture with all the enthusiasm of a wide-eyed child lapping up his new environment. He got the chance to go horse riding, which delighted him. He once laughingly confessed: 'I thought I was a cowboy after I came back from Cheyenne – a Brooklyn cowboy!'

In 1947, the Diamonds traded the wide-open Wyoming spaces for the urban, concrete sprawl of Brooklyn again, where Kieve resurrected his business by opening Diamond's Haberdashery. By now, New York had become the seat of the newly formed United Nations, and the city's already massive population had swelled to over 7 million. This significant influx of people did not seem to make all that much difference to the tenuous, threadbare nature of retailing for Neil's parents. Over the next several years the old pattern of continually moving home and business from district to district reasserted itself.

Of necessity, therefore, Neil's education was rather a haphazard experience, since he was constantly uprooted from a succession of schools. This continual dislocation formed a kernel of fierce self-reliance within him, and certain aspects of his identity gradually began to take shape. Invariably left outside each individual peer group he encountered, Neil Diamond increasingly adopted a loner attitude, and the seeds of non-conformity were sown. 'I don't fit in,' he has often declared.

Setting himself apart is not a stance he has always particularly relished, but he saw it as part of his arsenal for survival. Still, he once wistfully admitted: 'I guess I would have liked some friends to play with. Sometimes, I'd have liked to belong to a ball team or something like that.'

Although he was showing a distinct tendency to prefer his own company, when he was not at school he spent quite a bit of time with his father – having turned ten, he was expected to help out at the family garment shop. At the weekends, too, he would accompany Kieve to local flea markets to ply a clothier stall. 'I became an expert at putting girdles on women,' Neil wryly recalls. He also tagged along with his father on occasional weekend evening outings. Showing no signs of harbouring any musical leanings of his own, Neil was all the same curious about his father's penchant for public performing. He recalled: 'I don't come from a musical background, although some people in the family history have tried the stage. My father was an amateur entertainer – he mimicked old records. When I was young, I went around with him when he was appearing at events.'

According to Diamond, his father was so keen that the moment he discovered a show was being staged that was open to amateurs he would 'drop his tape measure and run to offer his services'. One offshoot of Kieve's avid interest in music was that Neil was soon steered towards the piano, and because of his onlooker's experience at his father's gigs, the idea of live performance was not at all alien to him. Still, as yet, no artistic nerve within him had been hit; indeed, he soon succumbed to a more primitive form of expression.

By the time Neil was 12, home was an apartment two floors above a butcher's shop on Brooklyn's Flatbush Avenue. Physically, his growth had more than kept pace with his age, and he was well on his way towards his eventual height of 6'1". Sparely built, he was at the gangly stage, and what caught the eye was the brooding, intense stare he now most often showed the world. There were accumulating reasons for this unsettling air. On top of harbouring a sense of dislocation, he was suffering from low self-esteem. Within the Diamond extended family there seemed to be a number of kids his age achieving an academic excellence that he did not.

Teachers would tell Neil's parents that he had the intelligence, but was simply not trying to apply it. Neil's young brother, Harvey, on the other hand, was clearly an eager and bright spark with a precocious aptitude for the complexities of electronics. Set against all this, Neil felt increasingly inadequate. His growing frustrations led to the adoption of a confrontational attitude. He managed to cap his rising reservoir of aggression while helping out at the shop, now located in Flatbush, and also as he earned nickels and dimes working as a shoeshine boy. When loose on the streets, however, it was another matter. Neil admits: 'I was sort of a black sheep. I tended to settle things with my fists. Not that I had to look far for trouble. There were always fights in Brooklyn.'

Although not a pack member by instinct, the dark, dodgy streets of Brooklyn were scarcely the place to go it alone. And the young, rough Diamond managed to inveigle his way into one of the dominant gangs that roamed the neighbourhood, vying to hold the balance of power among the local hoodlums. At 12, Neil was the youngest member of the gang, unafraid and keen to prove himself. Years later he revealed: 'Fear intrigues me and I always court it. That's what gives me a kick in life – being scared.' One bleak night, however, matters came to a nasty head.

Flatbush Avenue, built along the nine-mile-long line of the old Carnarsie Indian trail, virtually splits Brooklyn in half. Neighbourhoods to the northeast of this imaginary dividing line had been disintegrating because of deepening social problems, while to the southwest it was still solidly old residential and fairly prosperous. On the west side of Flatbush Avenue also lies

Prospect Park, by day a green oasis amid the grim, graffiti-covered buildings and rattling elevated trains. A favourite picnic spot for family outings, the park attracted the healthy, sporty type. Come nightfall, the complexion altered radically.

In the gang Neil ran with, all the high-school boys carried zip guns, crude home-made pistols powered by springs. Although the passage of time has dulled Diamond's memory on this particular point, he does not rule out having armed himself with an air gun during this period.

In mid-1953, the latest turf war erupted in Prospect Park; it proved to be Neil's last outing with the gang. He explained: 'We had a big rumble and I got shot twice in the face by CO_2 pellets.' Neil was hit just below the right eye, and could easily have been killed. Certainly, had the pellets hit him a fraction higher, there was a high chance of his losing the sight in that eye. As it was, he was injured with a hole in his upper right cheekbone; the scar is still faintly detectable, 50 years on. This frightening episode was an early defining moment in Neil Diamond's life, and he immediately reverted to keeping his own company. He never regretted it. Over the years he has seen from afar just how many of those gun-toting acquaintances ended up behind bars, some of them serving very lengthy sentences.

By the time Diamond turned teenager, in January 1954, he had well and truly left those brittle nights on the tough streets behind him. By autumn of that year, as a scrupulously neat schoolboy, with a severely short haircut, he began his secondary education at Brooklyn's Erasmus Hall High School. This was the eighth school Neil had enrolled in to date; hardly surprisingly, expectations of his scholastic performance were tempered. In other fields, however, he definitely found a niche.

His lean, lithe build and capacity for intense concentration made him a natural athlete. Away from the track, on the strength of his gravelly baritone singing voice, he was quickly drafted into the school's 100-member mixed choir. The school's music director, Adam DiPietto, had no way of knowing that he had two future music superstars in his charge – one of the stunning young sopranos was Barbra Streisand, with whom Neil Diamond would decades later duet on the number one hit single, 'You Don't Bring Me Flowers'.

At high school, Neil must have been something of an enigma to those around him. Palpably withdrawn, he clearly had a rich singing talent. Given to a moody demeanour, and hardly a rampant girl chaser, he proved to have an unusual way of winning female hearts – by writing poetry. To Neil, writing was the new, non-violent, outlet for his feelings and frustrations. Needless to say, given his perpetual intensity, his outpourings were far from being saturated in sentimental, hormonal drivel. He did write love poems, but in them he touched a nerve by expressing the aching depth of loneliness he carried inside himself.

With typical candour, Neil Diamond has dismissed his first poetic offerings as dire, but has acknowledged that he worked avidly on improving his technique. The reason why is simple. 'I was an introvert kid and found it a way of communicating with girls,' he confessed. He would pen a poem for a particular girl, in which he'd make it clear he wanted to ask her out, then surreptitiously pass it to the girl in class. Almost without fail this unusual chat-up approach found favour with the blossoming young lady in question. Suddenly, Neil not only found his feet with the female sex, he also discovered that he had a lot of new male friends, as his schoolmates tapped him up to provide poems that were guaranteed to work for them. Little did the girls in Erasmus Hall High realise that, in some cases, the same regurgitated poem was doing the rounds.

Neil later revealed that for a particular phase in his life he could sing the words 'I love you', a lot easier than he could say them. Certainly, progressing from writing poetry to expressing himself in song lyrics in time became his medium for communication. But not just yet.

At 14 he had a spell of working as a hotel porter at a holiday resort in the Catskill Mountains, northwest of New York City, before the family relocated again the following year, this time to

Brighton Beach, along the coastline from Neil's Coney Island birthplace. Because of the huge influx of Russian Jewish immigrants, Brighton Beach was impregnated with an east European flavour, and was popularly known as 'Little Odessa'. Attracted by the thronging trade around the main thoroughfare, Brighton Beach Avenue, Kieve Diamond opened up Diamond's Dry Goods.

A new locale, of course, meant yet another change of school for the teenager. But before that, Neil packed a bag for a brief holiday at Surprise Lake Camp, some 90 miles north of Brooklyn, in upstate New York. Here was a liberal environment in which the kids could harmlessly let off steam in the wide-open spaces, and could enjoy a temporary escape from the hustle and bustle of city life. Still very much a loner, Neil Diamond was perhaps not the most gregarious teenager there, and he tended to be a keen observer of goings-on, rather than a wildly enthusiastic participant. But it was nevertheless an experience he valued.

This brief break was also responsible for planting the first real seeds of Neil's attraction to music, when the folk singer Pete Seeger came to Surprise Lake Camp to perform. New York City-born, 36-year-old Seeger had recently faced persecution as a suspected communist in the McCarthy era. With hits to his credit such as, 'If I Had A Hammer' and 'Where Have All The Flowers Gone', he was nicknamed 'America's Tuning Fork'.

Viewing his visit as one of the highlights of the camping trip, the youth leaders had encouraged the teenagers to write songs of their own, which they would perform for the entertainer. The future songwriting superstar in their midst did not pick up on this opportunity. Instead, on the night, Neil stood well to the rear of the crowd; quietly intrigued, he simply watched and absorbed. He listened closely to the recording star and to the eager amateurs around him singing longingly about heart-rending, worthy causes or bleeding heart sentiments, and it took root with him that this was something he too could do, as an interesting hobby. As he later said: 'I wasn't thinking this could be my life.'

Come autumn 1956, life for Neil brought a switch from

Erasmus Hall High to Abraham Lincoln High School. He was seconded seamlessly into the choral group, and high-school life here promised to be much as before. Indeed, Neil called high school 'four years spent in a coma, wondering about my relationships with girls and why I never went to any parties'. In truth, it wasn't quite that bleak, for it was at Abraham Lincoln that he discovered a deep love of sword fencing.

It was not perhaps the most obvious weapon of choice for a streetwise Brooklyn kid, but the skilful finesse and stylish artistry required to master this intelligent sport appealed to Neil. 'It's physical combat in a classical sense and it's beautiful to see and do,' explained Diamond, adding frankly, 'and it's a terrific way to vent your aggressiveness. I needed that.' Fast on his feet, with his slender build, long arm reach and a supple wrist, Neil quickly showed an outstanding aptitude that impressed his sports teachers, and gave him his first ever sense of personal fulfilment.

Outside school, staying off the streets, in the privacy of his bedroom Neil found himself thinking back to Pete Seeger's appearance at Surprise Lake Camp. In Wyoming, as a young child, he had been vaguely drawn to the image of the guitar-slinging pop star, but this time the lure was different and more specific. He hadn't attempted to pen a composition to try out on the folk singer, but since then, back in Brooklyn, phrasing and partial storytelling lyrics had been running through his head unbidden. If he learned to play the guitar, he reckoned, he might just be able to articulate these thoughts.

He'd also absorbed how music made social interaction easier, and might help him overcome his innate shyness. There was one further attraction to Neil – there had never been a songwriter in the Diamond family. This would surely set him apart. Kieve and Rose Diamond read their elder son's heart's desire; on 24 January 1957 they presented Neil with a $16 second-hand acoustic guitar for his 16th birthday.

Not an easy instrument to persevere with, yet Neil took to it almost at once. He would be self-taught. He did go to guitar lessons initially, but only for a handful of sessions, because he disliked the tutor's traditional and restrictive approach. 'He wanted to teach me notes,' Diamond recalled. 'I wanted to learn to play from the heart and this no one could teach me.'

Although not till now focused on music, for years Neil had been passively exposed to a smorgasbord of sounds. The soundtrack of life at home was more often than not dominated by the Latin dance records beloved by his dancing fanatic parents. Flatbush, where he had recently lived, was a largely Caribbean community where the streets vibrated daily to the throbbing rhythm of reggae and thrashing steel drums. At his father's shop, the radio provided ever-present background noise.

Three years earlier, rock had spread through America like a contagion, sweeping in a new era in entertainment that was liberating, raw and exciting. At the cutting edge of this was the radically minded disc jockey Alan Freed. Fronting his hot show, *Rock and Roll Party*, on New York City's radio station WINS, Freed nightly wound up the nation's thrill-hungry teenagers by dishing them a diet of down and dirty sounds.

By 1957, a new breed of music stars had staged a coup on the charts with the emergence of Chuck Berry, often classed as the first guitar-playing rock star, Jerry Lee Lewis, the controversial wild man of rock, nicknamed 'The Killer', and rhythm and blues star Jackie Wilson, among others. The 20th-century's most influential solo artiste, Elvis Presley, a unique hybrid of a white singer with a black blues sound, and a dynamite stage performance style, consolidated his rocketing success with ten hits in that 12-month period, and easily swamped the radio airwaves from dawn to dusk.

For Neil Diamond, just tuning in, amid all of this two very diverse fledgling influences quickly began to emerge. One was Fats Domino, the New Orleans-born singer-songwriter and pianist. A pre-Presley star, the rhythm and blues artiste had already notched up a string of hits when, just months earlier, he'd made a huge splash by headlining a ten-day, high-profile series of gigs at an annual rock and roll show held at Brooklyn's

Paramount Theater, hosted by Alan Freed. The other influence was the Everly Brothers.

Genuinely related, Phil and Don – sons of radio stars Ike and Margaret Everly – had been child performers in the 1940s. They had been recording for a couple of years when, in June 1957, they took America by storm with their million-selling hit, 'Bye Bye Love'. The catchy number's impact lay not so much in the lyrics as in its radically new style of delivery, a strong feature of which was close Appalachian harmonies. It became the Everly Brothers' trademark sound, and was a major influence on a new swathe of aspiring recording artistes, not least on a budding teenage singer-songwriter at home in neighbouring Queens, named Paul Simon.

In Brooklyn, Neil Diamond started to soak up an appreciation of the composition and different textures of many musical styles. A whole range of rhythms and rhythm changes appealed to him; the idea of meshing various influences intrigued him. Apart from that, he mainly recognised the obvious potential for the evocative use of language in lyrics, when the writer can be blunt or subtle as the mood takes him.

None of this, it must be said, hit Diamond with the force of a speeding train. He had no burning desire to thrust himself conspicuously on stage to perform. The attraction lay in the internal craft of songwriting. As an established star Diamond would admit: 'I never really chose songwriting. It just absorbed me and became more and more important in my life as the years passed.'

Likewise, Neil enjoyed the solitude of learning to play the guitar. While to some, the instrument was more a prop, synonymous with the image of rock and roll, to him the acoustic, once mastered, would be a vehicle for expression. He began to put pen to paper the moment he conquered his first chord change.

Whatever his family made of his regular scribblings, songwriting finally gave Neil something he felt was uniquely his. It began to spill over into school time, when he would surreptitiously experiment with lyrical compositions rather than listen in class, where lessons bored him anyway. The upshot, not surprisingly, was that he often scored poorly in exams. In his own words, he clung on academically by 'the barest thread'. That didn't matter too much. To Neil, practically the only things to be said about attending Abraham Lincoln High School were that he was able to continue to excel at sword fencing, and that it was here that he met fellow pupil Jaye Posner.

Tall, slim, with a mane of strong, dark hair and well-defined eyebrows above intriguingly thoughtful eyes, at 17 Neil had the makings of an extremely handsome young man, and his self-contained demeanour hinted at attractive depths. Intense and given to moody spells that sometimes rendered him unpredictable, he nevertheless intrigued Jaye, a dark-haired, pretty and lively young lady with a scintillating smile. It wasn't long before she and Neil became sweethearts. Neil's first flush of feeling for Jaye inspired him to write his first complete song, a romantic gesture born out of necessity, as Neil frankly admitted: 'I really wanted to impress her but I couldn't afford to buy her a gift. So I wrote a song called "Hear Them Bells", which basically was a song saying, "Will you marry me?" And it worked.'

They wouldn't actually tie the knot for a few years yet. But still, for such a deep thinker, he was somewhat rushing his fences. Only much later, with the benefit of hindsight, was he able to acknowledge that they were both too young to become so intensely involved. Particularly when, as it would transpire, he had ambitions to pursue a less than conventional and uncertain career path. At the time, however, that didn't register. He was in love, and managing to write his first song spurred Neil into coming up with others, even going so far as to fork out a few dollars he had scraped together to record demonstration discs of a couple of numbers – 'Blue Destiny' and 'A Million Miles Away'. His highly critical ear told him that these were raw efforts, but he was not discouraged.

Come spring 1958, Neil had some important decisions to make about the direction of his life. He knew he was attracted to songwriting, but that hadn't quite crystallised strongly enough yet to be an all-out driving force. Academically, he was no high flier, though he had shown an aptitude for science. His most obvious talent, sword fencing, wasn't realistically something from which he could make a regular living. His parents' long-time dream had been for their elder son to become a doctor. With no pressing urge to do anything else, Neil found himself going down that road, applying for and winning a sword fencing scholarship which allowed him, when he left Abraham Lincoln High School in the summer, to enrol in a pre-med programme studying chemistry and biology at New York University's medical college, commencing that autumn. Diamond maintained that it was unlikely he would ever have gone to college if he hadn't secured a scholarship, adding that NYU was the only university that would accept him.

Never enamoured of the education system until now, Neil found college life more agreeable, especially the sword fencing activities. During his time there, the NYU Violets won two national college and three intercollegiate Fencing Association championships. 'We had the greatest fencing team in the country,' Diamond has since declared. 'I was proud to be ninth man on a nine-man team. Fencing made me feel, for the first time, like a winner.' He was fully entitled to that swelling self-confidence, for he had developed into an accomplished swordsman. Once, in two consecutive competitive duel bouts, he did not have a single touch scored against him.

It was tough going affording the fees and making ends meet, though. Neil worked at nights and weekends to support himself, taking a variety of odd jobs, including short-order cook and waiter at a number of Coney Island beach-front restaurants. Juggling demanding science classes with a robust sword fencing training regime and earning a crust, Neil had precious little time to spare to keep his romance with Jaye Posner alive, but somehow they managed to stay close.

There was another call on his attention, as trying his hand at songwriting, which had never died away, now took stronger root in him. He began to churn out love songs, very much aping the popular style of the day. Other times, he would pour his frustrations about life into numbers with excruciating depth. He kept up his guitar practice, and was more often than not to be seen lugging his acoustic around with him, wherever he went.

One college friend, Herb Cohen, recalled that on road trips to take part in sword fencing competitions, while the rest of the guys were busy playing cards down at the front of the bus, Neil was invariably perched at the back, with his feet up, his guitar balanced on his thighs, playing and singing for his team mates. Whether his preoccupied audience always noticed it when Neil would slip in an original composition is debatable, but to Diamond his songs increasingly meant more than just background noise.

Consequently, although his budget scarcely ran to it, he now began to shell out even more frequently to record demo discs of songs he felt had merit. Having looked up the addresses of music publishers in the telephone directory, he was soon heading across the majestic Brooklyn Bridge to Manhattan, seeking to sell his wares. 'I took to cutting classes and catching the train up to Tin Pan Alley to try to get my songs heard,' he recalled. This absorption was deepening all the time, and by the turn of the decade, sword fencing and songwriting were seriously threatening to swamp any intention he had of studying to be a doctor; albeit that out of the three interests filling his days, medicine was the only guaranteed profitable profession to pursue.

Diamond once offered an insight into his complex pysche when he revealed that had it been possible to earn a living through sword fencing, in all likelihood he would have opted for that, since through wielding a sword he felt able to vent the emotional aspects of his personality. In any event, his parents' great dream for him was inexorably going by the wayside. 'I wasn't inclined to be a good student,' Neil confessed. 'I didn't do well in organic chemistry. I didn't do very well in biology. So it didn't take very long for me to realise that medicine was not going to be for me.' But there was a more fundamental reason why Neil never became a medical Dr Diamond and, again, it came down to his sensibilities.

Taught from the start of this pre-med curriculum that a doctor had to be strictly professional and otherwise detached, Neil strongly suspected that he would fall down on the latter requirement – that he would be unable to prevent himself from becoming emotionally involved with patients' problems. That was shockingly brought home to him one day, completely out of the blue. He explained: 'During my years at college, one day a man had a heart attack in the street in front of me. I gave him mouth-to-mouth resuscitation, heart massage and everything else I knew, but he died in my arms.' It is likely that even a fully qualified doctor would have run a high chance of failing. But the acute distress Neil experienced at his inability to save the stranger that day signalled to him that emotionally he was not cut out to be a doctor. He kept at his pre-med course, but his attention now veered towards pursuing a music career.

In later years, Neil would refer in the song 'Shilo' to having as a child created an imaginary companion to offset his sense of loneliness. As a late teenager, he never sought to stand six-deep among friends. But at New York University he found one other guy whom he felt was in some ways a kindred spirit. Named Jack Packer, he too had ambitions to break into music, and relatively quickly he and Neil decided to team up to form an Everly Brothers-style duo, called Neil and Jack.

It was Diamond's only period as anything other than a solo performer, and this set-up probably never felt quite right to him. However, to acquire some polish and to earn much-needed money, the pair went out as a pub act, making their first public singing appearance at the Little Neck Country Club in Long Island. Although Neil continued to write songs alone and to make demo discs, he also collaborated with Jack on penning some numbers.

One day in 1960, Packer introduced Diamond to a man named Murray Millar, who subsequently steered Neil towards Allied Entertainment Corporation of America, a subsidiary company of Saxon Music. Eager to try out his latest solo compositions, as well as those he had co-written with Jack, Neil did his best to make an impact on the music executives, and he succeeded. The duo, Neil and Jack, landed a contract with Allied to record on the tiny New York City label Duel. Between 1960 and 1962 Neil and Jack released two singles: 'You Are My Love At Last'/'What Will I Do?' and 'I'm Afraid'/'Till You've Tried Love'. When both cuts were unsuccessful, this brief liaison with Duel Records fizzled out, as did Neil's professional partnership with Jack Packer. Pop music is littered with stories of false starts before finding success, but for a man with a propensity to look on the gloomy side, it was an experience Neil Diamond could probably have done without.

The 1960s would herald an explosion of musical talent, launching some glorious and long-lasting careers, and Neil Diamond was one of those future stars. There was no sign of it right then, however. None of the heat and energised excitement that would light up the decade could yet be guessed at. Far from it. Neil felt that he had lost his way at college, failed at song-writing, and that he was surrounded by an even more depressing environment than ever.

About the latter, he wasn't wrong. The growth and expansion Brooklyn had been experiencing had begun to ebb away, as a major economic downturn set in and began to bite hard. The deep waters around Brooklyn had been developed early on as a major shipping port, and had subsequently become a massive base for the US Navy. Now that yard shut down, along with breweries and other large industrial enterprises, throwing men by the thousands out of work, and contributing significantly to parts of Brooklyn degenerating rapidly into slumland. Prospects were grim enough for people seeking conventional employment, let alone for an aspiring songwriter.

That said, the hard-nosed New York borough of Brooklyn had a tradition of spawning great talent from the grassroots, including the actor/film director Woody Allen and the classical composer George Gershwin, who published his first song in 1916 while working as a song plugger for a firm of music publishers. So hope could spring eternal for the tenacious.

For what had seemed an age already, Neil Diamond had been rapping his knuckles on doors, desperately keen to sell his songs piecemeal to publishing houses. Getting any kind of toehold in the music world had become his goal as 1962 dawned. So when one company offered him a job as a staff songwriter, he was thrilled. Looking back, he candidly confessed: 'Man, I *ran* from school to take that job!'

CHAPTER 2

Desperate Days

DETERMINED TO BECOME a songwriter, 21-year-old Neil Diamond dropped out of New York University in spring 1962, just a few weeks shy of graduation, and embarked on what would be several consecutive years of severe hardship and struggle. It was a phase that would take its toll on him, but his resolve held firm, underpinned as it was by one basic spur. He revealed: 'Because I wasn't accepted as a kid at all, I always wanted to be something. That's why I took up writing so passionately.'

He needed that kind of myopic drive. The Tin Pan Alley system he entered was a notoriously bruising and testing one, mainly centred within the famous, multi-storeyed Brill Building at 1619 Broadway in Manhattan. Its impressive Art Deco façade covered an interior made up of labyrinthine corridors, all packed to over-crowding with cabin-sized offices belonging to different music publishing firms, record company executives, managers and producers. It was a factory, solely dedicated to churning out chart hits. The top echelon boasted such successful lyricists as Carole King, Gerry Goffin, Burt Bacharach, Hal David, Jerry Leiber, Mike Stoller and Neil Sedaka. But beneath that level, the tower block was filled with literally hundreds of anonymous, aspiring songwriters, who toiled daily from 9.00 a.m. to 5.00 p.m. in tiny cubicles.

Neil Diamond disappeared into one of those spartan cubicles when he picked up his post as a $50-a-week apprentice song-writer with a small publishing company called Sunbeam Music. Composing usually on piano, at this early stage Neil produced upwards of eight songs a day, none of which he recalls with any great fondness. In fact, he admitted bluntly: 'They were all bad. I had no sense of taste.'

From the outset he felt straitjacketed; it was mind-numbingly boring to write songs to order. Neil explained: 'A publisher would outline his ideas and expect me to translate them for a singer with a particular style. Like ... "This singer is coming up and he wants a positive song, mostly up tempo with a little hook in the middle and in a certain key."' Diamond loathed that formulaic approach. He also came to share the unending frustration of all his fellow songwriting workhorses, that the $50 he earned a week was a fixed salary, whether he wrote a chartbusting hit or a miserable flop.

For a young man who had hitherto felt fairly isolated, the upside to this new way of life was that, after hours, he had the chance to hang out with a bunch of like-minded souls. He partic-ularly enjoyed the company of the older generation of black rhythm and blues writers. He was eager to learn, not only about songwriting, but about who in the business would be best to know and who it would be wise to avoid.

During the four months that Neil worked for Sunbeam, he came up with a stream of easy listening numbers with such telling titles as 'I'm Nobody's Fool', 'On The Outside, Lookin' In', 'All I Have Is Me', and 'A Fool All Over Again'. Unfulfilled by writing bland songs for safe, middle-of-the-road artistes left over from the 1950s, Neil also worked surreptitiously on developing material that was more to his own taste. The publishers were looking for simple, catchy hooks; he liked to concentrate heavily on a song's lyrics. In the end, this personal preoccupation was said to have been the reason Sunbeam Music fired Neil by summer.

Now he flitted from one staff songwriting job to another. After Sunbeam Music, he pitched up at a desk for Roosevelt Music, only to be one of ten songwriters fired en bloc before the end of the year. These disgruntled lyricists promptly banded together and wrote a number called 'Ten Lonely Guys', which later scraped into the US Top 100 singles when it was recorded by America's Mr Clean Cut crooner, Pat Boone. In all, Neil found work with another three music publishers; one of them was Shell, a small label whose motto was: 'Our records are a gas.'

Life for Diamond, though, was hardly a gas. At one point, after Sunbeam Music, his wages dropped to $35 a week. Overall, it was a soul-destroying daily grind. He developed a near claus-trophobic aversion to the cubicle existence, and began to write songs at home, or as he rode the crowded subway train from Brooklyn into Manhattan – anywhere but in what felt increas-ingly like a battery farm. In the cut-throat world in which he operated, he imagined that the guys flanking him in their respec-tive coops were listening in to what he was composing, which made him terribly self-conscious. He later revised his view: 'I eventually realised, of course, that they couldn't have cared less what I was doing.'

When he couldn't get staff songwriting jobs, Neil plugged away at trying to place his compositions piecemeal with any music publisher he could get to listen to his work. Later, he talked of the sick sensation that stole over him whenever someone would take off his demo after only a few bars and show him the door. Sometimes, though, a song could be sold outright for $100, which helped to keep body and soul together, for his was an extremely frugal existence.

During this long period, Neil operated on a strict budget of 35 cents a day. This bought him a Hoagy (a bridge roll sandwich), a small bottle of Coca-Cola and a sweet, not leaving much cash to buy cigarettes – the lifeline for any nerve-shattered, struggling artiste. He couldn't ward off the physical cold, either. For years, Neil shivered through the harsh New York City winters in a woefully thin cotton coat. Throughout this testing time, he remained determined to go it alone. He had no inclination to team up with a creative partner, as so many of this era's most famous lyricists had done. Drily, Diamond takes pains to point out that he did not exactly have an army of would-be cohorts beating a path to his side. In any event, flying solo was very symptomatic of his nature.

There is no doubt that, for a select few, the production line system of songwriting synonymous with the Brill Building's heyday ultimately proved to be highly lucrative and was responsible for putting them firmly on the map. But looking back, Neil Diamond speaks out candidly against the whole fabled Tin Pan Alley set-up, stating: 'While I was there, it was restrictive, exploitive and had hardened arteries. Songwriters didn't have any artistic freedom or control. The publishers owned everyone they could.' This stage, when no one offered Diamond the opportunity to record his own material, when he had to make his music accommodate other people's vocals, was a time when he morosely considered himself an artistic failure. He said: 'Nothing happened properly for me, as far as public acceptance went, until I began to gear my music to my own point of view, to write what moved me.'

That state was still some years away, yet hope flared briefly for Neil at the start of 1963, when his persistence paid off and he landed a recording contract with Columbia Records. The good news was that this giant label had a strong distribution network. The downside was that the deal was for a one-off single only – not much leeway within which to prove himself. Those closest to Neil had been trying to bolster his confidence for some time; having heard a few of his demo discs, they were puzzled as to why he hadn't already been snapped up by a record company. And Neil himself knew that, with maturity, his voice was deepening distinctively. Even so, he was very nervous when, early in the new year, he recorded three original compositions for Columbia Records – 'At Night', 'I've Never Been The Same' and 'Clown Town'. The last number was influenced by Elvis Presley's 1956 classic rocker, 'Heartbreak Hotel'.

In July 1963 then, Neil Diamond's first solo single, 'Clown Town', backed by 'At Night', was released, but it was hardly cause for celebration. Although very introverted, and with no burning desire to be a performer, Neil did try to promote the single by lip-synching to the song at a succession of dances and small fairs. These solo public appearances were tough, especially when he suffered a humiliation the very first time he took centre stage alone. It was in Pennsylvania. He was trussed up in a sober Sunday-best suit, and felt awkward not knowing what to do with his hands, since he had not yet thought to include playing the guitar into his act. Stiff-limbed and concentrating too hard, he failed to notice a taut electric cable stretching across the stage, and duly tripped over it, falling ignominiously flat on his face, to the great amusement of his audience. This inauspicious beginning was borne out when 'Clown Town' bombed badly by not only failing to chart, but by earning royalties of just $15. Needless to say, at this stage, Columbia Records were not rushing to proffer any further record deals to the dedicated, intense singer-songwriter from Brooklyn.

By summer 1963, pressure was building on Neil. Back in the spring, after having dated for about five years, he and Jaye Posner, now a schoolteacher, had married. There had seemed to be inevitability to it. Diamond recalled: 'It was almost as though our destiny was preordained. We were to marry, have children, and live the lives our parents wanted for us.' Their highest aspiration was to be able someday to afford to live in a little house in Long Island, where they could get down to some serious nest building. It would not work out like that, however. As a newly-wed, Neil's main worry was that his desired career as a songwriter would not bring in sufficient funds to support a family single-handedly, should children come along quickly and necessitate Jaye giving up her employment. He had eked out a basic enough existence as a bachelor as it was. He was, in fact, in a strange position. He felt a deep, traditional obligation to be the main breadwinner, while yearning strongly to follow a far from conventional career path.

His struggles to date had not only been thoroughly un-rewarding in financial terms, but the years of failure had also sapped his emotional stamina; striving for success had caused him to withdraw into himself even more than was his natural wont. What gave Diamond crucial fuel for the fire was the changing environment around him. He had taken to spending quite a bit of his spare time in Greenwich Village, in Lower Manhattan. Known to New Yorkers simply as The Village, it lies between 14th Street and Houston Street, east of the Hudson River. Washington Square, in bygone days variously a place of public execution and a paupers' graveyard, was by the 1960s the hub of Village life, particularly at weekends, when the brimming bars and coffee houses resounded to a variety of live music.

In 1963, pop music was really just beginning to burgeon. In Britain, Beatlemania was the latest phenomenon, while the radio airwaves Stateside were being injected with a refreshing surf sound, mainly courtesy of the west-coast band The Beach Boys. At grassroots level on the east coast, within the walls of hip clubs such as Gerde's Folk City in Greenwich Village, a new musical messiah was emerging in the shape of Minnesota-born singer-songwriter Robert Allen Zimmerman who had legally changed his name to Bob Dylan.

Since Dylan's first New York live gig two years earlier, he had been causing a stir on the Village folk scene. In May 1963, *The Freewheelin' Bob Dylan* arrived, an album featuring major original compositions, including 'A Hard Rain's A-Gonna Fall', 'Masters Of War' and 'Blowin' In The Wind'. Dylan was fast establishing himself as one of the leaders of the growing youth protest movement. Within a few months more, as the folk-rock poet famously claimed, the times were a-changing, and in ways which struck a decidedly welcome chord with Neil Diamond. He said of such artistes as Bob Dylan and Joan Baez: 'They didn't want to be owned [by music publishers]. They wanted to write their own music, to say things that were pertinent. Everyone thought Dylan was crazy to begin with.'

The other impact on Diamond, in this respect, was made by

The Beatles. In January 1964, the four Liverpool lads achieved their US chart breakthrough with 'I Want To Hold Your Hand'. With hindsight, it is no more than a clanging, melodic, light-weight number, but at the time a *Billboard* reviewer hailed the single as 'a driving rocker with surf on the Thames sound'. Neil said of these British raiders: 'They proved that the artiste could have free rein of his instincts and still satisfy the business instincts of the record companies.' The combination of Dylan's influence and The Beatles' impact resulted in a whole revolution in popular music, in the way in which people received music and, Diamond felt, more important, in terms of what artistes and songwriters were able to do.

Closer to home that year, this new climate spurred Neil into taking action to detach himself from the detested Tin Pan Alley system. For starters, he set himself up with an office of his own. For $40 a month he sublet, from a printer, a tiny storeroom above the Birdland jazz nightclub on Broadway, Manhattan. There was just enough space in this storeroom for Diamond to cram in an old, repossessed upright piano, two spindle-legged hardwood chairs and a scratched second-hand desk. He also installed a pay phone, so that he could pay as he went and not be running up telephone bills. Musty, dusty and isolated it may have been, but this new set-up gave Diamond an almost giddy sense of freedom.

Initially, he still felt his songs were too samey and overinfluenced by the popular mainstream hits of the day, but that would change. He slaved away in his office, frequently well into the night, or on wintry days took himself off to nearby Greenwich Village to write in the warmer corners of its various cafés. The creative process itself had yet to be unlocked, had still to find its own voice. It is a general misconception that a writer leads a glamorous existence, idling in coffee houses, awaiting a few moments of blinding inspiration. As Diamond has been vocal in attesting, in reality writing is a lonely existence, made up of endless hours of hard work which, in his case, often rendered him incredibly tense by the end of the day.

Nevertheless, the change he craved did begin to kick in. Now that he was no longer constrained in his subject matter, interesting and more stimulating streams of thought showed signs of flowing. His efforts remained raw and unformed most of the time but, crucially, were different from anything he had previously penned. He believed he was seeing progress at last. For the first time, he would study his work and like what he saw – imperfections and all. Although he was years away from finding fame, this is the period when Diamond felt his career actually began.

He said: 'When I first started, I worked with three chords in every bar, but I found that tied me down. I'm not a chord-change writer. I'm a songwriter.' Diamond's method of composition, predictably, was never set in stone. He explained: 'I've always thought of music as something which gives words their wings. So often, music comes first. Although sometimes I'll have a concept, a title idea that I want to write, and the lyric then will come first. It never happens the same way.'

Despite being more invigorated, Neil continued to live on a shoestring. As a married couple, he and Jaye battled to make ends meet. At work, he had increased the meagre budget on his daily living expenses, but only from 35 cents to $1 a day. This meant that to meet the rent on his office and eat, he needed to find around $70 a month *before* also having to scrape up the cost of recording the demo discs of any potentially strong songs with which he hoped to impress. It was essential to his survival all round that, at least once a fortnight, he managed to sell a song or two to the inundated Broadway music publishers.

For long, concentrated periods, the only time Diamond ventured out of the ill-lit, poorly heated, storeroom office was to buy a sandwich and to go knocking on doors with his new material. Standout demo discs made during this time included ones for 'Flame' and 'Straw In The Wind'. With his nose firmly to the grindstone, no one could fault his dedication to his craft. He confessed: 'All I thought about was getting somebody to record one of my songs. There were long periods when nobody did.'

To plug these financial gaps, Neil picked up whatever casual work he could. For some weeks in summer 1964, in the early evenings, he sold vitamin pills door to door. He could also earn fees for gigging, and sometimes he performed folk songs in Greenwich Village bars, but the act of public performing still held little lure for him. He didn't, as he put it, 'have the hots' to be in the spotlight, a resistance rooted in being basically shy and self-conscious.

Diamond endured years of penury, and was never enamoured of money for money's sake. 'I'm not a materialistically minded person,' he has stated. 'I don't need that many things.' At the start of 1965, however, Jaye became pregnant. Apart from their joy at anticipating the arrival of their first child, it meant another mouth to feed, as well as the loss of Jaye's schoolteacher wage.

Partly out of sheer necessity, but more as a result of his artistic freedom bearing fruit, 1965 saw a decided upturn in Diamond's fortunes with regard to selling his songs for release by established stars. In America, Jimmy Clanton and the balladeer Bobby Vinton both recorded Neil Diamond compositions, as did major league UK artistes. Liverpool-born rock and roller Billy Fury, with a pedigree of 11 Top Ten hits by September 1965, that month released 'Where Do You Run?', penned by Neil Diamond (sharing the songwriting credit with wife, Jaye Posner). Most notably, in spring the flip side of Cliff Richard's number one UK hit, 'The Minute You're Gone', had been Diamond's 'Just Another Guy'. Part of the reason, too, for a shift in the wind stemmed from the dynamics of Neil's surroundings.

America was in a strange mood. The brutal assassination of Democrat President John F. Kennedy on 22 November 1963 had killed a dream in American society, smashing the illusion of the Camelot presidency, and plunging the nation into one of its darkest periods. The socio-political climate was strung tighter than a bow, especially as growing unrest at racial inequalities provoked angry protest on the streets. Things worsened considerably in February 1965, when the prominent Nebraska-born black nationalist leader Malcolm Little, known as Malcolm X, was shot dead during a rally of the Organisation for Afro-American Unity, held at the Audubon Ballroom in Harlem, in Upper Manhattan.

This running sore of dangerous discontent had found an articulate voice in music where, besides Bob Dylan, Joan Baez was something of a standard-bearer, having attracted enormous attention by leading the masses in singing 'We Shall Overcome' during a civil rights march on Washington, D.C. Protest heroes and worthy anthems were a hallmark of the era. To counterbalance this intensity, a new breeze was blowing, alleviating the unremittingly oppressive feelings of grievance, and invigorating that swathe of the younger generation that was not particularly politicised.

They wanted romance and drama from their pop idols, and among the forerunners of the dominant lyricists in this field was the husband and wife writer/producer team of Jeff Barry and Ellie Greenwich. By now, this couple had racked up colossal success, penning what became time-capsuled classics, frequently for all-girl groups. For the Brooklyn-born Crystals, Barry and Greenwich had written 'Da Doo Ron Ron', the 1963 million-selling hit now regarded as the first true example of legendary producer Phil Spector's famous 'wall of sound'. They followed this the same year with 'Then He Kissed Me'. Still in 1963, the Ronettes, again under Spector's auspices, had benefited from Barry and Greenwich's instinct for hitting the spot with 'Be My Baby'. In 1964, the couple's work had snared the top slot in the US singles charts with 'Leader Of The Pack', sung by the Shangri-Las, and 'Chapel Of Love', written in conjunction with Phil Spector for the Dixie Cups.

Come early 1965, with a baby on the way, Neil Diamond felt responsibility weighing more than ever on him. 'I couldn't afford to fool around,' he recalled. 'I had to get down to business and really make it.' That itself was problematic, for to stand a chance of succeeding he had to lay out more of his preciously limited cash on making increasing numbers of demo discs. Then fate took a hand. One February day, Neil entered a recording studio to make a demo of a song he had sold to Gil-Pincus Music, and found himself confronted by Ellie Greenwich, whom the music publisher had roped in to sing on the record.

With bouffant blonde hair and a fondness for the heavy kohl eyeshadow in vogue at the time, Ellie had an unusually husky voice which translated uniquely onto record. Professionally, the attraction lay the other way round at first, as Ellie Greenwich revealed years later: 'When Neil was teaching me the song, I thought, Gee! This guy really has an interesting sound!'

Initially, Diamond was somewhat in awe of the young beauty with the lyrical Midas touch. He was well aware that Greenwich and Barry were thought to be so infallible that music publishers practically bit their hands off even for partially completed songs, but he felt no envy – only respect. He knew, too, of the couple's successful association with Phil Spector, but for all that, he was given no reason to feel intimidated. On the contrary, Ellie was warm and openly encouraging. She discovered the knack of opening Neil up so that, almost from the off, they clicked.

Greenwich quickly became aware of the deep-rooted reserve in Diamond. She spotted at once that he was essentially an entity unto himself, but she found him frankly adorable. There was his rather 'Mr Sobersides' style – somehow endearing, considering it was in the midst of the swinging sixties – his deep, smooth, velvety speaking voice, and his doe-like, hazel eyes. Above all, his innate honesty shone out and appealed to her in an almost maternal way. She later explained that the Neil Diamond of those days was an intense, handsome young man of whom most women would find themselves fiercely protective.

Neil's memories of that first encounter are equally vivid. He has recalled the ease with which he, the struggling artiste, and she, the renowned hitmaker, laughed and relaxed that day, how after recording ended for that demo disc he was persuaded to let Greenwich hear some of his other compositions. Impressed by Diamond's potential, Ellie lost no time in asking him to come home and meet her husband, Jeff Barry. He agreed with Ellie that they believed they had discovered a strong talent, and they were adamant that there had to be a way in which they could help him.

The year before, Greenwich and Barry had helped the Shangri-Las to sign up to Jerry Leiber and Mike Stoller's Red Bird record label. Now they also helped Neil to be signed as a staff writer at Leiber and Stoller's company, but it would prove to be an unproductive move. Neil recalls that he scarcely saw either of his bosses at Red Bird – the top-flight lyricists were always busy in their office, and normally quite separate from all their staff writers.

For some time now, Neil had composed on piano. Lately he had taken to accompanying himself on guitar while he wrote, and he felt that caused some of the others at his level to look askance at him. Virtually nobody in his experience of working for music publishers wrote with an acoustic on his knee, and although he was a city kid through and through, there were occasions when some people seemed to treat him like a country bumpkin for it. Characteristically, Diamond chalked it up but said nothing.

When it became obvious that his time at Red Bird was not panning out, there had to be a rethink. The upshot was that Jeff Barry, Ellie Greenwich and Neil Diamond formed their own music publishing company, which they called Tallyrand Music. Neil promptly intensified his efforts, and came up with numbers such as 'Don't Go Away Mad'. By now, royalties were trickling in from songs he had placed in the past. In spring, of course, he'd had 'Just Another Guy' recorded by one of Britain's top pop acts, but as a B-side. He yearned for success in writing an A-side.

A taste of that success came his way, albeit at a modest level, in the second half of 1965, when his melodic ballad 'Sunday And Me' was taken to number 18 in the US singles chart by Jay & The Americans. It was not yet the start of something big, however, and when no momentum resulted, Diamond became deflated again. Like most New Yorkers, he looked at life pretty flat on, and was only too aware that all his struggles to date had produced very little in real terms, which made it hard for him to see a light at the end of the tunnel.

Come summer 1965, pop music was undergoing an exciting revolution, with styles rapidly shifting and developing. The most invigorating new trend was emerging from California, with the beginnings of what would become the incredible West Coast sound. Electric folk-rock, far too commercialised for purists like Diamond's earliest inspiration, Pete Seeger, was about to sweep all in its wake when the Los Angeles-formed band, The Byrds, burst onto the scene with a cover version of Bob Dylan's 'Mr Tambourine Man'. This global chart-topper was an innovative and stunning blend of harmony-rich arrangement and astounding 12-string acoustic guitar accompaniment, anchored by strong percussion.

The Byrds paved the way for the likes of The Mamas and the Papas to follow. Around the end of the year, bristling at the top of the US singles chart was 'The Sound of Silence' by Simon and Garfunkel. This was written by Paul Simon, a songwriter almost the same age as Diamond, from neighbouring Queens, New York, who had likewise begun his career endlessly rapping on doors in the Brill Building, trying to peddle his wares. It was Paul Simon's launch pad. Ellie Greenwich spoke for many like her at the time when she described rock as being in its infancy and how being part of the growing process was enormously thrilling. Neil wasn't thrilled. He felt left behind, not part of it. Even so he did not contemplate abandoning his love of songwriting, to melt anonymously into the conventional workforce, to lead a life of traditional conformity. Not even when, in September 1965, Jaye gave birth to their first child, a daughter, whom they named Marjorie.

Given Diamond's dedication to songwriting, and his dogged pursuit of breaking into a notoriously ephemeral world, which was right then already sprouting with talent, there was very little opportunity for either Neil or Jaye to nurture their relationship properly. Starved by lack of progress, Neil must sometimes have been in an impenetrable mood when he arrived back in Brooklyn, often late in the evening. It was scarcely the best ground upon which to build a sound marriage. A certain stability came from the fact that they had known each other since high school; having been raised to believe in the sanctity of marriage, both parties would hang in for some time yet. But cracks became inevitable as each one came to want more from life than they were getting.

Near the end of 1965, Neil found renewed zest for the fight. In one particularly fertile period he produced 'Solitary Man', 'Cherry Cherry' and 'I Got the Feeling (Oh No No)'. He sat up and took heart when Ellie Greenwich and Jeff Barry agreed that these three songs were his best offerings so far. So confident was Barry in the new material, in fact, that he took Neil along to audition for Jerry Wexler at Atlantic Records in New York. Reining in his nerves, and toting his black six-string acoustic guitar, Diamond duly performed his latest clutch of songs for the influential executive, who was impressed enough to offer Neil a verbal deal, there and then. By the very next day that offer had slipped somewhat sideways, in that Jerry Wexler had decided to recommend Neil Diamond to a fledgling label called Bang Records, for which Atlantic Records handled distribution. But, in early 1966, Neil was only too happy to sign to the New York-based label, with Jeff Barry and Ellie Greenwich as his producers.

Bang Records, with its distinctive logo of a revolver, was owned by Bert Berns. Only in his mid-thirties, he had already led a colourful and varied career in and around the fringes of the music scene. He had been a very young nightclub owner in Cuba in the late 1950s, until Fidel Castro, the 32-year-old rebel leader, won his 25-month-long revolutionary struggle and forced the corrupt dictator General Fulgencio Batista to flee.

Berns was among those who quickly quit Cuba as Castro became a premier bent on a rigorous programme of reform. He headed for his native North America, where he became more specifically involved in the burgeoning music scene, first as a song plugger, before he rapidly discovered talents that would take him further. Berns's instinct for the commercial potential of raw and raucous rhythm and blues led him to produce records for Solomon Burke, Wilson Pickett, and The Drifters, all big names at that time. Then he struck gold as a lyricist in the early 1960s.

His most recognisable songwriting success was 'Twist And Shout'. It topped the R&B US charts in mid-1962, courtesy of the Isley Brothers. Two years later, the classic dance hall favourite claimed the number two slot, when it was covered by The Beatles for the American market. While working in London, in early 1965, Berns also scored a UK number two hit with 'Here Comes The Night', recorded by Them, fronted by Irish-born singer Van Morrison.

When Bert Berns, buoyant and ambitious, returned to the States that summer, he launched his own label, Bang Records; almost immediately he signed up the four-piece band, The McCoys. They picked off the US number one spot with 'Hang On Sloopy'. By the time that Jerry Wexler steered Neil Diamond his way, Berns felt on the cusp of big things.

Diamond's contract with Bang Records was for four singles over the next 12 months. In spring 1966, Neil concentrated as never before, cutting songs in three separate New York City recording studios – Dick Charles Recording, A&R Studios and Century Sound. Century was a renowned facility part-owned by Brooks Arthur, who also worked as principal engineer at Bang Records; he vividly recalled these early Neil Diamond sessions. 'What Neil brought was a great attitude and, as Bert Berns used to say, "the feel of Neil". It's hard to put your finger on what that was. But you knew it when it was happening.'

It was in Neil's nature to be thoroughly prepared when he walked into any recording studio, and he would have it set in his head how the sessions ought to go. Even at this early stage, he also exuded an infectious confidence while he set about laying down his songs with the recording engineers, and his style of delivery was memorable. He didn't merely sing the song. To the surprise of those in the control room, he performed it, and in such a way that the strong sense of rhythm running through him was channelled visibly in the way his body and his acoustic guitar would sway in perfect harmony with each other. Brooks Arthur called it 'a kinetic thing happening', and from his own position behind the soundproofed window, it frankly fascinated him. For their part, operating as producers, Jeff Barry and Ellie Greenwich injected a joyous enthusiasm into proceedings. The first release from these recording sessions was the single 'Solitary Man'.

In spring 1966, hits from US artistes were more than holding their own against their British counterparts in the singles charts. Upbeat numbers like The Beach Boys' 'Barbara Ann', and 'California Dreamin' by The Mamas and the Papas, were offset by doleful songs such as 'The Sun Ain't Gonna Shine Anymore' by The Walker Brothers, and Bob Dylan's caustic 'Rainy Day Women Nos. 12 and 35'. 'Solitary Man' came into the doleful category. An introspective song, delivered in a sombre style, 'Solitary Man' had a haunting quality that still stands up. A melancholic mistrust of the female sex nakedly pervades the piece, in which Diamond talks of someone determinedly shielding himself against inevitable hurt.

Being composed in a minor key gave the number an unusual sound. And by dint alone of it becoming Neil's first record in his own name to chart, 'Solitary Man' remains one of his personal all-time favourite discs. Diamond would become an autobiographical songwriter, but he wasn't conscious when he wrote 'Solitary Man' that the guy he sang so soulfully about bore any relation to himself. He has admitted: 'It wasn't until years later, when I went into Freudian analysis, that I understood that it was me.' He added: 'It was an outgrowth of my despair.'

The period prior to the single's release was an exciting time for Neil Diamond as he became exposed, for the first time, to the preparation that goes into launching a new recording artiste with promotional photo shoots and the like. Before the single went to press, when Bang Records set about preparing PR material for distribution to the music media, the possibility of Neil changing his name was floated. It was not driven by the question as to whether it might be commercially advantageous to de-ethnicise his name. Bob Dylan had changed from Zimmerman, but Simon and Garfunkel, who had retained their given names, were going from strength to strength. Once a change was mooted, though, Diamond mulled over various options, one of which was to call himself Eice Cherry. Mercifully, at the last moment, he decided he could not do it, and retained his own name.

In May 1966, Neil Diamond's 'Solitary Man', backed by 'Do It', was released on Bang Records and peaked two months later at number 55 in the US singles chart. A modest showing, certainly, but as far as Diamond was concerned it changed him from an unknown lyricist scouring the streets for success via established stars, to a legitimate recording artiste in his own right, with his first chart position under his belt. 'Solitary Man' would not prove to be typical of his material at this point – his next numbers were appreciably jauntier – and it was not a hit single. Still, for many, it would define Neil Diamond for a number of years.

Diamond does concede that the songs he went on to record for Bang Records had a stark simplicity to them. He progressed to deeper and better things when his emotional connection to certain songs would keep him motivated but, at that stage, he had nothing to live up to. He also had less time to linger over agonisingly meaningful lyrics. What he had to concentrate on was trying to promote this first single. At the end of March, Neil received a royalty cheque from Broadcast Music Inc., on New York's 5th Avenue, for all of 73 cents – paltry recompense for months and months of writing material for other artistes to record. Clearly, he looked for better things from 'Solitary Man'; to that end, he knew that gaining visibility was essential.

His ingrained reservations about performing live had not diminished. By now he had begun to play a regular gig at the Greenwich Village pub, The Bitter End. It was managed by Fred Weintraub, who had lately been enlisted as his manager; Weintraub's memories of these appearances reveal how incredibly nervous, even insecure, Diamond was. Neil's chronic unease didn't betray itself so much while he was singing, but his gentle attempts to converse with the audience between numbers had to be tactfully curtailed by Fred Weintraub because they were excruciatingly shaky.

Neil has owned up to this unease, admitting further that for gigs he would deliberately wear all black so as to make himself, he thought, less conspicuous on stage. Considering that he is a superstar who has become internationally renowned for his glittering glass-beaded shirts, it is an interesting insight into him at this time. It is also a measure of Diamond's early professionalism that, despite his private resistance to the limelight, he was prepared to thrust himself into a series of live performances in an attempt to get his name and face known.

Initially, he played at the thin end of the wedge, appearing at bowling alleys, and performing in all weathers aboard flatbed trucks, stationed in car parks. He would scrape up a local scratch band to back him at each individual pit stop. With the barest time for any semblance of rehearsal, he lived in daily dread that he and the band would not stay in step for the duration of his set. This ramshackle beginning went by the wayside, however, once Bang Records began to land their signing some proper engagements. In summer 1966, Neil Diamond made his first Bay Area appearance on America's west coast when he played the Red Rooster Lounge in San Leandro. He was backed by a group calling themselves The Mothers of Invention, fronted by a future star, Frank Zappa. Then, in June, he took part in a concert held at San Francisco's Cow Palace.

By this time, sporadic gold dust TV opportunities were coming his way. If appearing live before an intimate club audience had been tough, subjecting himself to scrutiny on television must have been an ordeal. Nevertheless, Diamond performed 'Solitary Man' on a programme which went out locally in Washington, D.C., and was a precursor to his national television debut on 25 June on the hit show *American Bandstand*.

By the time he guested on *Hullabaloo* he was finding his feet, confident enough even to proclaim that rock music would overtake the still immensely popular folk movement. Exponents of pop, Diamond declared with unusual boldness to the masses watching at home, 'are the torchbearers of the new American culture'. Inwardly, he burned to be one of those pioneers.

Meeting the promotional obligations for his first single had involved a deal of travel, which had further eaten into the time

Neil had available to spend with Jaye and young Marjorie at home, which was now in Jamaica, in Queens. The strain this was placing on his marriage and family life was only part of the problems that were beginning to percolate through his private world. More serious were changes occurring intrinsically in Neil.

It is true that songwriting had already absorbed him deeply for some time, but now it was becoming his lifeblood. Years later, he would describe songwriting as his shield, passionately claiming that to him the difference between writing and not writing was the difference between living and dying, and that he could let nothing stand in its way. Extreme sentiments to many, but for Neil a deep-seated belief. He also realised for the first time that the real Neil had, until now, lain undiscovered. By travelling, breaking from the nightly ritual of going home to domestic life, getting his first taste of what succeeding in music would mean, glimpsing the alternative life that could open up to him – it all conspired to make him face up to the stark fact that he wanted different things from life. As a result, the preordained path he had hitherto accepted was coming under serious threat.

'Things began to deteriorate from that point,' he has said. A hunger for success would take Neil Diamond far, professionally. But he would very soon begin to pay a high personal cost for it.

CHAPTER 3

Mixed Fortunes

FROM LATE SUMMER 1966, for the next six years, roadwork came to dominate a large portion of Neil Diamond's life. As a hesitant performer yet to develop the magnetic stage aura with which he would become synonymous, live gigs were initially an emotionally debilitating experience – not helped by critical complaints and low turnouts in places.

Diamond's manager, Fred Weintraub, had organised a backing band and fixed up ten concerts to take Neil across America over the remaining months of the year. In Virginia, he played at the Manassas National Guard Armory and at Alexandria's Roller Skating Rink, with an appearance at the Sam Houston Coliseum, Texas, in between. But the lion's share of the gigs took place in December at Dave Hull's Hullabaloo on Sunset Boulevard in Los Angeles, where the west coast music critics were very hard to please. One review of Neil's first night at the Hullabaloo suggested not so tactfully that he should stick to songwriting and leave live performance to others. It must have cut extra deep with Diamond to read that, then to turn up that very night to the venue to find an audience of only six people for his second show. As he headed back to New York City at the end of a seven-night stint just prior to Christmas, he was able to console himself with the knowledge that there had been an upturn in the success of his record releases – at least in terms of his two recent singles.

To follow his thoughtful ballad 'Solitary Man', Neil had changed direction with 'Cherry Cherry', a bouncy, uncomplicated, boy-dates-girl number delivered in a strident, three-chord thrashing melody. Diamond's guiding principle this time had been to let the rhythm flowing through him have its head. The infectious freshness that this had bred had been interpreted well by the team of top New York session musicians with whom he had worked, and would continue to work on most of his early recordings.

Talking of the skilful arrangements and the whole ambience of tracks such as 'Cherry Cherry', engineer Brooks Arthur later likened the resulting sound as similar to Phil Spector's. Backed by 'I'll Come Running', this second single on Bang Records was released in August 1966 and, bolstered by Neil's performing it on *American Bandstand* in September, by mid-October it had peaked at number six, giving Diamond his first major hit in his own name. The following month came 'I Got The Feelin' (Oh No, No)'/'The Boat That I Row'. Again, Neil had executed a turnaround. Compared with the plethora of songwriters churning out teenage-oriented pop tunes, he invested a distinctly adult tinge into his lyrics on this single. The poignantly sorrowful lyrics on the A-side, expressing the agony of a fragmenting love affair, were partnered by those of a song about a self-contained individual who is prepared to answer to no one. The upbeat, near hand-clapping, musical style of 'The Boat That I Row' disguised the strongly independent sentiment hammered out in this number.

Chalking up a number 16 hit in December with this third single helped dilute Neil's deep disappointment at the dismal performance of his debut album, *The Feel Of Neil Diamond*, which had been released the previous month. Of the 12 songs featured on this album, five were cover versions. 'Cherry Cherry' was anchor to the album's lead track 'Solitary Man'. On the front sleeve, a full-length shot showed Diamond darkly dressed, standing against a wall with one knee bent and his arms folded confidently over his chest as he stared moodily at the camera. Neil's name was given clear prominence. Still, it was not enough to capture the imagination of the record-buying public in anything like large numbers. When it was also critically ignored, the underexposure led to the album grinding to a halt well outside *Billboard*'s Top 100, at number 137. It was early days, and Diamond had merely put a toe in the water when it came to recording in his own right, but it was scarcely the progress he craved.

What was interesting, but bittersweet, was the comparison between the performance of his own recordings at the end of 1966, and the enviable success his songwriting attracted for other artistes, most notably for The Monkees. In autumn 1965, eye-catching adverts had appeared in the *Hollywood Reporter* and in *Daily Variety* for 'four insane boys, age 17–21' to take part in a new TV sitcom series, roughly inspired by the loony goings-on in The Beatles' film, *A Hard Day's Night*. The 440 applicants had been whittled down to the requisite four – Mickey Dolenz, Mike Nesmith, Peter Tork and Davy Jones.

In January 1966, NBC-TV had bought *The Monkees* series, and it was scheduled to air in the autumn. Once filming had got under way, by summer The Monkees' producer, Don Kirshner of Aldon Music, had asked a number of lyricists to write suitable songs for the show. Gerry Goffin, Carole King, Barry Mann, Cynthia Weil and Neil Sedaka were among those approached, as was Neil Diamond. When the goofy Monkees – the world's first ever manufactured boy band – hit TV screens in September 1966, they elicited a variety of reactions from within the music business. Some established artistes, on both sides of the Atlantic, were distinctly unimpressed. Brian Jones, the musical genius and founder of The Rolling Stones, caustically dubbed the lightweight Monkees 'The Prefab Four'. But they became phenomenally popular, instantaneously.

The Monkees' debut single, 'Last Train to Clarksville', written by Tommy Boyce and Bobby Hart, rocketed to the top of the American singles chart. Don Kirshner found the hot follow-up he was looking for when he listened to Neil Diamond's offering, 'I'm A Believer'. In content, 'I'm A Believer' was typical Diamond. The song's subject was a jaded pessimist with a store of bad life experiences behind him, who has given up on ever finding true love, until he encounters one particular girl. In line with his remit, taking account of the fluff nature of *The Monkees*, he had wrapped these partly cynical lyrics in a catchy melody for an easy-listening-style delivery by the parent-friendly new band. The Monkees recorded Diamond's song at RCA Studios in New York with producer Jeff Barry at the helm. When it was released in late November 1966, advance orders of 1,051,280 ensured that it went gold within two days. By the end of the year, it lodged at the top of the charts, where it reigned for seven weeks.

Three days before Neil Diamond's 26th birthday, his song was also bristling in pole position in the British singles chart. In all 'I'm A Believer' eventually sold over six million copies for The Monkees, and was Neil Diamond's first number one triumph as a songwriter. Neil provided The Monkees with four more songs: 'Look Out (Here Comes Tomorrow)'; 'Love To Love'; 'A Little Bit Me, A Little Bit You', another multi-million seller in spring 1967; and one song which was not recorded, 'Black and Blue (From Kicking Myself)'.

Although deriving some self-satisfaction from writing such a colossal hit as 'I'm A Believer', Neil didn't immediately get loads of cash in his pocket. Financially, things remained a strain, and while he awaited a return on his songwriting royalties, he made money by recording some commercial sessions for the Coca-Cola Company. As 1967 got under way, there was nothing for it – the tour circuit had to loom once more. Fred Weintraub believed in this tried and trusted method of an artiste plugging away at making an impression on live audiences across the country, and it was the only realistic route open to Neil Diamond right then. While Neil knew that his manager had his best interests at heart, at first he felt pushed out on the road.

Earlier in the decade, the collegiate circuit had provided a good hunting ground for Simon and Garfunkel to build the bedrock of a fan base. Over the course of 1967, Neil Diamond played universities and even high schools, in the likes of Wichita, Kansas, South Bend, Indiana and Winnipeg in Canada. Town halls, gymnasiums, ski lodges and open-air fairs also featured. Kicking off in late January with eight straight gigs at the 40 Thieves Club in Hamilton, Bermuda, he visited Ohio, Tennessee, Illinois, Florida, Iowa, Alabama and Virginia, among other states. All this junketing about required him to travel by air, which was a problem, as he discovered that he had a fear of flying.

He worked hard at perfecting an act, but wasn't wild about the repetitiveness of jumping nightly through the same hoops. He recalled: 'My performances were about fifteen songs, some patter to get the audience to like me, trying to get the audience to enjoy themselves, coming back for a few encores and that was that. It's a shame the thing was so limited.' It was a pity, too, that Diamond's lack of self-confidence was such that he refused to take a small break halfway through a gig, just in case his audience got up and left!

That said, his travels did throw up some amusing, eye-opening experiences when at one stage he joined a bill including a couple of UK acts. One was Herman's Hermits, a band basking in the glow of its million-selling single in America, 'There's a Kind of Hush (All Over The World)'. The other was the British bad boy outfit, The Who, on their first US tour. Fronted by Roger Daltrey, The Who had by then notched up a string of Top Five hits at home including 'My Generation', 'Substitute', 'I'm A Boy' and 'Happy Jack'. They and their raucous reputation for destructive behaviour were completely unknown to Neil Diamond, who was astonished by drummer Keith Moon's manic mannerisms as he watched The Who's set from the wings. But his eyes almost sprang out on stalks when Pete Townshend began swinging his electric guitar like a club, thrashing it off the stage and walls until he broke the instrument's neck. Neil had never witnessed a band wildly beating up its own amplifiers until they were smashed to pieces.

Such antics were mildly diverting, then boring; Neil focused instead on his own performances. While he slogged it out on the road, his first two singles of the year were released, the love song 'You Got To Me', backed by 'Someday Baby', which peaked by spring at number 18, and 'Girl, You'll Be A Woman Soon'/'You'll Forget', released in April. 'Girl, You'll Be A Woman Soon' once again centred on a young man with a sizeable chip on his shoulder, a misunderstood outsider, who feels got at in life. It struck a chord with enough teenagers to land Diamond a number ten hit. On the strength of this, Neil began to attract more offers to appear in guest slots on various regional television programmes.

He had started the year not particularly enamoured of live performance, but a need to absorb the increasingly appreciative feedback from attentive audiences began to take hold. Applause is a drug to a performer, and the more Diamond came to realise that this was his time, the more it pumped into his bloodstream to go out there and pursue success. It was in some ways inevitable that Neil's marriage to Jaye would become a casualty of this pursuit. The couple's family grew with the addition of a second daughter, named Elyn. But nothing could prevent the steady disintegration of their relationship – a process that proved to be very painful for them both.

In the 12-month period since Neil made his chart debut as a singer-songwriter with 'Solitary Man', four of his five single releases had become Top 20 hits. Come July 1967, a DJ poll in the American magazine *Cash Box* named Neil Diamond as the Most Promising Up and Coming Male Vocalist. By the year's end, another *Cash Box* survey had Diamond tying with veteran star Frank Sinatra as the nation's number one singer for 1967. Neil has openly assumed the lion's share of the blame for allowing this change in his fortunes to undermine, then lay waste to, his first marriage.

He knew that with his increasing absences from home, touring and performing on television shows around the US, he was asking for trouble on the domestic front. His wife was hardly seeing him, and his first daughter, Marjorie, was growing up largely without him. But his need to do it was stronger than anything. With sad candour he once admitted: 'I can barely remember that marriage.' This was not intended as a callous swipe at his former high-school sweetheart, nor did it reflect a lack of love for his offspring. He has confessed that although he had been chasing success for years, when it began to happen for him at 26, he was still too young to handle it. 'I couldn't cope with the sudden pressure,' he said. 'It was all happening so quickly and I was so unused to it.' Diamond described his actions then as akin to leaping onto a wild horse and single-mindedly setting off for the ride, regardless of the personal consequences. His marriage staggered on its last legs for a while yet – both Neil and Jaye aware of the futility of trying to hold it together. When it came to the final break, Neil took the responsibility on his own shoulders. He revealed: 'I decided to split and leave it all behind. In a sense, it was running away.'

With his personal life crumbling, Diamond concentrated on work, acutely aware that his singles had not yet broken him into even the shallows of the British charts. Cross-pollination between the US and UK markets in the booming mid-1960s music scene was rife, but Neil was missing out – as a recording artiste in his own name, that is. As a songwriter, he continued to rack up the hits.

Eighteen year-old Lulu, from Strathclyde in Scotland, had notched up a UK number six hit in May with Neil's 'The Boat That I Row'. This was the raucous singer's highest chart position at that point, since her most famous number 'Shout' had stopped at number seven in 1964. Britain's prince of pop, Cliff Richard, had lately scored a Top 30 hit with the double A-side, 'I'll Come Running'/'I Got The Feelin' (Oh No, No)', both written by Neil Diamond.

Within the American rock scene, Diamond felt that he had entered another sphere into which he didn't easily fit. The year 1967 saw Brooklyn being scarred by race riots, yet this was the so-called 'summer of love' when the drug culture was meshing with a music scene in which groups or duos were predominant and, it seemed to Diamond, the solo artiste was rarer. He declared: 'People didn't know exactly what to make of me. The critics and the press paid absolutely no attention to me. They weren't looking to some guy with a guitar. It was like I didn't exist.' When it came to drugs, Neil not only had no interest in taking mind-altering substances, he soon adopted an overt stance against drugs, which further alienated him from circles soaked in psychedelia.

Accustomed to ploughing his own furrow, Neil made his next single the gospel-flavoured 'Thank The Lord For The Night Time'. It was not the last time that his music would hold religious connotations – Diamond valued his willingness to appreciate a whole range of such influences. He had loved singing in the school choirs, and already felt that there was a connection between gospel and choral music. As far as incorporating a gospel influence into his own compositions was concerned, he can trace this to a specific event. He explained: 'I had one experience that had quite an effect on me. I went up to a church in Harlem one day and sat in for the service to hear the singing. It was extraordinary, raw and powerful. It made my hair stand up.'

'Thank The Lord For The Night Time', continuing the thread of a guy who is frank about the fact that he has no money but does have an open heart and is looking for love, was partnered with 'The Long Way Home'. Released in mid-July, it peaked six weeks later at number 13.

As summer segued into autumn with yet another consecutive Top 20 hit to his credit, Diamond had fairly high hopes for the performance of his second album when it hit the shelves in early October. Called *Just For You*, its 11 tracks included Neil's own rendition of the chartbusting 'I'm A Believer'. There had already been three cuts off it that year, and a fourth spin-off single emerged the following spring. While performing markedly better than his debut album, *Just For You* stalled at a lowly number 80.

Diamond was disappointed to be trailing in the dust album-wise, when his singles continued to give him firm grounds for encouragement. But at least he was gaining yet more profile through television appearances. In September, he made a guest appearance on *Live From The Bitter End*, a show staged at his stomping-ground club in Manhattan, and hosted by Fred Weintraub. Other performers on the night included The Lovin' Spoonful.

Not long after that, Neil took on his first 'acting' role when he played a nightclub singer in the episode titled 'The Many Deaths of Saint Christopher' of the new CBS-Paramount private investigator series *Mannix*, created for television by Richard Levinson and William Link, and starring Mike Connors. Acting would ultimately draw Neil Diamond, but for now he stuck to experimenting with musical styles, and soon came up with the country-tinged ballad 'Kentucky Woman'. Previously recorded in the summer at New York's A&R Studios, this cut, coupled with 'The Time Is Now', charted in November 1967 at number 22 and went on to become a strong favourite among dyed-in-the-wool Diamond fans.

'Kentucky Woman' came to represent a watershed in Neil's professional life. Not enough that his first marriage was splintering on the rocks, his association with Bang Records was beginning to come unstuck too. Instead of 'Kentucky Woman', Neil had wanted his follow-up single to 'Thank The Lord For The Night Time' to be a song called 'Shilo', but Bert Berns had flatly disagreed.

'Shilo' meant a great deal to Neil. For really the first time, its hauntingly personal lyrics cast a bright spotlight onto the inner workings of Neil Diamond, the man. With courageous clarity, he had written about the loneliness he felt while growing up, and about how, in order to combat that, he had created an imaginary friend in his head as a comfort, someone to whom he could turn for company and a sense of continuity in a constantly shifting world.

It is easy to put Bert Berns's attitude towards 'Shilo' down to the record company executive trying to cater for Diamond's best interests. Berns was not attached to this new song, and did not see it being a hit for an artiste whose second album had floundered well down the charts, and who needed to stick to a proven formula and not diversify again. For Diamond, passionately possessive of 'Shilo', this was not what he wanted to hear. It also felt like another straitjacket was threatening to clasp around him. He rebelled instinctively against the attitude that he ought to settle for churning out predictable material. 'They began to expect music that I'd already gone past,' he explained.

Neil was never a man to tolerate feeling stifled for long. A parting of the ways was inevitable. But separating from Bang Records proved to be a fraught business. Indeed, the whole period covering the split, as far as Neil Diamond is concerned, was – to say the least – an extremely testing time.

The tussle over Bert Berns's refusal to release 'Shilo' as a single in 1967 left Diamond first frustrated, then thoroughly disgusted. One day he walked out, telling the record boss that he was not prepared to record for him any more. Diamond has said that it was from that point that he felt heat coming his way. Over the years he has stated more than once that he began to feel threatened. He has claimed that a fortnight after his quarrel with Bert Berns, 'somebody threw a bomb into the Bitter End'. Neil took this attack on the Manhattan club to be a not-so-subtle warning directed at him. It's impossible to know if this interpretation was accurate. It has to be said that Fred Weintraub, who managed Diamond and the Bitter End, has commuted 'bomb' to 'stink bomb', which rendered the place uninhabitable for a short space of time. However, Weintraub has admitted that exactly around this time 'I got beaten up very badly, but it would be impossible to pin things down. There's no proof of anything.'

Bert Berns's widow, Ilene, later declared that any implication that such activities had anything to do with her late husband was absurd. But that does not negate the fact that Neil Diamond clearly felt that his personal safety, and that of his family, was under threat from some source. And it seems that the judge hearing legal arguments in a New York court case in connection with Neil's bid to break free of Bang Records was also prepared to entertain the possibility that Diamond's unease ought to be taken seriously. It has been reported that the court was poised to give the singer bodyguard protection just before the increasingly bitter court battle was temporarily derailed by Bert Berns's sudden death at the end of 1967. According to Neil Diamond, even the FBI became involved.

In 2002, Diamond told the London *Evening Standard*: 'I carried a .38 for six months after I left Bang Records in 1968. I had a warning from the FBI to protect myself. So I sent my family away and started carrying a gun. Was I scared? I was scared 24/7.' Neil had ushered his family to a location in Long Island, where they stayed for several weeks.

While all this drama was going on, Neil somehow had to find the nerve to carry on with his career. In mid-January 1968, during an interview on *The Merv Griffin Show*, Neil demonstrated his sword fencing skills, which he continued to keep honed. The following month, 'New Orleans'/'Hanky Panky' was released. 'New Orleans' was Diamond's first non-original single release. The song had been recorded in 1959 by Gary 'U.S.' Bonds, when it had been a Top Ten hit. Diamond's cover version ran out of steam at a dismal number 51. His worst chart position for two years, however, came with 'Red Red Wine', which Neil had penned some time back, while sitting in the storeroom behind his father-in-law's haberdashery shop in Massapequa in Long Island. This number later came to be firmly associated with Neil Diamond. At the time of its first release, however, 'Red Red Wine', backed by 'Red Rubber Ball', petered out in April 1968 at number 62.

By that time, Neil's life had changed dramatically. His touring had taken him from New York, through Nova Scotia to Indiana, Tennessee, Illinois, Texas and Ohio. For all his inner anxiety about his personal safety, he was aware of a new freedom dawning, and his live act had flourished substantially. He was still dressing in sober black for stage performances, which continued to signify a core lack of self-confidence. Yet at the same time he was finding a deeper intuitive communication with his audiences; Neil knew he was now discovering a niche as a solo performer. Over time, Diamond would acquire the nickname 'the Jewish Elvis', and would attract a Presley-type devotion among his massive loyal fan base. In spring 1968, he reflected on this shift up in gear: 'People started to tire of groups, and a single guy like me was a throwback to someone who they could accept as an Urban Elvis.'

It was also that spring that Neil's private life took an important turn. By now his marriage to Jaye was over. They had separated and were heading for divorce when he encountered Marcia Murphey, a slender beauty who worked as a television production associate in New York City. Diamond saw them as soulmates from the start. He is adamant, too, that he and Marcia connected on first eye contact alone, before a single word had been exchanged. Certainly, he was attracted to what he perceived as an unhappiness in her eyes that day. To him, it meant that she was a young woman who understood great pain, and that was important to him. The vital spark between them was very real, and they quickly became passionately involved with each other at a juncture when so much was happening for Neil.

In March, his court dispute with Bang Records had finally wound up; the result was that he was free to pursue a new recording contract elsewhere. By April, Columbia Records and Warner Records were among the labels considering signing Diamond. In the end, in May 1968, he struck a five-year, $250,000 deal with Uni Records, a division of MCA based in Hollywood, to deliver eight albums. The deal did not demand that Neil uproot from New York, but he was ready to make that move, and it seemed like the logical next step for him. His life in New York was over, at least as he had known it thus far.

His first marriage, made on the east coast, was finished. He had successfully severed from his first New York City-based record label, even as he also parted company now from Fred Weintraub, who had acted as his manager. As he assessed his position at this point, he was 27 years old, with a new record deal and a new woman at his side who was happy to move with him. A new location was immensely appealing after all the stress and strain of late. So Diamond quit the east coast for California, eager to open a new chapter in his life. He later said: 'The pace of life in New York was very fast, and the west coast gave me time to relax and plan where I was heading.'

The geographical shift away from his past was pivotal for Diamond. In Los Angeles, where everything was so very different, he figured out that he could discard former shackles in songwriting and concentrate instead on producing material that would challenge him more. For the first time, too, he discovered a love of recording.

That said, not everything about being a native New Yorker was left behind. Crucially, Neil has confessed: 'The fact that I'm from New York is reflected in everything I write. All my songs have the tensions, the loves, the hates and nostalgia created by a big city. It's inborn.' Nostalgia was rife in 'Brooklyn Roads', Neil's first composition written for Uni Records. 'Shilo', as yet unreleased, was his first consciously autobiographical offering, but 'Brooklyn Roads' became his first such song to be released.

This slow number reinforced his boyhood propensity to create an illusionary setting for himself, and it spoke of how, academically, he had regularly vexed his parents. But in contrast with the dark shadows thrown by his earlier tale of an imaginary friend, and of empty, lonely stretches in his life, in this new number Neil primarily conjured up a warm, glowing picture of the other side of family life, growing up *chez* Diamond. With naked affection he evoked the tempting smells of tasty home cooking, and the flat above the butcher's shop in Flatbush, Brooklyn, of racing his young brother home, of his loving mother's care and his father's hearty bear hugs. Neil confessed: 'I never thought the song would be a hit, but that's the last thing I'm thinking about when writing a song. I'm just trying to let the emotion speak for itself.'

Backed by 'Holiday Inn Blues', when 'Brooklyn Roads' was

released in June, sure enough it climbed no higher than number 58. It was not quite the flying start Uni Records were looking for. Indeed, worse chart performances were to follow before the year was out, but the label was happy to keep faith with its new signing.

It was perhaps predictable that Neil Diamond would not be entirely happy with every aspect of his new life and environment in the sun-drenched state synonymous with golden beaches and beautiful bodies. By summer 1968, Diamond's darkly handsome looks were now very well defined, and he had grown his abundant hair well down over his collar. But although he looked the part, he was no long-haired hippy, or into drug taking.

There is a blanket tendency to look back on this period as a halcyon time, to associate it – particularly in terms of west coast America – with the harmless image of smiley people wearing patterned kaftans, waving joss sticks and slotting roses into the gun barrels of US Army troops in protest against the Vietnam war. Reality was very different.

Dr Stephen Perrin of Liverpool Hope University, a 1960s/1970s counterculture specialist, explains: 'In 1967 you had had Scott McKenzie singing about people coming to San Francisco wearing flowers in their hair. But then the original hippies moved out of Haight-Ashbury and the Mafia moved in and controlled the drug supply. They caused an LSD famine and flooded the place with speed and heroin. So where we had the flower children before, we now had a bunch of very strung-out people.

'A little later, in 1969, came the Charles Manson murders, and all of the associations of the young people had gone. Even if the mainstream population had not agreed with the hippy students' messages of love and peace, still they could see the point of it and they had not considered these people to be a terrible threat.

'On top of the horrific Manson murders, the Rolling Stones' Altamont concert went hideously wrong when Meredith Hunter, an 18-year-old black youth in the audience, was savagely beaten to death by a handful of Hell's Angels. And it turned the whole hippy thing on its head. Suddenly, you couldn't even hitch-hike any more. Before, young people would have been picked up easily, without a thought, but the murders ended that overnight. Now, nobody would give anyone a lift who had long hair, for fear that they were a psychopath in the Manson mould. It all got very dark, very fast.'

Neil had not needed to wait for it to turn so bleak to recognise the scourge of drugs. In New York City, he had long since met the people who ran a drug rehabilitation centre called Phoenix House. Over the years, as a successful artiste, Diamond has frequently contributed the proceeds from gigs towards the work done there to help addicts get clean. Without fanfare, he has also spent time personally visiting the centre, talking with the dedicated counsellors and listening to the addicts tell him about their individual struggle to straighten out their lives. It gave him a very different, in-your-face view of drugs. 'I'm not a moraliser about drugs,' Diamond has insisted, 'but I've seen so many of my friends going down the tubes because they've been led on to experiment with hard drugs.'

What Neil had witnessed at Phoenix House led him, in 1968, to become involved in founding an organisation called MAD (Musicians Against Drugs), which quickly changed to PAD (Performers Against Drugs). He had already taken part recently in a MAD benefit concert at New York City's Philharmonic Hall. His switch of base to the extremely laid-back west coast changed nothing. He was resolute about his stand on drugs and was unafraid to pin his colours to the mast, even though it won him few friends in the music industry out there. In Los Angeles right then, rock stars were rapidly usurping movie stars as the new feted royalty, slavishly adored and emulated. With his anti-drug stance, Neil Diamond stood outside the favoured circle.

Diamond was no mouthpiece, bent on attracting attention by being controversial. But when he felt strongly enough about something, he usually came right out with it. In August 1968, he revived an old theme when he said that the American culture of

his generation '...picked up the torch from the nothing generation which gave us World War II, the Korean war, the Vietnam
war, alcoholism and more mental illness than ever before.
Thanks to them, these days it takes nerves of steel only to be
neurotic.'

Rebellion for the sheer sake of it never hit the spot with Neil
either. Maybe the fact that he had been married, was a father and
was not a footloose, giddy teenager also had something to do
with it, but he quickly found his off-duty society in California
comprised a party of two – himself and Marcia. Neil had been a
loner all his life, so it didn't trouble him not to be hanging out.
As far as he was concerned, being hip was a frivolous pastime for
those who had nothing constructive to do with their lives. He
simply became absorbed with building a new relationship and
developing his craft.

Uni Records appreciated that Neil was searching for a lyrical
freedom that would lend a new, mature dimension to his material. With 'Brooklyn Roads', he had given vent to his need to be
inward-looking. But he went almost too far out on a limb with the
anti-drug number 'The Pot Smoker's Song'. His association with
Phoenix House had prompted the song, which contained, spliced
between verses, spoken testimonials from young drug users who
made a distinct connection between starting on grass and
finding it was all too often a slippery slope to experimenting with
the harder stuff, thereby risking potentially fatal consequences.
The song went down like a lead balloon; worse, it made Neil
Diamond an object of ridicule to a sizeable section of the drug-
oriented hip music scene.

Candidly, he has since confessed: '"The Pot Smoker's Song"
almost cost me my career. People just laughed at it.' Fairly soon
afterwards, he admitted that the song had perhaps been misdir-
ected. Considering the source of its inspiration, he also came to
realise that it had even been misnamed. The addicts he felt for
were not on pot – heroin was the greater enemy, by far. 'The
Pot Smoker's Song' simply confirmed how much Neil Diamond
was an outsider in the west coast musical fraternity, and did

nothing for his popularity in social circles. Again, Diamond was unconcerned. He came to accept that he had scored an own goal, an error that he would privately analyse later. As to the rest? He had no burning desire to be gathered into the bosom of the in-crowd.

It wasn't essential to Neil Diamond to be loved by everyone, all of the time. To expect that, he figured, was setting oneself up for an inevitable fall. He *had* craved to be taken seriously, however, and felt that that was eluding him – which did get under his skin a bit, no matter how philosophical he managed to be. And all in all, growing as an artiste was proving to be an arduous business.

It was also hard to pigeonhole Neil Diamond. The glaringly obvious comparison was, of course, Paul Simon. But Diamond has long ago doused that one. He will acknowledge that a similarity exists in their respective backgrounds, and that Simon started some years before him which, as Neil once phrased it, puts Simon 'further ahead than I on the evolutionary scale'. But he has asserted of the legendary lyricist who provided a soundtrack for an entire generation: 'I always thought of Paul as being much more of an intellectual than I. I was a sheer emotional guy. Paul is a standard of excellence.'

Carving his own creative path in such a highly competitive industry was risky, to say the least, and Diamond was reliant on the record label's continuing patience. 'The Pot Smoker's Song' was not a single – it was only briefly an album track. His single, come August 1968, was 'Two-bit Manchild'/'Broad Old Woman (6 a.m. Insanity)', which creaked to a premature stop at number 66. A couple of months later, 'Sunday Sun'/'Honey Drippin' Times' fared slightly worse, halting at two places lower still. None of this augured well for the chances of Neil's first album for Uni, which was released in November.

Velvet Gloves And Spit was ambitious. Neil had made seriousness his watchword when Uni magnanimously gave him the green light to do an album purely on his own inclinations. As an attempt at a progressive work, it included 'Brooklyn Roads' and the two most recently released singles, plus the controversial 'Pot Smoker's Song', but the latter only on original pressings of the album. On later pressings, this track was deleted.

Velvet Gloves And Spit had an intriguing cover concept. The front sleeve showed an extreme close-up shot of Neil Diamond's face from his fringe to the bridge of his nose only, rendering his intense stare even more compelling. Inside the gatefold album, Neil was pictured in a leather jacket, standing with an arm propped somewhat incongruously on the shoulder of one of several naked female shop mannequins.

If it was difficult to figure out the thinking behind the image, it was even harder, it seems, for many to take to the material, for *Velvet Gloves And Spit* failed even to scrape into *Billboard*'s Top 200. It was his worst album performance yet, and Diamond puts his hands up to a gamble that did not pay off. He said soon afterwards: 'It was a failure as an experiment and was even embarrassing in spots, but the experience allowed me to set new reference points for myself.' Determined to view this album privately as an artistically valuable move, he had also enjoyed dabbling with various musical styles from pop through to rock, and had been bold enough to include comedic touches as well as some social commentary. But, bottom line, he was very conscious of having notched up another mishit.

He had also clocked up that in September Bang Records had released an album titled *Neil Diamond's Greatest Hits* which, although performing poorly, had at least registered on the charts by reaching number 100. Neil knew that although 1968 had been a dire year for him chartwise, he would move on to a better game. To find his individual identity as a lyricist, what he needed was new stimulus. He got that stimulus while he completed the last handful of a series of live gigs that had taken him around the country, playing mainly colleges, gymnasiums and fairs through-out the year. He had played a concert at the Biester Auditorium in Lombard, Illinois, at the end of November and was due to perform in Wichita Falls in Texas in a fortnight's time when, like millions of others, he found himself glued to a television screen on the evening of 8 December as NBC-TV aired a TV special, called *Elvis*.

Throughout the sixties, Elvis Presley's once sizzling sexuality had systematically been neutered as he had become mired in making a stream of vacuous Hollywood musicals, so banal in content that one film's threadbare plot simply ran seamlessly into the next. Elvis himself had found the inane scripts mind-numbingly boring, sadly only too aware that his intrinsic light and energy were in danger of being permanently extinguished. The stunning firebrand who had transformed popular music had not, however, been snuffed out. Looking leaner and fitter than he had done in years, dressed in slinky, soft black leather, with his jet-black hair quiffed fifties' style once more, Presley erupted onto the small screen that night in what has forever since been known as the '68 Comeback Special', and took the nation's breath away.

In January 1969, Elvis started long recording sessions at Chips Moman's American Sound Studios in Memphis, Tennessee. Invigorated by the massive response to his TV special, he was eager to re-engage with his exhilarating roots. Presley's scintillating rejuvenation, as it was seen at that time, in a wider sense also provided a vitalising spur to several jaded palates in the music industry.

Neil Diamond had not been in the business long enough to be jaded. But he was demoralised after a bad enough year in the charts, when Uni Records issued the song 'Practically Newborn', off *Velvet Gloves And Spit,* in the dying weeks of 1968. The single was stillborn, racking up the dubious distinction of being Diamond's first single in nearly three years not to chart at all. It meant that Neil acted on the uplift of Presley's blistering TV appearance. Soon after he had played his final gig of 1968, at the Haynes Gymnasium in Shreveport, Louisiana, he hightailed it to Memphis to start recording sessions in American Sound Studios, just prior to Elvis's imminent occupation.

This fresh environment, an inspired new attitude and a comforting awareness that the record company was not harrying him, all contributed to these sessions throwing up the songs that would give Neil Diamond the long-awaited big break he desperately needed. The work ethic in Memphis, too, operated in a more laid-back style that Neil was right then ready for. 'We had a ball,' he recalled. 'We cut a track and we went fishing. We'd cut another track, then go and have some beers.' That's not to say that Neil was not deeply involved in articulating his thoughts and emotions. His brain never really switched off. And it was in his Memphis hotel room one day, near the end of his stay in the Deep South that, with at least two future hit songs already in the can, he came up with what would become arguably his best-known song worldwide, 'Sweet Caroline'. While there was still no rigid format to the way Neil composed, by now he worked largely by first acquiring a sense of the *feel* of a song, sure that from there would stem the melody and the lyrics. 'A good song has a life of its own,' he has stated. 'It tells you when it's ready to come, and you have to sit there and try and catch it when it does.'

That day, Neil sat strumming around with his guitar, aching to hit a riff on which he could go to work. For long enough, teasingly, nothing would quite crystallise between the semi-formed notions running through his head and what his fingers were actually doing with the strings. Then, repeatedly humming and strumming the bare beginnings of a melody, trying to break the block, unable to articulate his next need, suddenly the fingers of his left hand involuntarily positioned themselves on the slender fretboard of his guitar in a pattern that was unfamiliar to him, but he strummed anyway and a sound rang out which stunned him. He had found a chord he had not even known existed, but which was the key to what became the distinctive sound of 'Sweet Caroline'. To this day, Neil finds it a mystifying moment. 'I have no way of explaining it,' he said.

From finding that breakthrough sound, Diamond took a mere one hour to write 'Sweet Caroline', and there are precious few countries in the world now where this song is not instantly recognised. He remains touched by that fact. 'It makes you feel that all the stupid things you've done over your life and career have a little bit of meaning,' he reflected.

Brimming with confidence in the quality of the songs he had recorded for his next album, Diamond left Memphis with a decided spring in his step to embark on his next round of live television and stage appearances. Early in the new year, he was one of a number of guests taking part in a round-the-table discussion about contentious current affairs on *The David Susskind Show*, during which Diamond gave his opinions and also upheld his open opposition to drugs. By now, he was more informed on the subject of drug abuse, and had even altered his views a little on marijuana; acknowledging that the real bogey was the harder stuff like cocaine and heroin.

This slightly more relaxed attitude to grass came at a time when, for a brief period, he took to smoking the odd joint out of sheer boredom when he hit the road again. Before any whiff of hypocrisy could waft in Diamond's direction, he was equally open about his own use of marijuana. Talking about this in 1976, he told *Rolling Stone* that he had at least been of an age at which he could distinguish between occasionally enjoying grass and being led onto anything harder.

The tedium Diamond found in touring lay in the endless travelling and being away from Marcia. When it came to showtime, though, he was thriving. The colour of his stage clothes continued to be a curious, but reliable, barometer of the state of his self-confidence, and in 1969 he was definitely blossoming. From wearing funereal black he had moved into browns, reds and blues – still dark, but definitely edging towards being less inhibited about drawing attention to himself as a performer. He still played songs with virtually no break in between them, for fear of hearing a deafening silence when he ended each number. And he still would not go off stage for a small intermission in case his audience took the chance to abscond before the second half got under way.

Kicking off on 26 January at the MSU Auditorium in East Lansing, Michigan, Diamond played Cleveland's Public Hall in Ohio before returning to the halls of academe with a gig at the University of Windsor in Ontario, Canada, just prior to taking a spell off the road, during which time his first single of the year was released. Called 'Brother Love's Travelling Salvation Show', and backed by 'A Modern Day Version of Love', it peaked in April at number 22, thereby restoring Neil Diamond to the Top 30. Betrayed by its title, the A-side was a heavily gospelised, rousing rocker, which winkled out the hidden rhythm soul inside most people. A notable exception was America's Bible Belt, where radio stations chose en masse to deny the single the oxygen of any airplay.

Highly individual, and delivered in a loud revivalist style, 'Brother Love's Travelling Salvation Show' included a lengthy sermon midway, in which Diamond, casting himself in the role of enthusiastic preacher, calls on everyone to join together to become spiritual brothers and sisters, complete equals, with no distinction based on skin colour, religious creed, sexual proclivities, social status or age. It was an all-out message of inspirational love, and an expression of hope that the world's population could unite to share life's gifts.

Initially, it was an easier number to have created in the recording studio than it was to perform live. Still, the sheer fact that stage renditions of the song required a strong theatrical grip to pull off effectively meant that Neil was pushed even harder into developing his growing communication skills with his audiences. It took confidence and a commanding stage presence, and was the first of several such melodramatic songs to form the core of Diamond's famously dynamic live sets.

When the single's parent album, *Brother Love's Travelling Salvation Show*, was released in April, while it charted, it stalled at number 82. The album proffered a mix of musical styles, from the wake-me-up title track at one end of the spectrum, to the softly sensitive ballad 'And The Grass Won't Pay No Mind' at the other, in which, while showcasing the rich timbre of his deep voice, Neil conjures up images of a pastoral love scene that captures a fleeting moment in time.

The landmark release of the year, however, was indubitably the single 'Sweet Caroline'. Backed by 'Dig In', with its soaring style and stirring arrangement, 'Sweet Caroline' simply stormed up the US charts until it lodged at number four in late July. Neil Diamond's highest chart placing yet also became his first million-plus selling single, and at last it catapulted his name firmly onto the musical map.

It was a moment of immense satisfaction for Neil. But as the praise and plaudits suddenly started to come his way, Diamond displayed his ingrained modesty about his lyrical skills. Not long after the release of 'Sweet Caroline', he told reporters: 'I am constantly amazed that I'm able to write a song – to just take a piece of paper and at the end of an hour, a day, a week or a month, to have a song on it, a lyric that makes sense and a melody I enjoy. I never considered myself creative as such. The songs just say something I feel.'

This sudden change in fortune meant that when Diamond took to the road again in September 1969, there were certain changes – the size of some of the venues he played for one, and also a new touring band to back him. In Los Angeles, Neil's manager was Joe Sutton, who had been helping to bring this band together for some time. Finally, he and Diamond had plumped for experienced musicians Randy Sterling on bass guitar, Eddie Rubin to play drums and Carol Hunter as lead guitarist.

In accepting to work with Neil Diamond, Carol Hunter became the only female in an otherwise all-male domain. She had already played in a number of bands in New York, earning a crust at one point by performing in what were termed 'basket joints'. These were bars and coffee houses in Greenwich Village where the management did not pay the entertainers a fee for their services. Instead, a basket sat beside the artiste, who depended on a generous crowd being sufficiently impressed to dig deep into their pockets. After a spell at the prestigious Julliard School of Music, Carol Hunter had quit New York for Los Angeles, where she had acquired a fine reputation as an excellent session musician. In August 1969, she had been lined up for some studio work with another singer. But just as that project fell through at the last moment, she was tipped off by a producer who knew through Joe Sutton that Neil Diamond was looking for a lead guitarist to join his band for an upcoming tour.

Initially, Carol wasn't interested in the post because she wanted to concentrate on playing bass guitar, but the guy persevered, and she finally agreed to meet Neil, although their first encounter was scarcely auspicious. They met one morning at a rehearsal studio in Hollywood, too early in the day for either of them. Carol Hunter recalled: 'Neil had been mixing all night, and I had just woken up. I think we were just about in equally bad moods. I really bungled it and the audition really wasn't much. I played "Rudolph The Rednosed Reindeer" and a couple of ragtime pieces. He was so taken with the ridiculousness of it all that he decided to take me on.' It was meant to be a three-month stint, but Carol would be part of Neil Diamond's backing band for the next two years, during which time they became friends.

Diamond preferred to have an amicable, informal rapport with all those around him professionally, while at the same time making it known that he expected his band and road crew to provide a reliable foundation for him. Carol Hunter later described Diamond as a lovely man who did not resort to pulling rank but who was, without a doubt, the boss.

It had been four months since Neil wound up his last tour when he got back in harness towards the end of September with six sell-out LA shows at the Troubadour in West Hollywood. The difference a million-selling single made was easy to see. Where critics had been scathing before, or had ignored him altogether, now it was safe to praise him. In fairness, some music critics did only now come upon Neil Diamond for the first time, and immediately recognised his talents. When that happened, Neil appreciated their supportive comments.

Robert Hilburn for the *Los Angeles Times*, writing after the first of the Troubadour gigs, weighed in with: 'Neil Diamond is an excellent reminder of what made early rock such an exciting sound.' Neil would never live or die personally or professionally by the critics' favour, but good reviews ringing in his ears helped set him up for the rest of the trip. Before the year's end, Diamond trekked to Utah, Massachusetts, Mississippi and Alabama, pitching up at Memphis in October to play the Mid-South Coliseum, before reverting to a college visit in Beaver Falls, Pennsylvania, and completing gigs in Maryland and Texas.

When Neil set out on this tour, Marcia was pregnant, but it was never his way anyway to lead a wild after-gig existence on the road. There were rarely get-togethers after a show. Neil and his crew were usually tired and hungry, and since there was inevitably an early rise next morning, before catching the next plane as the tour crisscrossed the States, partying was the last thing on his mind.

The end of this tour virtually dovetailed with the official end of a personal era for Neil when, days after returning home to Los Angeles, on 25 November 1969, his and Jaye's divorce finally came through. Nine days later, on 4 December, Neil and four months' pregnant Marcia Murphey were wed in their LA home, both believing that this marriage would last for ever. There was scant time to savour married bliss, however, as the wheels were turning fast for Neil.

At the end of November, he made an appearance on the famous *Ed Sullivan Show*, performing 'Sweet Caroline' and his latest release 'Holly Holy'. Backed by 'Hurtin' You Don't Come Easy', this new single peaked around the time Neil remarried at number six in the US charts. Of his songs thus far, 'Holly Holy' was Diamond's personal favourite. He felt it had a kind of magic, and a huge chunk of the record-buying public agreed when they made the poignant portrayal of pure love between a man and a woman another million-plus seller. Alongside a number called 'And The Singer Sings His Song', which promotes the impressions of hazy, carefree summer days, 'Holly Holy' proved to be one of the most noteworthy tracks on the album *Touching You, Touching Me*, which gave Neil his highest-charting album when it peaked at number 30, early in January 1970, and earned him his first gold album award, just in advance of him facing his busiest tour schedule yet.

By the end of the decade that was just dawning, Diamond declared: 'I could survive without the road. Each live performance feels like some part of my life is being torn away.' Right then, though, he was determined to consolidate his new-found profile. He was also becoming frankly addicted to the adrenalin rush of walking out on stage to the resounding reaction of his increasingly voluble, devoted followers. Neil's friend, songwriter Ellie Greenwich, described the sensation of walking out on stage as 'the ultimate orgasm'. Neil would never quite couch it in such earthy terms, but certainly, over time, legions of his fans would come in their droves to genuflect at the altar of Diamond.

Neil was also becoming a more familiar face on network television, and he took time out to guest on *The Glen Campbell Show*, days after he had picked up his tour in Michigan. Playing civic arenas and huge auditoriums was now the norm, and while Diamond enjoyed the fact that his songs were reaching out to larger numbers, he was at the same time conscious of the risk of losing touch with his fans. He said: 'I hate performing to an audience with my back on them, when about a fifth of the seats are behind the stage. I'd rather play to two thousand personally, than six thousand impersonally.'

While he gigged around New Mexico, North Dakota and Wisconsin in February, his next single was released – 'Until It's Time For You To Go'/'And The Singer Sings His Song'. The A-side, taken from *Touching You, Touching Me*, was a cover version of a song by Buffy Sainte-Marie, the Canadian singer who scored a universal hit with the theme song to the controversially violent 1970 western, *Soldier Blue*. Hard on the heels of two consecutive million-selling singles, this cover version disappointingly dropped anchor at a sobering number 53. But Diamond's focus switched when he realised that his old record label, Bang Records, had released 'Shilo' onto the market to take advantage of his rising status. Ironically, 'Shilo'/'La Bamba' scored a number 24 hit, belatedly vindicating the trenchant position Neil had taken, more than two years earlier, when he had staunchly believed in this very personal song, and Bert Berns had not.

As spring progressed, live performance nailed Neil's attention. Throughout March, he concentrated keenly on impressing the Canadians, turning in memorable performances in Ontario, Alberta and Manitoba before returning to the States to whisk through Tacoma in Washington, before heading to California, where he ended the month once again with a run of half a dozen shows at Los Angeles's Troubadour. It was no accident that he had deliberately kept April clear of bookings and wound his way home before the start of the month. He needed to be free of commitments to be with Marcia for the birth of their first child. Obligingly, at the end of April 1970, Jesse Michael Diamond made his entrance into the world, giving Neil his first son to add to the two daughters he had had with Jaye. Thrilled as he was with the new arrival, Neil had only ten days to dote on the latest star in the family before he headed to Austin in Texas for a concert at the Municipal Auditorium that would start the tour carousel off again.

Perhaps fatherhood and/or a rare sense of contentment had something to do with the new direction Neil's songwriting took around spring 1970. Certainly, he felt the confidence to experiment, and his leanings were towards the percussive sound of African rhythms. He pursued this intriguing path in more depth later in the year; but early on, he had come up with a haunting number called 'Soolaimon'. According to Diamond the title was intended to be an interpretation of the word 'salamah', which in several tongues means hello and welcome, as well as goodbye and peace be with you. There was also a religious flavour to the song's lyrics, and an overall soaring, optimistic tone. 'Soolaimon'/'And The Grass Won't Pay No Mind' was different, but it took Diamond back into the US Top 30 in May.

After relentlessly clocking up the miles through June and July, following a gig at the Merriweather Post Pavilion in Columbia, Maryland, Neil took nearly the whole of August off, retrenching to spend time with his wife and three-month-old baby. Home was now a luxurious property in Coldwater Canyon, built in the style of the renowned architect Frank Lloyd Wright;

the estate had formerly belonged to a vice-president of Universal Pictures. Privacy was provided not only by the impressively long walkway up to the front of the house, but also by the massive grounds. Neil was particularly taken by a pepper tree in the luscious garden, and a stone statue of a frog. A forest of flowers and shrubs complemented the verdant lawns and provided a tranquil paradise in which to unwind and relax.

In addition to settling into life as an attentive husband and father, Neil enjoyed the cut and thrust of sword fencing practice. He also liked to take off on horseback, to be alone with his thoughts; there was a part of him that was still strongly solitary.

As it happened, his first chart single, 'Solitary Man', teamed with 'The Time Is Now', had been rereleased by Bang Records in the summer and climbed to number 21 by September 1970. When 'Do It'/'Hanky Panky' emerged before the year was out, sticking at number 36, it became obvious that Bang Records had decided to compete for the money in the pockets of Neil Diamond fans by releasing a stream of old records when Uni Records were producing his new material.

Diamond, though, was determined not to look back. He had a new wife, a new child and a new home to go with his hard-won, new-found fame. He also had a new song up his sleeve for his next single that would bounce old Bang Record releases well into the shade.

CHAPTER 4

Between Two Shores

THROUGHOUT 1970 the musical map had been inexorably altering. In spring, Simon and Garfunkel had split just as their landmark album, *Bridge Over Troubled Water*, was taking the world by storm, and The Beatles publicly imploded. On 18 September, the dynamic lead guitarist Jimi Hendrix, whose flame had briefly burned bright, died. Three weeks later strident rock chick Janis Joplin was found at a Hollywood hotel with fresh needle marks in one arm; both were victims of an accidental drug overdose.

In the case of Simon and Garfunkel and The Beatles, individual solo careers would rise from the wreckage, but for many of their staunch devotees things would never quite be the same again. As one era went twilight, however, the next dawned, bringing with it an emerging new echelon of stars among whom, Neil Diamond was pleased to see, solo performers were at last coming more strongly into vogue.

Country-folk singer-songwriter John Denver soon landed his debut chart hit with 'Take Me Home, Country Roads'. Canadian singer-songwriter Neil Young, once a folk circuit favourite, then part of Crosby, Stills, Nash & Young, struck out solo in September 1970 with the hit album *After The Gold Rush*. And a new face in town on west coast America, come that August, was Elton John, then just a piano player from across the pond.

On one level, there were some similarities between the short, flamboyant musician from Pinner, Middlesex, and the tall, handsome New York-born songwriter. Elton John was already teamed up with lyricist Bernie Taupin, but, like Neil, he had started out working as a staff writer for a few pounds a week for music publishers. Lulu had performed one of John's songs, 'I Can't Go On Living Without You', and Elton had recently signed to Uni Records. 'Border Song', from the album *Elton John*, gave the future star his US singles chart debut when it made it to number 92. He had yet to embark on his first Stateside tour when, on 25 August 1970, Neil Diamond introduced his fellow record label signing to his first audience at the famous Troubadour club in West Hollywood. Just as Elton John was still an unknown quantity in America, so Neil Diamond was unfamiliar to the British public. But that would change with Neil's next single release.

The first step in Diamond's elevation to superstar status came with 'Cracklin' Rosie', an up-tempo song which was instantly infectious but which actually had subtle, hidden depths. Superficially, it appeared to be about a goodtime woman – maybe even a hooker, if 'store bought' was interpreted as paying for the pleasure of her company. The truth is, Cracklin' Rosie referred to a cheap red wine.

For some time, Diamond had had squirrelled away in the back of his head a folk tale he had heard about a native American tribe living on a north Canadian reservation, where the men well outnumbered the women. Come the weekend, not all of the guys got themselves a girl; those left on their lonesome sought solace in a potent red wine called Cracklin' Rose. The idea that getting a high from this liquor was a substitute (and one with fewer complications) for bedding a woman had prompted Neil into composing a song which seemed to be saying one thing, while having a unique subtext.

Backed by 'Lordy', 'Cracklin' Rosie' sufficiently hit the spot by October 1970 to propel it all the way to the top of the singles chart. Along with revelling in his first number one hit, Neil also racked up his third million-seller. As he had done in the past, he still looked to Britain to see how the song would fare there. To date, he had a dismal track record – a run of 14 flops – in the buoyant British music scene and he was becoming somewhat resigned to it. 'I was concerned about not breaking into the UK,' he said, 'but I just felt I was fated and that my music would never be heard in Britain.'

He was wrong. At the end of the first week of November, 'Cracklin' Rosie' tagged on to the tail end of the UK Top 40. Four weeks after that, the single peaked at number three, sandwiched between the number two hit 'Voodoo Chile', by the Jimi Hendrix Experience, and Don Fardon's 'Indian Reservation'. Diamond had competed with top-notch company. Riding high at the top of the chart was Dave Edmunds, with what would be 1970's Christmas number one, 'I Hear You Knocking'. And in the Top Ten were T-Rex, McGuinness Flint and Elvis Presley, whose single, 'I've Lost You', had shot its bolt at number nine. 'Cracklin' Rosie' held on to the UK number three spot for four consecutive weeks.

In late summer Diamond climbed once more onto the busy tour circuit. Stopping in Bob Dylan's birthplace of Duluth, Minnesota, mid-September to play the Arena, a fortnight later he played a particularly successful show at the Convention Center in Anaheim, California, about which the *Hollywood Reporter* said: 'Neil Diamond received a standing ovation from 9,000 fans on Saturday night. It was spontaneous and deserved. Diamond is a great artist and a dynamic and warm performer. In a smaller room, such as the Troubadour, his every body move and nuance makes the place come alive. He's not a mover in that tasteless, blatant sex symbol trick. He has taste. In a big concert, it is difficult to achieve a rapport with a crowd and make each member of the audience feel as if you are singing to him, but Diamond does.' Praising renditions of several numbers, the review singled out 'Brother Love's Travelling Salvation Show', highlighting that when Diamond went into the song's sermon, it provoked the crowd into cheering at the top of their lungs.

By the end of the first week of October, having just performed at the Pershing Auditorium in Lincoln, Nebraska, Neil took a ten-day break to promote his hit 'Cracklin' Rosie'. On 16 October he then hit Tempe, Arizona, commencing a two-month trek designed to take him from coast to coast across America. While out east, before the end of the month, he played his most prestigious engagements to date – two sell-out nights at New York City's Carnegie Hall. His parents, Rose and Kieve, attended; appearing at this world-famous venue is a high spot for any New York-born entertainer.

For Neil Diamond, however, the rush of live performance – especially in evocative venues – was often immediately followed by a drastic feeling of anti-climax. To try to cushion this drop, Neil let it be known through a press release that members of his various swelling fan clubs would be welcome to stay behind after the shows ended, to spend time with him backstage. He stated: 'I don't just want fans asking for autographed pictures of me. I would like them to be there, to share with me the elation I feel after a good show. Sometimes, it gets lonely after the audience leaves.' In addition to live performance, Diamond stepped up his television appearances. He was on a roll, which was consolidated with the release of his first live album.

Called *Gold*, it featured ten songs, including 'Sweet Caroline', 'Cherry Cherry', 'Kentucky Woman' and 'Holly Holy'; they had all been recorded months earlier during a particularly dynamic performance at the Troubadour. Reaching number ten, *Gold* gave Neil Diamond his highest placed album yet. This proof of his burgeoning popularity lent Diamond added impetus towards taking a gamble he had been working on for some time.

That gamble was a body of work, released as his next album, called *Tap Root Manuscript*. In the mid-1980s, after repeatedly listening to an audio cassette of accordion and drum-driven South African township jive music, Paul Simon had set out on a musical journey of discovery which culminated in the controversial but award-winning, multi-million selling album *Graceland*. A full 15 years before that, in early 1970, Neil Diamond had become drawn to exploring African-inspired music after a friend had let him hear a record of an African tribal mass – a 'missa' – which had knocked Neil out. He had become obsessed with gathering in as many examples of this music as he could, and soon knew that he was destined to experiment with these evocative sounds.

The first rock star with the vision to record ethnic music and to see its intrinsic worth was Rolling Stones founder Brian Jones. In 1968, Jones wanted to bring Moroccan music to the masses by recording the Master Musicians of Jajouka, but world music, as it would become known, was not universally embraced then. Two years on, at the dawn of the 1970s, it was no different. Nevertheless, the perennial fear of feeling hidebound in any way had played its part in prodding Neil Diamond in this risky direction. He revealed: 'I needed a specific and immediate point of departure. I had tried to write one song that would encompass my feelings and love for African music, which was "Soolaimon". I quickly realised, though, that four minutes wasn't going to be nearly enough. Hence it grew into "The African Trilogy".'

In reality, the trilogy was six numbers; Neil labelled it a folk ballet, and it centred around the three phases of life: childhood; adulthood; and old age. Needless to say, *Tap Root Manuscript*, on which Diamond worked with Hollywood arranger Marty Paich to orchestrate the African themes, was an ambitious project. It was also split in two halves, in more ways than one.

Side one contained more conventional tracks, such as 'Cracklin' Rosie' and the slow ballad 'Coldwater Morning'. This rather melancholic song, with its prominent piano work, held a strong longing element both vocally and musically. It was unusual in that, in places, Diamond reached for a far higher register sound than he had ever done before, to contrast with his deep baritone. Side two, on the other hand, showcased just how experimental he had been with, in addition to 'Soolaimon', the tracks 'Missa' and 'African Suite' as well as 'Madrigal', 'Childsong' and 'I Am The Lion'.

That Neil was very proud of this musical exploration was made clear in the liner notes for *Tap Root Manuscript*, where he wrote about falling in love with 'a woman named gospel', of soaking up what 'she' had to offer, by attending Harlem churches and revivalist meetings in the black south. He stated: 'I found a great yearning to know of her roots. I found them in Africa and they left me breathless. "The African Trilogy" is an attempt to convey my passion for the folk music of that black continent.'

Diamond could easily have fallen on his face commercially with such a radical departure, at a time when common sense might have screamed at him to hold the line that was only newly gaining true strength. However, he got away with it. *Tap Root Manuscript* peaked in December at number 13. Critically, it even prompted Britain's *Melody Maker* to declare: 'Things are changing for Neil Diamond. Now, his name can be mentioned to intellectual friends.' Diamond no doubt permitted himself a wry smile at the snobbery implicit in that intended compliment.

Something Neil had no snobbery about – even as his star as a lyricist was rising – was recording cover versions of popular songs for his albums. On *Touching You, Touching Me* he had included his interpretations of Fred Neil's 'Everybody's Talkin'', Jerry Jeff Walker's much-covered 'Mr Bojangles', and Joni Mitchell's folksy song, 'Both Sides Now'. On *Tap Root Manuscript* he had included the Bobby Russell and Bobby Scott-penned ballad, 'He Ain't Heavy, He's My Brother'. Featuring session piano work by Elton John, this had been a summer 1969 smash hit single on both sides of the Atlantic for the British band The Hollies. By spring 1970, the number had notched up a million-plus seller for The Hollies. When Neil Diamond's version was released that December as the second cut from *Tap Root Manuscript*, with 'Free Life' on the flip side, it halted at number 20.

Throughout the year, Bang Records continued to release Neil Diamond recordings, including an album titled *Shilo*. But, before the year's end, it was for the success of his new material that Neil picked up three *Billboard* magazine awards. He came second in the Singles Artiste category, runner-up as the Easy Listening Artiste of 1970, but was voted the number one Male Singles Vocalist of the Year. By the time Neil graciously accepted these trophies, he had already ended his live gigging for the year, winding up on 11 December with a concert in Dallas, Texas. He was stepping back from stage performances for a short while, to spend time with Marcia and the children, and also to take stock of his career.

Creatively, he was restless again, in need of a challenge, some new horizon to explore that would stretch him. He had a project in mind, but before he could tackle it, he hiked off at the turn of the year to Britain on a four-day whirlwind promotional drive to boost 'Cracklin' Rosie'. It was his first blitz on the UK, and the British press welcomed him with open arms. After one media scrum, Gillian Saich for *New Musical Express* wrote: 'Neil Diamond arrived in this country to be greeted by the acclaim he has long deserved.' Diamond's inbred politesse and impeccable manners clearly bowled over the female journalists in particular. Commenting glowingly on Neil's handsome looks and gentlemanly style, Saich waxed: 'He seems to speak in calm, thoughtful, flowing poetry.' Diamond realised he would not always bask in such warm waters with the critics, so he absorbed their approbation while it came his way.

By the time he returned to the States he was already in some inner turmoil. *Time* magazine had featured him in an article titled 'Tin Pan Tailor'. Pictorially in the piece, his image was that of a Brooklyn tough, oozing edgy street cred, when in reality his life was spent in conspicuously luxurious comfort in the exclusive and rarefied celebrity sector of Los Angeles. Of course, he *did* come from Brooklyn and *had been* streetwise, but that was being steadily sanitised the further he climbed up the ladder of success that he craved. The question of just where he belonged now was beginning to get under his skin to a serious degree. A deep thinker and prone to tormenting himself, Neil approached his 30th birthday on 24 January 1971 with a full-blown identity crisis brewing.

Matters came to a head when he tried to explore that challenging horizon he'd had in mind by attempting to break into acting. His ambitions in this field went beyond popping up in an episode of a TV series, such as he had done in *Mannix*. This time he wanted the works – to take on the lead role in a feature movie. It would have been a tall enough order even had he not been wrestling with unease as to his roots and future direction. Arguably, auditioning for any major acting role right then was a recipe for trouble – let alone for a role that was guaranteed to be controversial.

By the start of 1971 a film project based on the life of the iconoclastic comedian Lenny Bruce was under way; it was never going to be an easy one to bring to the silver screen. In the late 1950s/early 1960s, Lenny Bruce had been a much troubled stand-up nightclub comic whose largely obscene humour and dialogue drew him to the attention of the authorities. In 1964, Bruce was charged by the police under US obscenity law after having used more than 100 obscene or offensive words in a single performance. After a six-month-long trial he was convicted. But, before he could serve any jail time, he was found dead in Hollywood in 1966 of a drug overdose.

Although it is hard for most people to find much artistic merit in scatology, some came to champion Lenny Bruce, or at least to view him as a victim of unacceptable and relentless harassment by the state. In 1981, Bob Dylan released a powerful tribute to Lenny Bruce in which he openly railed against the pressures placed upon the comedian. The single did not chart – perhaps a sign that public distaste for Bruce's style had not much altered. Indeed, it would take nearly 40 years for Lenny Bruce to be granted a posthumous pardon by the state of New York. On Christmas Eve 2003, State Governor George Pataki stated that the pardon represented New York's commitment to the fundamental right of freedom of speech.

In early 1971, Neil Diamond was not drawn to depicting Lenny Bruce on screen because he either championed or rejected the controversial comedian. He saw the intriguing film role as something into which he could sink his teeth. For Diamond, the prospect of acting was no mild distraction. His audience communication skills at gigs were developing rewardingly, but he wanted more. Believing that there were several levels on which an artiste should try to touch an audience, he said: 'Maybe films can do it for me. My attitude to films is the same one I had towards songwriting in the beginning. I want to do so much and I think I'm going to be good at it.'

For months he had cast his eyes over possible screenplays, but his adrenalin pumped when he read the script for the proposed Lenny Bruce biopic. His attraction was an unusually profound one, even for him. 'Bruce's language and thoughts were so violent,' he said. 'It was almost an intellectual form of vomiting. He was saying all the things I had been holding in, "fuck", "shit", "death" and "kill". And all of those things that he was getting out, I found that they were coming out with me. It was all the anger that was pent up in me.' The intense connection Diamond felt would have a disturbing consequence, but he was determined to be put forward for the role.

The screen test he landed in early 1971 did not go well. Neil was fired up about the part, and properly prepared, yet when he did his scenes he was aware of an abject hollowness deep inside that told him he had failed. After one scene, he trudged off set straight to his dressing room thoroughly depressed, sure that he had made a miserable mess of the take. He was being unnecessarily harsh on himself. The film-makers actually thought more highly of his screen test than Diamond did. But, as it happened, the entire project soon foundered.

Market forces were controlling the purse strings. The movie blockbuster drawing in huge box-office receipts right then was the schmaltzy *Love Story*, the Paramount-made, Arthur Hiller-directed film starring Ali MacGraw and Ryan O'Neal, in which the beautiful young heroine dies tragically. The powers behind the vastly different Lenny Bruce project saw the way the wind was blowing, so in spring 1971 the biopic was put on ice. Diamond said at the time: 'The movie company backed out, thanks to the publicity afforded to *Love Story* and the romantic trend it is heralding. They think by the time the Bruce film would be out that no one would want to go see it.'

It was another three years before this biopic saw the light of day. *Lenny*, scripted by Julian Barry from his play, and directed by Bob Fosse for United Artists, hit US cinema screens in 1974. It was shot in atmospheric black and white, and starred Dustin Hoffman, who had already been Oscar-nominated twice for his roles in *The Graduate* and *Midnight Cowboy*. It is hard to say if the passage of time had made the Lenny Bruce biopic any more successful than it might have been in 1971. Of the 1974 movie, the *New Yorker* film critic wrote that it was 'for audiences who want to believe that Lenny Bruce was a saintly gadfly who was martyred for having lived before his time'. *Halliwell's Film Guide* classed it 'Filmically extremely clever, emotionally hollow.'

In the first quarter of 1971, 'emotionally hollow' was a good summary of how Neil Diamond felt. His identity crisis had been building before what he felt was the debacle of his film screen test. His personal sense of failure then only fuelled that, and worse. Through auditioning to portray Lenny Bruce, Neil had discovered a wildly intoxicating liberty in being able to articulate violent, unrestrained thoughts and words that he would never have otherwise expressed. But the experience had a worrying backlash on him.

It was curiously stimulating to Neil to climb inside the skin of a man so unlike himself, but he was frightened by what it had unlocked in him personally. He had uncovered a side of his personality that he was unwilling to admit existed. 'I couldn't deal with that,' he confessed. He quickly put himself into professional therapy to help him work his way out of that fear. His own self-analysis, meanwhile, actually began during his screen test experience when, sunk in dark despair in his dressing room, he picked up his guitar and began to write what would become one of his most famous songs. Where 'Sweet Caroline' had rushed upon him in a single hour, this time giving voice to his deepening sense of internal isolation would take months.

It was not uninterrupted time. On 12 February 1971, Neil was committed to restarting an extended series of gigs, which kicked off at the Milwaukee Auditorium in Wisconsin. On the face of it, his frame of mind might not have seemed the best in which to handle stage work. Yet perhaps live performance was, in fact, part of what he needed to help unravel the intense tussle going on inside him. For Neil was no more than a handful of concerts into this new tour, when the state of his self-confidence as a public performer passed a milestone. It happened when he took to the stage at the Gill Coliseum in Corvallis, Oregon, dressed all in showy white. He later described that decision as a break-through. He saw wearing white symbolically, as a conspicuous sign that he was finally lowering his defences.

It augmented his returning self-confidence when he picked off more recording success in Britain ahead of making his debut European concert appearances. The albums *Tap Root Manuscript* and *Gold* simultaneously chalked up number 19 and number 23 placings respectively in the UK chart in April, following on the number eight hit he had freshly scored with 'Sweet Caroline' on its reissue in Britain to capitalise on the popularity of 'Cracklin' Rosie'.

For all that, spring 1971 was not an easy time for Neil Diamond. He continued to feel conflicted on different fronts. Taking just one issue – whether to aim to please the audience or the critics – on the one hand he declared: 'I felt that it was more democratic to try to please the audience.' On the other, he was adamant that: 'If an artiste follows the dictates of his audience, he is slave to a thousand masters.' It was tough enough satisfy-ing himself.

During a period of intensive inner reflection, while away from the stage, Neil continued to concentrate on writing that one song that he had started in January, aware that it had become his most arduous lyrical test yet, but unable to shelve it. For his need to express himself this time around was even more paramount than normal. He once claimed: 'I can only write when I feel in the mood and I write my best songs when I'm happy. When I'm down, I'm too busy feeling depressed and worrying to get the chance to write.' This song would be a spectacular exception to that school of thought.

When Neil had picked up his guitar that day in the dressing room at the film studio, within fifteen minutes the unusual title,

'I Am...I Said' had suggested itself to him. Intriguingly then, he had quickly come up with a line about a frog who fantasised about one day turning into a king. From that point on, Neil hadn't been able to let go. Every day, he had locked himself in a room and struggled with his thoughts. 'It was extremely difficult,' he admitted, 'because I had to spend such a lot of time thinking about what I was, before the song could be written.' He has described how he fought with the material, even cursing thoughts out of himself. He went so far as to liken the song to an adversary who refused to submit. His involvement with it was clearly his most mentally intense.

He can vouch that: '"I Am...I Said" is a very complicated song because my feelings were very complex when I wrote it. It tells of feelings lost, and is full of questions, doubts and insecurities.' He later admitted that the crux was an underlying need he had harboured at the time to leave Los Angeles and go back east, to go home to his roots, even while he had just come to realise that there was no going back, that times and circumstances had changed things for ever. Conflicts, frustrations and fears made up the mosaic of a song that, taking four months to come to fruition, encapsulated his current view of life. The number had been agonisingly personal to write, but he later described the lyrics as easily the most satisfying he had written at that point.

Since starting to write songs in his teens, Neil Diamond had primarily wanted lyrics to reflect his place and direction in life, but never before had his lyrics quite so nakedly exposed the depth of his innermost demons. In recording this number, too, his stringent need to articulate his disturbingly profound sense of dislocation was hauntingly conveyed by the skin-tingling depth of his resonating voice, and was especially evident in the occasional unique crack in his voice, which came across almost as a tormented cry from his soul.

'I Am...I Said'/'Done Too Soon' was released while Diamond gigged across America, and peaked in the US singles chart in May 1971 at number four. In Britain, after ten weeks in the Top 40, 'Sweet Caroline' had just dropped out of the charts when, still in May, 'I Am...I Said' entered at number 33. Initially, it was a slow mover, then it started to motor. On its sixth week on the charts, in mid-June, 'I Am...I Said' nudged out 'Brown Sugar', the best Rolling Stones' single in years, and Free's rousing rocker, 'My Brother Jake', to leapfrog comfortably into the number four spot.

Where Neil Diamond had consciously shone a public light onto a very private state of mind with 'I Am...I Said', in the case of the single's B-side song, 'Done Too Soon', he had taken a far wider view. In doing so, he had come up with a number that ranks among his most unusual compositions. Diamond saw his job as a lyricist as trying to say something a little different, to be thought-provoking when he could. In 'Done Too Soon' he had been moved to highlight just how many talented people, down the years, had died too young.

Among the 25 names he crammed into the two-minute, 45-second song, starting with Jesus Christ and ending with the silent movie star Buster Keaton, Diamond also mentioned Alan Freed, the influential disc jockey who had died aged 43 in 1965, but omitted the highest profile celebrity casualty of recent times – Rolling Stone Brian Jones, who had been murdered in the swimming pool at his beautiful Sussex country home in July 1969.

With uncanny timing, 'Done Too Soon' had not long been released as a single A-side in its own right, in June, when almost exactly two years to the day from the Stone's demise, on 3 July 1971, The Doors' frontman, Jim Morrison, added his name to the roll-call of premature death. With slight echoes of Lenny Bruce, the overtly sexual singer, nicknamed The Lizard King, had run foul of his country's decency laws on more than one occasion before he was found dead in a bathtub in Paris. Like Hendrix, Joplin and Jones, he was just 27 years old.

Diamond was pleased with the uniqueness of 'Done Too Soon', but felt that it was esoteric. And indeed the song's limited appeal was revealed when it wallowed well down in the lower reaches of the US chart, rising no higher than number 65. By then, having fulfilled a string of concert dates across America throughout spring, Neil had at last embarked on his debut UK and European tour, and was viewing it with a mixture of rife anticipation and cautious wariness – the latter because he had been given to believe that British audiences were a lot more reserved than American ones.

Diamond's UK gigs numbered only two, both staged on the same day, 29 May 1971, at London's Royal Festival Hall. What he found first relieved, then surprised him. He said: 'People in Britain are very warm and seem so genuine. If they like you they show it, if not then you'll find that out too.' Turning in performances that stood as probably his best yet, Neil drew an astounding and immensely satisfying response from his new congregation. So much so, that he quickly vowed to the still supportive UK press that he would come back again soon, and would be sure to play many more concerts next time, not only in the capital. During this brief stay in London, he took part in that week's episode of *Top Of The Pops*, performing with vibrant intensity his hit, 'I Am...I Said'. Neil's fellow guest performers that night included Peter Noone, recently split from Herman's Hermits, The Hollies and Stevie Wonder.

Days later, Diamond arrived in Germany to play Munich, Frankfurt, Berlin, Hamburg and Stuttgart for the first time. He ventured no further around Europe than that, content for now that he had spread his wings this far outside America. Along the way, he had acquired a new attitude towards performing in large venues. 'I find I prefer to avoid playing small halls and clubs now,' he said. 'They upset me generally and I can't give my best. What happens really is that you get spoiled by doing concerts. In a concert, the audience is held more. Clubs tend to have bars so you get chatter, laughter and glasses clinking.' The larger stage, too, was becoming a far more attractive platform to Diamond, upon which his performance and vocal techniques were steadily blossoming.

By June 1971, he had come to realise that he was not frightened of changes occurring, externally or internally. Around this time he acknowledged: 'I've been running through life, taking it *so* seriously.' That said, Neil had not turned inside out overnight. He may have been living on, and working out of, the west coast of America for a few years now, but he could not be described as having become laid back.

When asked repeatedly by journalists to explain what was by now a very famous lyric about a frog yearning to be a king, Diamond finally admitted: 'When I speak of dreaming about being a king in "I Am...I Said", the king is my representation of acceptance.' One of the striking aspects of 'I Am...I Said' was that Diamond half spoke, half sang the lyrics. Neil pointed out: 'I've always thought of myself as a writer whose work has to be either spoken or sung to make its maximum impact.'

The scope of his writing was something he also aimed to expand. The once shy guy who used rhyming couplets to woo dates with the fair sex at high school had, for the past two years, been turning privately to poetry again, this time to help express himself in a far deeper vein, and he was considering making this material public. Although his poetry closely resembled song lyrics, there was fundamentally a different feel to this work, which was in essence an accumulated wealth of personal and highly reflective insights into his life, and into life itself. That summer of 1971, he was talking openly of hoping to publish these insights in a book.

Concentrating on his live performances had to be given priority, and these concerts were enhanced by the changing set-up of his backing band. By this time, these skilled musicians included Dennis St John on drums, bassist Emory Gordy, Jr., Alan Lindgren playing keyboards, with Richard Bennet as one of the guitarists. Reinie Press, Danny Nicholson, Jefferson Kewley and others would also feature, and Diamond depended on their understanding of, and solid commitment to him. 'Some of them have been with me for two years and some for about three months,' he explained to the British rock press. 'They've changed with me.'

It was imperative to Neil that the people who made up his backing band were completely suited to the sort of music he was into. But he was about to lose a valued member of the team – guitar player Carol Hunter. After two busy years with Neil, Carol wanted to move on. She had no intention of leaving him in the lurch, and waited until he found her successor. But, by June 1971, she was talking publicly of being ready to break away. Without speaking out of school, Hunter was most forthcoming about the fact that the changes being effected in the backing band set-up that pleased Neil so much, did not – as an artiste – find favour with her. In *Melody Maker* she is said to have described the bigger band as over-tight and shortsighted. She opined: 'Neil's band is essentially made up of session men who play the same notes every night.' Having previously been a performer in her own right, Carol recognised the worth of such an efficient bedrock, but personally found it too restricting to be bound to a rigid formula. Hence her need to move on.

At this mid-point in the year, Diamond was on the move himself, back to America, where his own single version of 'I'm A Believer', backed by 'Crooked Street', had faltered just outside the Top 50. But that scarcely registered with Neil, for he was coming home to concentrate on using his recent experiences as modelling clay for his next album. The days of huddling in a cold storeroom above a noisy jazz club were a fast-fading memory. Now, he could closet himself in one of the luxurious rooms set aside for him to work in his palatial home. His practice during those spells had become to work most nights from midnight till around 5.00 a.m., while his wife and young son slept – no disturbances, no sounds, except for those he created as he articulated his thoughts and ideas through his acoustic guitar or his piano.

He had a whole reservoir of stimulus to draw on, ensuring that it was an enjoyable and fairly profitable process, even when long nights writing and the start of the subsequent studio recording sessions had to be juggled with a return to stage work. Starting in late July, Diamond was committed to a series of US and Canadian concerts that would stretch into early December. Admittedly, each month was individually watermarked with, for example, September and November featuring only two or three gigs, while for the remaining months his schedule was packed. Wherever he went, audiences for these live shows were nightly left gasping at the confident, brilliantly dazzling performer Neil Diamond had become. His stage act had evolved into an extension of his personality; as such it combined an unassailable strength, which appealed to men, with a touching vulnerability that went straight to the heart of a growing army of female fans. He depended on no gimmicks, no visual theatrics.

By 1971, the highest paid solo singer in the world was Welsh-born Tom Jones, whose snake-hipped gyrations on stage were unsubtly orchestrated to render him knee-deep in knickers by the end of the night. Elvis Presley, the original purveyor of overtly sensual body language in performance, had become wedded to incorporating simulated karate moves into his act. Diamond's flashy, flared, white stage tunics were not dissimilar to Presley's dress style. Neil had also realised for some time that certain ways in which he thrust the neck of his guitar out while playing were reminiscent of particular sword fencing moves. Overridingly, though, it was the uniquely dynamic magnetism he projected, with commanding authority to match, that was earning him slavish adoration now. When Diamond thrust his right arm compellingly upwards to the sky, while singing movingly into his microphone with head bowed, the passion he poured into his heartfelt, very personal lyrics made him an arresting figure. Emanating powerful intensity and charisma, he sucked his audience into his world of pain, self-doubt, hope and optimism. Increasingly, the masses were only too willing to be entranced.

Away from the cauldron of performance, as a consummate professional about every aspect of his work, Neil had begun to take an even keener interest in his stage arrangements. Never more so than when he approached his longest stint in any one place that year – seven sold-out nights to end August, at the Greek Theater in Los Angeles. In fact, it would be his return appearance at this venue the following year that would be immortalised, but these 1971 concerts were still ground-breaking.

The Greek Theater, a small, long-established outdoor venue situated in LA's Griffith Park, has as its logo: 'Live music under the stars in the heart of Los Angeles.' It prided itself on having created a tradition of showcasing the finest in all forms of musical entertainment. When Neil Diamond took to the stage on his opening night, on 23 August, it was the first time that a stereo sound system was used at the theatre. Diamond had also bolstered his backing band with a 35-piece string orchestra, and had enlisted the services of six backing singers.

For the duration of the concert, Neil sang out soul-baring sentiments, or thrashed his acoustic guitar to blood-pounding, rhythmic rock numbers. He alternately swept his audience to a hushed attentiveness, or blatantly whipped them into a frenzy of unrestrained enjoyment. The *Los Angeles Herald-Examiner* next day reported that the gig was 'the finest concert in Greek Theater history'. Amid a lengthy write-up titled 'Diamond In Debut At Greek', Robert Hilburn told the *Los Angeles Times'* readers: 'The important thing to realise about Diamond at the moment is that he is interested in exploring his potential as both a performer and writer. He is concerned with artistic growth. Thus, he is interested in winning respect as well as applause. He got both from his audience.'

Sue Cameron, music reviewer for the *Hollywood Reporter*, described Diamond as having been one thousand per cent better than flawless on this opening night. She went on: 'The reason for the success is Neil Diamond's attitude on stage, an inner feeling of intensity that comes across to the audience like a laser beam. He showed many sides of his personality. He spoofed some of his "dumb" songs, written during his starving songwriting days in New York. Watching Neil Diamond work is like watching the parts of a $5,000 watch work!' The boost this reaction gave to Diamond's morale was invested right back into every Greek Theater performance thereafter, as well as beyond when he took his show back out on the road. It proved to be an especially invigorating, creative period all round for him.

In quiet spells, when he was not wowing the crowds at

Coliseums in Texas, Virginia, Wisconsin, Arkansas and the like, he avidly channelled his energies into a brand new challenge. Since spring, he had been sketching out a film screenplay, the details of which he kept to himself, and he had been waiting until rest-up periods in the autumn for the chance to develop this, in the hope that it was a project with legs. He also had to knuckle down and put the finishing touches to the new songs he had penned for his next album.

Presumably, all the hours he devoted to his screenplay had squeezed out time for writing this original material, because fewer than half the eventual ten tracks on the album turned out to be his own compositions – and one of those was 'I Am...I Said'. This lower percentage contribution didn't trouble Diamond much. Since his Tin Pan Alley days he had had a pathological resistance to churning out songs for the sake of it. Quality was preferable to quantity.

He was insistent that: 'My music says who I am.' It reflected, he maintained, what he dreamt about, hoped to achieve, ached for, loved and laughed at. Plus, music pinpointed when he felt weak or strong. So, therefore, it should not be mass-produced. 'I'm a dyed-in-the-wool songwriter,' he said. 'I am not a rock 'n' roll songwriter. To me, rock 'n' roll was never substantial enough for me to devote my life to it.' He had always prided himself on the ability to appreciate all styles of music – dubbing himself 'the Will Rogers of pop'. He wanted to make his body of work as broad as possible. 'I don't want to be tied to one style,' he stressed. This partly explained why, apart from expediency, he included a variety of cover versions in the album he called *Stones*.

Of the cover versions Diamond put on to *Stones*, the ones which stood out as his favourites started with the Tom Paxton number 'The Last Thing On My Mind'. Its very delicacy had appealed to him, and it was a song he already loved singing. Joni Mitchell's 1969 number 'Chelsea Morning' had been chosen more for the songwriter than the song. Neil was frank: 'I guess I'm partial to Joni Mitchell's lyrics because they show me a slightly different perspective on life. She's a fine lyricist and I think that, in a sense, women see things from a slightly different perspective. I find that refreshing.'

As far as the Randy Newman song, 'I Think It's Going To Rain Today', is concerned, Diamond said: 'It's my favourite outside song of all on the album. It leaves me with goosebumps.' When Diamond had finished recording this particular track for the album, he sent a copy of the acetate to Newman, along with a note; Randy wrote back saying how much he liked Diamond's rendition. For all that, Neil focused most on his own efforts; among these the standout song, besides 'I Am...I Said', had to be the title track itself, 'Stones'. 'I'd call it a desperate love song,' Diamond said. 'To me stones are things that hurt people and cause them pain.'

'Stones', backed by the quirkily titled Diamond composition, 'Crunchy Granola Suite', managed to make number 14 in December, while the album itself peaked later that month in America, and then in Britain, at numbers 11 and 18 respectively.

The year 1971 climaxed for Neil when *Cashbox* voted him Top Male Performer of the Year, ahead of Elvis Presley, who had had a busy, high-profile twelve months, and George Harrison. The ex-Beatle was also riding high, having followed his solo number one hit, 'My Sweet Lord', with organising the much publicised, all-star charity Concert For Bangladesh that had been held at New York City's Madison Square Garden. Diamond was going from strength to strength as an artiste, and the momentum continued unbroken into the new year. By this time he had hit the road again, kicking off in America and soon landing back in Britain, as he had promised months earlier. Likewise as pledged, although he played a memorable gig in May at London's Royal Albert Hall, he took himself off to both Manchester and Birmingham to make his impression further afield. After visiting Germany, France and the Netherlands, he returned to Britain for gigs in London, Bristol and Southampton.

Prior to this European trip, British rock journalist Ray Coleman caught up with Diamond in Los Angeles, posing the question that since his popularity was soaring sky-high, would it not be sensible to make himself a little scarce now, less accessible to people, thereby creating a mystique around himself. Diamond replied bluntly that the audience was his patron, and that his uncomplicated goal was to seek their appreciation. He added: 'I have never understood the kind of artiste who thinks he has some kind of divine right to play, and the audience has to work to get inside what he is trying to communicate.' He also stated baldly that if you are absorbed with being impenetrably enigmatic, it might be very arty, but if a bewildered audience doesn't clap, then basically you're finished.

There was scant chance of Diamond being subjected to a deafening silence at the end of his songs. By now his powerhouse performances were electrifying. With the rhythm driving him, his acoustic guitar would be rocking back and forth on the edge of his right hip as he belted out numbers that had the crowds swaying in their rows of seats like a field of corn waving in the wind. His delivery of some songs held an almost invincible tone that winkled out a primitive chord in many. Actor Jack Black once described Diamond's voice as having a grandness. 'It's like he's getting ready to save the world, or something,' he said. Black attributed Diamond's attracting such a large female following to that supremely confident tone. It was a male journalist, however, who went way out on a limb to applaud the visiting American star.

In 1972, *Record Mirror*'s Lon Goddard enthused: 'On stage, Neil Diamond is a shattering, exhausting experience which literally drags you, or softly sweeps you, across the spectrum of emotions from song to song. As powerful and intense as Elvis Presley, yet as defenceless as a kitten, Diamond is the biggest example of talent, professionalism, sex and mystery since Valentino.'

A growing number of international music commentators were queuing up to point out that Neil Diamond radiated a magic that was unusually also apparent on record. Neil had not started out as a natural-born spotlight seeker, yet he had grown immensely in stature as a live performer, to the point where he had now come to class his stage appearances as the easiest aspect of his professional life. Come the 1970s, his attitude to song-writing – always his lifeblood – had undergone something of a change in one respect. Or so it seemed when he announced: 'Songwriting is the only real discipline I've had in my whole life. That's why I hate it so much. I don't like imposing that kind of discipline on myself, but it has to be.'

The next product of that discipline would be 'Song Sung Blue'. After sifting through the new material Neil was laying down in the studio, it was Russ Regan, head of Uni Records, who primarily pressed for this song to be released as the first cut from Neil's pending new album; Regan was convinced that it would be a massive hit. For his part, Diamond seemed to have a slightly ambivalent attitude towards the song. It only had two verses, he said, because he never got around to writing a bridge for it – this, from a man who would put himself through an emotional wringer for a song. Although it lacked a lot of body, he knew that the lyrics expressed all he had intended.

Perhaps conscious of his reputation for intensity, Diamond had begun to make the distinction that he didn't analyse *all* his songs. 'Song Sung Blue' was always supposed to have been simple, light and so easy-going that he had not for a second considered it to be single material. On the other hand, he had found an intrinsic pleasure in putting the song together. 'There was a continuity, a flow in those words that was very rare for me to find,' he explained at the time. 'You always look to be able to say something so concisely and tellingly. And occasionally those inspirations come up in songs. "Song Sung Blue" was one of those moments.'

It took Diamond 20 years to confess: 'I probably said more, in less words in "Song Sung Blue" than in any other song I've ever written.' The concise, simple message he seemed to be conveying in the number was that when he is able to express sadness through a song, it somehow lessens the pain of his problems. 'Song Sung Blue' was backed by 'Gitchy Goomy', an incomprehensibly titled, upbeat song that made several references to contented fatherhood. By the beginning of July 1972 it had peaked at number 14 in the UK singles chart.

Before becoming a song-writer, Neil Diamond, pictured here in May 1967, excelled in the elegant sport of sword-fencing. Often thought of as an elite and expensive sport, only indulged in by the privileged, it seemed an unlikely choice of pastime for the tough, Brooklyn-born star.

In London for his first British concert, May 1971, during a tour of Europe.

Neil Diamond attends the Arista Records Pre-Grammy Celebration in 2000, held at the Beverly Hills Hotel, California.

A private moment before going on stage at New York's Winter Garden Theater in October 1972, with his wife Marcia, and baby son, Jesse.

While broadcasting in one of the BBC studios, December 1974, Neil affectionately squeezes the cheeks of British radio DJ, Tony Blackburn.

Neil Diamond's live concert album, *Hot August Night*, solidified his reputation as a compelling and energetic performer. This hallowed open-air venue had hosted its share of memorable performances in its illustrious 70-year history, but Neil Diamond's August 1972 shows were arguably among the finest.

In America, record boss Russ Regan's judgement was vindicated when, that same month, 'Song Sung Blue' gave Neil Diamond his second number one hit. The single's parent album, *Moods*, released weeks later, also clawed in the star's highest album placing to date, when it reached number five in the States and number seven in Britain. *Moods*' playlist lived up to the album's title. Among the varied tracks there was the ultra slow 'Walk On Water', the cheerful-sounding 'Captain Sunshine', which spoke of striving for a hopeful optimism, 'Canta Libre', a distinctive ode to the cleansing and redemptive power etched into the process of songwriting, alongside the light-on-lyrics 'High Rolling Man'.

It was becoming noticeable that Neil Diamond's lyrics were now sometimes harder to decipher. In contrast to the winning simplicity of the chart-topping 'Song Sung Blue' came the far less understandable 'Porcupine Pie'. 'Morningside' was a tribute to one of Neil's grandmothers, who had died in a New York hospital. For many, the most popular song on the album was the emotive ballad, 'Play Me'. This was the cut Diamond had anticipated being the first single off *Moods,* and was one of those numbers that perfectly showcased his maturing voice.

Moods appeared to critical acclaim in August, having spawned Diamond's second number one single. Although there were still several months yet to run on his recording contract with Uni Records, Neil began to be headhunted by other labels keen to poach him away to their stables. Some of the music industry's most influential record companies began openly vying for the star's attention, dangling what were in 1972 very substantial sums of cash under his nose to entice him. Among the labels leading the field, Columbia Records offered a $2.5 million advance for ten albums. Warner Records promptly placed a $4 million deal on the table. Weighing up his options – although these were still in principle only, as his Uni Records contract remained firmly in force – Neil Diamond eventually told Columbia Records he would sign with them if they were prepared to equal Warner Records' offer. Columbia rose to the challenge, and an agreement was reached that would see Diamond move record labels in the following spring, after the official expiry of his existing deal with Uni/MCA.

This contest to win the business Neil Diamond generated had made the music press throughout. And so all eyes were already on the star when, in launching the new US leg of his tour in Illinois in mid-July, he began to attract even more comparisons to Elvis Presley. Jack Hafferkamp for the *Chicago Daily News* declared: 'Neil Diamond is a strange cat. He looks like the missing link between Elvis Presley and James Taylor – greasy, but sensitive. His voice, too, is peculiar. He sings like a newly awakened man with a head cold.' Diamond spent five consecutive nights performing to sell-out crowds at Chicago's Arie Crown Theater. Hafferkamp mused: 'I was somewhat at a loss to understand his appeal, until I realised that the audience was four-fifths young women. One girl perfectly summed up Diamond's attraction when she said: "He's sexy, cuddly, gorgeous and *so lost!*"'

It was in high summer 1972 that Neil Diamond made the leap up to true superstardom, starting with a ten-gig stint at the Greek Theater in Los Angeles, almost exactly a year on from his previous triumph there. The moment it leaked out that Diamond was returning to Hollywood's 5,000-seater Greek Theater, there was such a stampede for tickets that all ten shows sold out in a blur at the box office. This stint would gross $278,923, a new house record for the theatre.

Opening night was 18 August 1972. Determined to improve on his stage shows given there 12 months earlier, Neil was prepared this time to experiment with the pioneering use of quadraphonic sound. It was such a success that Diamond, already fired up, blazed brighter than ever, and gave a string of blistering performances that are still talked about in the new millennium. One particular performance, a week in, on 24 August, was recorded not only for posterity but for what would become a history-making, colossally successful, live double album called *Hot August Night*. Said Neil later: '*Hot August Night* captures a very special show for me. We went all out to really knock 'em dead in LA.'

Indeed everything about the double album – from the dynamic live renditions of so many of his already much-loved songs, to the classic cover which depicted a lean, long-haired Neil Diamond in full pulsating throttle on stage – ensured that the artiste was immortalised in that moment in time. *Hot August Night* is unarguably a landmark album in rock music annals, as well as one of the most popular live albums of all time. It was released in America towards the end of the year, when it went gold in its first month. By early December 1972, the album was fast heading towards its number five peak in *Billboard,* and had started a chart run that would last an impressive 78 weeks.

In Britain, curiously, *Hot August Night* only managed number 32, but in Australia the double album reached sales in excess of $2 million. No other album had done that there. In fact, Diamond's phenomenal popularity Down Under prompted *Time International* to reveal in the late 1990s that Australia has the most Neil Diamond fans per capita in the world. From November 1972, *Hot August Night* stayed in Australia's Top 20 bestselling albums chart for two years.

Back at the ten-gig stint at the Greek Theater in August 1972, Neil Diamond knew that he was making history, just as he had set out to attempt. What he had not bargained for was becoming hot in more ways than one. He was struck by a summer fever midway through his run of performances. He refused to let feeling unwell hamper him, though, to the point that he performed one night to an ecstatic audience who had no idea that the rivulets of sweat dripping off the star's brow owed much to the fact that he was running a raging 102-degree temperature.

By the conclusion of the Greek Theater gigs, *Time* magazine described Diamond as 'a smooth, inventive composer-performer with various talents that have enabled him not only to bridge the generation gap, but to leap all the way from commercial pop to rock stardom'. Fresh from this gold-plated triumph at the Greek

Theater, and after five days' rest, Neil took his show to the Denver Coliseum in Colorado to kick off September's gigs, which came to an end with two appearances at the Grand Ole Opry House in Nashville, Tennessee.

He was accustomed now to playing the world's most prestigious venues, but he had long harboured an ambition to do a show on Broadway. Earlier in the year, he had said: 'I suppose I won't get around to it for another two years or more.' In fact, October 1972 would be dominated by a season of 20 sell-out shows at the Winter Garden Theater in New York, starting on the third. Located at 1634 Broadway, between 50th and 51st streets, the Winter Garden Theater did not have a large seating capacity – 1,608, to be precise. But it had the name. Not only that, but only Al Jolson, the great 1920s/1930s entertainer, had ever played a one-man show on Broadway, and then over scattered nights rather than a series of concerts. That meant that Neil Diamond's 20 one-man performances at the Winter Garden Theater made him the first rock era star to headline in the world's most famous theatrical heartland.

With his name literally up in gigantic neon lights on Broadway, Neil Diamond's cup seemed to be overflowing. Especially when he lived up so far to expectations in live performance at the Winter Garden that the *New York Times*, whose arts critics could make or break an artiste, was induced to say about his opening night: 'Neil Diamond's one-man show seemed, on the face of it, to be a brash idea. One-man shows have traditionally been associated with talents like Judy Garland and Danny Kaye. But Mr Diamond is clearly a brash young man and one with both the musical track record and the performance macho to bring it off.' Complimenting his commanding stage presence, his immaculate timing and the fact that he had oozed self-confidence, the critic decided that Diamond 'needn't worry about comparisons with the likes of Garland and Kaye'.

In October, 'Play Me'/'Porcupine Pie' reached number 11 in the US singles chart. Two months later, 'Walk On Water'/'High Rolling Man' lodged six places lower. Just as the latter record was

Neil's last single release on Uni Records/MCA, so was *Hot August Night* his final album for that label.

In October 1972, *Life* magazine ran a lengthy feature on the star, titled 'Diamond In The Smooth', when he was still taking a public anti-drug stance. Speaking of the drug culture, Diamond had recently announced: 'Those people are simply turning their lives off, not turning themselves on.' He was named Entertainer of the Year by the American Guild of Variety Artists, not least on the strength of his live performance triumphs, and the fact that every one of his albums to date had gone either gold or platinum.

But what would be most remembered about Neil Diamond, as at October 1972, was that just as he reached the pinnacle of his power, at the end of his blisteringly successful, 20-night Winter Garden Theater shows, he startlingly announced that he was taking a break from live work. His flabbergasted fans felt pole-axed; the music media were caught completely on the back foot. And certain Columbia Record executives were doubtless more than a little stunned, not to say downright nervous, considering the hugely lucrative recording deal they had agreed in principle with the now much feted singer.

The only person guaranteed to have known Neil's news in advance of it being made public was Marcia. Despite his efforts to build in frequent breaks in his touring schedules to allow him to be with his family, Neil knew by autumn 1972 that it hadn't been enough, and that his personal life was once more in jeopardy. For that reason then, he made it clear that he was withdrawing from the spotlight. When pressed for an idea as to how long he intended to be away, Neil's reply was vague. He wasn't being coy or disingenuous. He honestly had no way of knowing. It is likely that he ended up as surprised as many others that this unexpected sabbatical lasted for more than three years.

CHAPTER 5

Restless
Reflection

THE **SPECTRE OF** other women would never haunt Neil
Diamond's wives. His constant, threatening mistress was
always his deep devotion to his music. He had undoubtedly
tried to take measures that were designed to avoid his second
marriage being eroded by the demands of his success. Yet, when
talking of the periods when he did sidestep work to be with his
family, he confessed: 'I play a little chess now and then. I like to
play with my son, and I enjoy making love to my wife. But music
is my life.' Remarks like the latter may have expressed an extra-
ordinarily candid sentiment, but it was one that was fraught with
potential trouble.

Neil's was not a normal life. It was an occupational hazard in
his line of work, and at his elevated level, that he would
frequently miss Christmas, birthdays and important develop-
ments in his loved ones' lives. But that didn't stop it from taking
its toll on those close to him. In October 1972, when Diamond
announced his break from live appearances and from travelling,
Jesse was just 30 months old, but Neil had become painfully
aware of the dicey state of his home life. He confessed: 'My son
was in very bad shape while I was touring. He was a fragile child
and I was haunted by the memory of him when I would leave. He

and Marcia would be standing in the window, both of them crying.' The joy of performing was dimmed by the knowledge that he had left serious heartache at home. 'I realised I was shirking my responsibilities as a father,' he said.

Neil was haunted, too, by memories of the disastrous break-up of his first marriage. One wife and two daughters had already largely been sacrificed on the altar of his success. Beneath it all, he was angry with himself for having dared to risk lightning striking twice. Hard as he was on himself, he was determined that it was not too late to save the situation. He set enormous store by the sabbatical period he had gouged out for himself. He had a goal firmly fixed in his head. It could no longer be enough to strive to be what he called 'a complete songwriter and performer'. He also wanted – *needed* – to be complete as a person, a husband and a father.

In a weird way, his mental and physical exhaustion helped him make the transition when he set out on this new course. The relentless dynamo which had driven him so far for so long had at last run down, leaving him more malleable than he had ever been, more open to viewing life in a different light. He embraced a new daily existence, which he grew to relish. Reconnecting fully with Marcia, sharing the parental load and being more accessible to his three children were all top priorities. He took to going fishing with Jesse. Till now, Neil had been unable even remotely to contemplate whiling away hours on something as unproductive as fishing. The fact that he could amble home with the child from the riverbank, having thrown back any fish they did catch, with no notion of the time spent with rod and line, was a new experience and a major breakthrough.

He also became an avid bookworm. He had always had an interest in books, but had never given himself time out to relax and read. He had, however, kept a running list of potentially interesting reading material. Now, on a spending spree, he set out to track down over 100 of these books. Over the sabbatical period, he ploughed through them methodically. Diamond mused: 'Most were biographies, but I think I enjoyed *The Cells of Life* by C.E. Lewis the best.' During this idyllic hiatus, Diamond's reading gradually went beyond the recreational. He called it pursuing the college education he had never quite finished. Along the way, he also studied music theory. In one corner of his mind he recognised the germ of a notion that he might someday be capable of writing symphonies. He developed his piano skills and even once took a singing lesson, but decided it was an unwise road to go down.

Vocal coaches, he felt, tended to have a somewhat clinical approach to their work, and while Diamond appreciated that these specialists could train a singer to use his voice better, and in ways that would avoid putting enormous strain on the vocal cords, he feared that in his case such training would erase the valuably raw emotional quality of his singing, which differed according to mood, and was an integral part of his unique sound.

It quickly became apparent that while Neil's decision to back away from the limelight at the height of his fame had been an unwelcome shock for his fans, for the Diamond family unit it was a godsend. In addition to the healing effects on his wife and son, for Diamond personally one of the best benefits of this break would come from entering a period of spiritual and psychological introspection.

He had realised that: 'The music business is always in one long hurry, and when you're moving up as a person in the limelight, you run the risk of losing your original self. It hit me that I hadn't been brought up to live the life of a celebrity.' He faced up, too, to the fact that he had to learn from scratch how to ease off. His complex nature made that hard. Music had always been his motivation, alongside a desire to understand himself. He described himself at this point in the early 1970s as: 'an imperfect emotional being, trying to figure out some substance and meaning to my life'. He pondered whether writing, recording and performing his songs was a strange, or even a shallow way in which to obtain a sense of acceptance, while at the same time being adamant that, along with his children, his songwriting was precious, the single justification he had found thus far for his life.

To look at the public figure of Neil Diamond in 1972, few would have guessed that there were still ways in which he felt unable to interact with people. His concerns went a deal deeper than that. He declared: 'It was difficult to face the reality that the things you have been told will make you happy – money, success, security – do not, in fact, get you straight inside. That's something you have to work out for yourself, in your own way.'

In the circumstances, Diamond sensibly chose not to do it alone. Instead, he sought help by undertaking therapy sessions again. Asked which specific kind of analysis he underwent, Neil proffered that it was probably Freudian, but that he had never actually discussed the particular technique with his therapist. Whether he confided as much in his therapist, it took Neil nearly four years to admit publicly that when he had played his last encore at the end of his final stage appearance at the Winter Garden Theater on Broadway, New York, in October 1972, he secretly hoped that he would never again have to go back to live performance.

That did not prevent him, however, from taking part in a political fund-raising benefit in mid-October. Neil does not consider himself to be a prominent political animal, but his persuasion is firmly Democrat. Specifically, he feels an attachment to the Kennedy dynasty. It was the Kennedys' entrenched sense of family loyalty that appealed the most to him. That, and their innate belief that they had an obligation to make life better for people.

The year 1972 was an election year in America, and the Democratic presidential candidate, who had been tirelessly out on the stump for months, was George Stanley McGovern. A portion of the receipts for Neil's opening night gig at the Winter Garden Theater had already been donated to a couple of charities that were championed by the Kennedy family. Around $18,000 went to the memorial fund set up in the name of the late Senator Robert F. Kennedy who, in June 1968, had been ambushed while leaving a Los Angeles hotel and shot dead by a young Palestinian, Sirhan Sirhan.

Throughout the summer, various celebrities, including Paul Simon and heart-throb film star Warren Beatty, took part in benefit gigs to aid the 50-year-old South Dakota-born Senator McGovern. On 15 October, yet another fund-raising event was held, this time in the grounds of the Shriver family mansion in Rockville, Maryland. It was hosted by RFK's widow, Ethel Kennedy, and Eunice Kennedy Shriver. Taking to the platform stage that day, Neil Diamond turned in a warm, charismatic set during which, at Eunice Shriver's request, he sang 'Sweet Caroline'.

It was reported that, while Diamond was in full flight, a mischievously high-spirited Ethel Kennedy made a sudden appearance on stage and, in front of everyone, poured a glass of beer over his head. It was meant in jest, and Diamond is said to have taken it entirely in good part. Such high-jinks behaviour from a senior Kennedy clan member has been seen as granting Diamond favoured recognition from the famous family. For his part, Neil Diamond is patently not prepared to claim any actual closeness with these iconic political figures. He told *Rolling Stone* years later: 'I'm not sure whether you ever really know that you're friends with the Kennedy family.'

In the end, all the fund-raising activities for Senator George McGovern were to no avail when, to the disgusted dismay of Democrats nationwide, in November 1972, Richard Nixon was returned to power, again by a very skinny margin. While 1973 saw no change on the political landscape, in Neil Diamond's world a sea change occurred in early summer when his agreement with the giant Columbia Records label finally came into effect. The ten-album deal, negotiated with label boss Clive Davis, guaranteed Diamond more than $400,000 per album, and was the industry's most lucrative recording contract at that time.

On the quiet, Diamond would have been forgiven if he had permitted himself a small smile. Ten years ago Columbia

Records had looked at him askance after his single with them, 'Clown Town', had struggled to rake in $15 in royalties. Although the company could not know it yet, this time around it would recoup its entire advance of $4 million with Neil Diamond's first two albums for them. It's fair to assume, though, that executives at Columbia Records needed nerves of steel in the long period between Diamond's hand-grenade announcement the previous autumn that he was dropping out of sight, and the deal being formalised.

When the deal had been talked through in principle, in summer 1972, Neil Diamond was the best-selling male recording artiste in America, which in effect meant the best in the world. So to say that his decision to depart from front-line visibility caused consternation must be an understatement. One can only imagine, then, the initial scare Diamond sent straight into the same executives' hearts when he told them that he intended his first album for Columbia Records to be a soundtrack to a film about the life of a seagull!

In 1970 Richard Bach, an ex-US Air Force pilot who had written books on flying, as well as a shedload of magazine articles mainly on the subject of flight, had published *Jonathan Livingston Seagull: a story*. In three sections, the slim volume runs to 93 pages, almost half of them given over to illustrations of airborne seagulls.

While most people see the raucous seagull as a screeching, aggressive scavenger, Bach chose to portray the common yet distinctive bird in a sympathetic, even intelligent light. Naming the seagull around which he crafted a philosophical study Jonathan Seagull, he sought to promote the liberating, mind-expanding value in being different, and the reward in being ready to stand out from the crowd. Bach championed those who make their own rules in life, in the sturdy belief that they are right, and he praised the depth of ambition that drives the uniquely minded individual to test his or her own mettle.

The dedication inside the book was to that individual spirit which hopefully resides, even deeply hidden, inside everyone. At its heart, the book's feathered hero was that loner, that fiercely independent creature who was an enigma to his peers, a being who sought, and found, a higher purpose in life, even if along the way he had to pay the price of ostracism from the flock and an isolated exile.

The turn of 1969/1970 was just the time for such a book to find popular favour, especially among college students, and it became a best-seller. This ode to individuality also caught the attention of director Hal Bartlett, better known for his melo-dramas. Within a year or so of the book's release, Richard Bach had been commissioned to write the screenplay of his story. Produced and directed by Bartlett, *Jonathan Livingston Seagull* was set to become a 114-minute movie for Paramount.

The nature of the subject matter quickly made it clear that the film required a strong musical score by someone who could implement the need to convey a sensitive understanding of the tale's four-pronged theme of love, hope, compassion and indi-viduality – someone who could 'see' the music in cinemascope scale. In the dying weeks of 1972, Hal Bartlett approached Neil Diamond to offer him the job. The producer-director was so eager to enlist the star's services that, in what was an unusual provision at the time in films, he's said to have guaranteed that 48 minutes of the music composed would be utilised in the film.

Hal Bartlett's timing in reaching out to Neil Diamond with this particular project had been perfect, dovetailing as it did with Diamond's recent personal quest for a new meaning in his life. It was not difficult for Neil to see a metaphorical match between himself – intrinsically a loner, bent on carving his own path – and the seagull at the centre of the story. Long before the ink had dried on his contract with Columbia Records, he said yes to Bartlett and began work on the musical score, working alongside experienced arranger Lee Holdridge.

Although Neil's imagination and enthusiasm had him all fired up, the project was not without its problems when he began to concentrate on it in early 1973. He knew he needed a purely orchestral prologue as a base. Beyond that, he had to come up with songs that were an inspired blend of contemporary and orchestral music – songs that would epitomise the ethereal, searching and spiritual qualities required. For three months he experimented with material and ideas that might have been promising but were proving elusive, to the point where he felt that nothing tangible was happening, or was even likely to in the foreseeable future. Disappointment was about to set in, no doubt chased by a feeling of failure, when everything changed almost literally in the blink of an eye.

Diamond explained: 'One day while I was sitting at the piano, I wrote down on a pad the words "God is being". I said aloud, "That's odd! Where did that come from?"' He stared long and hard at those three words, and began to fill up with a great rush of excitement. 'My heart began to palpitate and I said, "My God, that's it! That's the crux of the story – be!"' He meant that he felt the sentiment he had been looking for and had now found was as straightforward as that – be the best you can possibly be; be what essentially you are without façade, be true and honest in life and in the curious pursuit of experience. He made that the cornerstone of the songs and the music he went on to compose for the soundtrack.

After that pivotal moment, everything fell nicely into place, and he encountered little difficulty in transferring his aims onto paper. 'I wrote the rest of the music over a period of three months,' he revealed, later also confessing: 'When I was writing the lyrics, I wasn't always sure what they meant.' But even those traces of uncertainty felt appropriate, coming as they did in the early throes of his sabbatical when, in his ongoing therapy sessions, he was seeking answers to several questions.

As part of those sessions, it transpired, Diamond and his therapist delved into an analysis of some of Neil's more impregnable song lyrics. It is a tactic that has worked with other songwriters, and found great favour with such an introverted individual as Diamond. On top of everything, the spiritual-cum-religious element of the work he was doing on the film soundtrack was right up Diamond's street. He maintains: 'There's definitely a spiritual point of view in most of the things I do. Whether it's religious or not is another question. But I do tend to be philosophical about things. I think that attitude, coupled with a strong sense of drama, gives a lot of what I do a spiritual quality.' Diamond declared that although he had been brought up in the strict Orthodox Jewish faith, as an adult he did not feel the need to be rooted only in a formal religion. His curiosity allowed, even encouraged, him to be interested in and to tolerate all forms of worship.

It was while he was laying the foundations of the film sound-track, contemplating philosophical questions, exploring spiritual influences and querying religious connotations, that he was visited, uninvited, by a youth who was immersed in the Hare Krishna teachings. It was rare for strangers to turn up un-announced at the Diamonds' Malibu beach property, especially ones who were savvy enough to get around the stringent security measures. One would imagine that they were treated with a great deal of caution. Fortunately in this case, the young man seeking Neil out came armed only with Hare Krishna literature, in which he hoped to interest the songwriter.

Unfazed by the intrusion, Neil welcomed the youth into his home, where they spent some time talking. No doubt much to the young man's surprise, Diamond offered him the chance to read the film screenplay for *Jonathan Livingston Seagull,* and even invited him to offer his thoughts on it. The youth ended up stick-ing around for about six weeks. For that time, Neil arranged for him to be put up in an apartment, provided him with a rented car to travel back and forth, and when the guy eventually decided that it was time to head off for India, the plane fare came cour-tesy of the star too.

After his visitor left, Neil Diamond settled down to complet-ing his work on the soundtrack. Certain tracks, such as the heavily religious sounding 'Anthem', and 'Dear Father', which was sparse of lyrics, placed strong emphasis on the effect of the musical arrangement crafted for each. The lilting lyrics of

'Skybird' conjured up the feel of floating in a cloudless blue sky, wafting lazily around with fresh air under light wings. For many, the track that best captured the film's mood was 'Be'. Optimism, curiosity, spirituality and soulfulness, as well as a hint of a tantalising glimpse of a better world, were all embroidered into this single song.

The soundtrack had to be recorded for release in the autumn, and was not without a degree of controversy. But Neil, confident that his new record label would be happy with his first album, found his attention snagged elsewhere. Back in January 1973, *Moods*, released the previous summer, had attracted two Grammy Award nominations, as had 'Song Sung Blue'. *Moods* had been nominated for Album of the Year, as well as for Best Engineered Recording – Non Classical. 'Song Sung Blue' was up for Song of the Year, which is a songwriter award, and for Record of the Year. Come 3 March at the annual Grammy Awards ceremony, however, out of the four potential trophies the only award ultimately bagged was for *Moods*. And it was landed in the Best Engineered Recording – Non Classical section, which went to Armin Steiner.

By early May, a live version of 'Cherry Cherry', backed by 'Morningside', and taken from *Hot August Night*, reached number 31 in the US singles chart. Six weeks later, Diamond stepped back into the limelight briefly to perform his very first hit single, 'Cherry Cherry', on the show which marked the 20th anniversary of ABC-TV's *American Bandstand*. As Neil retreated back home, to focus on his forthcoming new release, recordings from his past associations with both Bang Records and MCA mushroomed during the summer, albeit mainly levelling out in the lower reaches of the charts. Backed by 'Monday Monday', 'The Long Way Home' (originally the B-side of the 1967 release, 'Thank The Lord For The Night Time') was released in August, only to stall at number 91. The following month, MCA trotted out the single 'The Last Thing On My Mind'/'Canta Libre', which made it to number 56 in America. The best placing among this small flurry of releases was achieved by *Rainbow*. The eleven-track MCA album climbed to number 35 in America and lodged inside the UK Top 40 the following year.

Neil Diamond's whole attention that autumn, however, was centred on *Jonathan Livingston Seagull*. The film had its world premiere on 24 October 1973 at the Sutton Theater in New York City. Six days later, its Los Angeles premiere was held at Mann's Village Theater. The film was a box-office flop, and was not well received by critics. Benny Green for *Punch* commented cuttingly: 'It may be that the creature best qualified to review *Jonathan Livingston Seagull* is another seagull.' *Halliwells Film Guide* called the movie 'A weird family fantasy that clearly could not translate easily to the screen.'

The *Leonard Maltin Film Guide* found *Jonathan Livingston Seagull* unique, and praised the cinematography but otherwise found fault: 'The dialogue doesn't work nearly as well, nor does Neil Diamond's overbearing score.' Neil Diamond's 'overwhelmingly successful' film score would have been closer to the mark. The soundtrack album *Jonathan Livingston Seagull* – Diamond's first release for Columbia Records – became a gigantic international hit, ranked as one of the world's top-selling albums at that time and, taking the number two position in the US charts, went double platinum, grossing around $12 million – several times the box-office take for the film.

If anyone's palms had been sweating nervously before, commercially all was more than well now. However, the pleasure provided by this triumph was tarnished to an extent by behind-the-scenes disputes involving some of the main players in the film's creation. Almost two decades later, *Record Collector* maintained: 'Many observers reckoned that these conflicts prevented Diamond's work from being nominated for an Oscar.'

If that is true, glittering consolations still came the star's way at the end of January 1974, when at the 32nd Golden Globe Awards ceremony held in Los Angeles the *Jonathan Livingston Seagull* soundtrack won the coveted trophy for Best Original Musical Score Written for a Motion Picture. A little over a month later, on 2 March, the album repeated this success by picking off the prestigious Grammy Award in the equivalent category at the National Academy of Recording Arts and Sciences' 16th annual awards ceremony.

It was an immensely proud period for Neil Diamond; it helped to offset the lukewarm performance of individual singles from the soundtrack, which itself had newly halted in Britain at number 35. 'Lonely Looking Sky' was nominated for a Golden Globe Award for Best Original Song but did not win. In December, Neil's first single for Columbia Records, 'Be'/'Flight Of The Gull', ran aground at number 34; 'Skybird', backed by 'Lonely Looking Sky', then limped to a stop 41 places lower still.

Winning two such prestigious industry awards had put Neil Diamond's name back in the spotlight. But the glare was still not to his taste; after these high-profile celebrity-packed events were over, he slipped back into his self-imposed retreat. There were too many benefits to be gained from this sabbatical to wind it up just yet. Furthermore, he had no intention of putting a time limit on himself as to when he would do so. It must have been a source of comfort, all the same, to know that he had a very satisfied record label behind him, which now had proof positive that Neil Diamond did not necessarily need to be seen in order to sparkle in the market place.

Columbia Records *were* obviously keen to hear of his next recording project. Indeed, Diamond's thoughts soon started turning towards the framework of a new, so to speak 'normal' album. But he was in no hurry. He also felt he ought first to consider his options fully. Having earned himself this relaxed breathing space, it seemed an appropriate time to examine the possibility of expanding his horizons. One unusual notion stirred persistently within him. For a long time, his fascination with sword fencing had intrigued him into the idea of writing a swordplay ballet, set to the complementary motions of attack and parry. Along with his back-burner ambition to write symphonies, though, the ballet idea was put on hold when a potentially very exciting project came his way in springtime.

Since his attempt to enter the world of acting three years

earlier, portraying the late comedian Lenny Bruce, Neil Diamond had never ditched his interest in appearing on the silver screen. So he was ripe and available when he received approaches to take one of the leading roles in a Frank Pierson-directed movie, *A Star Is Born*, for which Barbra Streisand had been cast as the female lead. This film would be a second remake of the original 1937 romantic melodrama of the constructive, then destructive relationship between a beautiful, talented young actress on the rise and an ageing, alcoholic, formerly famous lead man on the skids. In its day it was a powerful story, dubbed: 'the most accurate study of Hollywood ever put on film', and it had attracted rave reviews. So did the first remake, released in 1954, starring Judy Garland and James Mason.

Twenty years on, this well-known story was again being dusted off and given a revamp, in that the setting was changed from the film world to the rock world, and the filmmakers had decided that they wanted to see Neil Diamond take on the male lead. Frustratingly for Diamond, the role conflicted him. On the one hand, the chance to get his hands on this supercharged tale of love, fame, depression and tragedy invigorated him. But on the flip side, the closer he studied the role, the more he felt an unshakeable unease about portraying the part of a screwed-up, burned out, doomed singer. The character was a highly destructive person; concerned about the level of negativity, Neil was not sure that he wanted to be identified with it.

As it happened, this very role was one that, after years of making dreadfully flimsy movies, Elvis Presley had desperately wanted, seeing it as a vehicle in which to show the world that he really could act. However, he was unable to land the part, partly because some of the film studios put obstacles in his way. Neil Diamond was offered it on a plate, and was master of his own decision making. After due consideration, though, he listened to his qualms and decided not to accept the role.

Barbra Streisand's lead man eventually proved to be the Texan-born singer-songwriter Kris Kristofferson, and this third version of *A Star Is Born* was released in 1976. Critically, the film certainly suffered in comparison to its two predecessor versions. *Village Voice* said of it: 'A bore is starred.' But for all that, Kris Kristofferson won a Best Actor Golden Globe for his perform-ance in the role that Neil Diamond had turned down. One wonders if, in hindsight, Diamond ever wondered if he had made the right decision.

Throughout the months leading into summer 1974, while enjoying family life, Diamond settled into his songwriting, still at an unhurried pace. In July, MCA once again released a Neil Diamond album, this time a compilation of songs recorded between 1969 and 1972. Called *Neil Diamond / His 12 Greatest Hits*, its front sleeve photograph of Diamond by Harry Langdon was so glamorous that it went out of its way to project Neil as Hollywood matinee idol material. In America, the album entered the Top 30 and made number 13 in Britain.

Travelling to and from various Los Angeles recording studios, Diamond found himself in an inward-looking frame of mind. The relative privacy of the recording studio was always an inti-mate setting in which he could flourish and find expression for his feel for music. Songwriting, he said around now, 'comes not only from a person's experiences but from his fantasies, his dreams, his fears and frustrations – everything that makes up a person'. The human voice itself intrigued him. As an interpretive vocalist he believed that the voice was far and away the most important tool at a person's disposal. Yet he felt it was one of the most difficult instruments to comprehend or to define. 'You either hear it, or you don't. It either moves you, or it leaves you cold,' he said.

By November 1974, after nine months writing and recording the songs, Diamond's next new album was released. Called *Serenade*, it quickly claimed the number 11 spot in the UK, but hit number three in the States. Once again, his work here consti-tuted an interesting mix of material. For many, 'I've Been This Way Before' proved to be among their all-time favourite Neil Diamond numbers. But the reflective song about being given a second chance in life would, for years, give the songwriter a faint but gnawing disappointment. He had written it for *Jonathan Livingston Seagull,* but had been unable to complete it in time to include it on the soundtrack album. To him, 'I've Been This Way Before' was intended as the decisive end statement in the film score. Instead, it had trailed over into a different album altogether, so Diamond felt a niggling sense of dislocation.

Other standout numbers on *Serenade* included 'Lady Magdalene', a majestic yet yearning song with completely undisguised religious overtones shown in its references to God and Abraham, the infectiously rhythmic 'The Last Picasso', and 'Rosemary's Wine'. Then there was 'Longfellow Serenade', an emotive love song which, paired with 'Rosemary's Wine', was the first cut released from *Serenade.*

Having spent so many years writing songs, Diamond had an ever deepening pool of half-formed numbers which had never quite come to fruition but which held enough potential never to be completely discarded. 'Longfellow Serenade', in one shape or another, had been incubating in his subconscious for some time. Having completed his work on *Jonathan Livingston Seagull,* Neil had felt it essential to face up to this growing reservoir of raw material in his head; apart from anything else, he desperately needed to separate the wheat from the chaff. He has described this phase as washing out his brain, and he had sat down and begun to experiment with some of these semi-crystallised songs.

'Longfellow Serenade' held a particularly fond place in his heart, because in an obvious way it was a throwback to his teenage schooldays, when he was too shy to ask a girl directly out on a date, so would write her a poem. He said: 'I imagined the poet who writes the words he cannot speak to the woman he wants to woo and win. "Longfellow Serenade" is not about a guy who writes poetry, but who reads some of the beautiful poems of Henry Wadsworth Longfellow. And it reflects my own experiences too.'

By late November, 'Longfellow Serenade' made number five, giving Neil Diamond his first US Top Ten single since his chart-topping 'Song Sung Blue' in summer 1972. Although Columbia Records would doubtless have liked the star to take to the stage again, Diamond still would not contemplate returning to that sort of live performance. He was, however, prepared to help promote *Serenade* and his latest single by undertaking television appearances. For the last two months of the year, therefore, Diamond set out on a busy round of interviews and guesting on a variety of shows around Europe, work that was not always to his liking, for he had an interesting almost love/hate relationship with TV. As a promotional tool he knew it was unrivalled. But talking of American TV, in 1971 Diamond had said: 'I've deliberately been laying off. I'm not happy with the way I'm presented. American TV is too concerned with schedules. They don't relax enough. There's this pattern they follow, all the time.'

Three years on, the European experience felt little better. In particular, he was left with no great opinion of guesting on variety shows. He found it deeply frustrating when time and again he encountered programme producers who were determined to have him sing duets with show hosts, regardless of whether the respective voices had even the remotest chance of blending. And he often cringed at being expected to take part in contrived and unhumorous comedy skits. He recalled an absurd occasion when he had to insist that the diminutive host of a particular TV show (disguised by the camera angle) actually stand on a prop staircase while they sang, so that the ridiculous mismatch in their heights did not turn the already awkward spot into a completely embarrassing farce.

When Diamond returned to home soil, the first quarter of 1975 hinted at a continued slow pace for him. First, 'I've Been This Way Before'/'Reggae Strut' from *Serenade* peaked in the US singles chart at number 34. Then in April, 'The Last Picasso'/ 'The Gift of Song' failed to register at all. Neil had no plans to release any new studio material that year. Being unstructured was still the name of the game for him, but he had not accounted for fate taking a hand. In early summer he ran into someone who would be instrumental in starting to end this long sabbatical from the music scene. He was renowned songwriter Robbie Robertson.

Jaime Robert Robertson was born in July 1943 in Toronto, Canada, to a Jewish father and a Mohawk mother from the Six Nations Reservation. Passionate about a wide range of music from a very young age, before he was 20 he had already run through country and big band music to root firmly in rock, playing with a band called The Hawks. As backing band to a 1950s rocker named Ronnie Hawkins, The Hawks consisted of piano player and vocalist Richard Manuel, organist Garth Hudson, bass player Rick Danko and drummer Levon Helm.

In 1964, having parted from Hawkins to start performing as a unit in their own right, The Hawks had quickly drawn the gimlet eye of Bob Dylan. By the following year, Dylan had hired the five-piece to back him in what would become his much celebrated world tour. It was while The Hawks were closely associated with Bob Dylan that they renamed themselves The Band, an outfit that gained a reputation as one of rock music's seminal acts. Robbie Robertson, in particular, quickly accrued widespread respect as a unique, intuitive and evocative songwriter.

In the early 1970s, Neil Diamond and Robbie Robertson had casually crossed paths in Woodstock, New York, where Robertson was living. But it was not until years later, by which time Robertson had moved out west, that the pair met one day by chance and realised that they were near neighbours in Malibu. On the face of it, it was not the most obvious meeting of minds. Robbie Robertson had greatly admired Neil Diamond's very early material. To him, the Brooklyn-born lyricist had been responsible for songs and melodies that had become near branded on the public's collective consciousness. Diamond, he believed, filled the musical vacuum between Frank Sinatra and Elvis Presley. Said Robertson once: 'This huge audience adopted Neil. When you see him in performance it's like, "What's going on here?" These people are hypnotised!' For his part, Neil Diamond candidly confessed that The Band's music had never managed to make any mark on him.

Nevertheless, enough spark occurred between the lyricists to get the pair talking; the more time they spent together, the more a friendship began to take on a life of its own. They talked mainly about their respective backgrounds, their experiences in the music world, and they discovered that they had some acquaintances in common. What possibly impressed Diamond most vividly was finding out that his fellow songwriter had had his own share of problems on the road to fame. Said Neil: 'This was a personal relationship between us and a mutual respect for what we'd each been through – commonly shared disasters along the way.' Before long, it became obvious that it might be a stimulating experience for them to collaborate on something. For months, the two men met roughly once a week, usually at weekends; sitting or strolling on the luxurious golden beach in their privileged haven, they got deeper and deeper into each other's lives.

Their discussions largely came round to what they were each aiming to do in the future. But Robbie Robertson found himself particularly intrigued by the past, specifically the long-defunct Tin Pan Alley scene. It was in this scene that he and Diamond had acquaintances in common, but Neil was not enamoured of being closely reminded of that whole phase in his life. It ought to have seemed no more than a distant memory now, a stressful, demoralising world, aeons away from his secure, status-rich life. In fact, those early days were still all too horribly imprinted on his brain. They had not been his happiest years. He wanted to leave everything about them well behind. And so, despite his new friend's determination to delve into the renowned production line songwriting institution, initially Neil had a resistance to going into any depth about the whole Brill Building syndrome.

The root of Robbie Robertson's fascination lay in his view that this period in modern music's history represented both a beginning and an ending – that Tin Pan Alley's death throes hallmarked the birth of a new mood and movement towards creative independence on the part of songwriters and musicians, amid an exhilarating, even scary, period of social and political change. Robbie's enthusiasm was such that it wore Neil down. It wasn't too far into their spirited discussions that they came up with the idea of putting together a concept album around the Tin Pan Alley experience. Diamond would draw on his days as a penniless songwriter struggling to operate within, yet never fitting within, the structured system of churning out songs to order. Robertson would be the record's producer.

For Neil it was a big undertaking, in more ways than one. It had psychological implications. Having first resisted taking this long look over his shoulder, he had now committed himself to staring probingly into his past. That meant reliving a different life, one that had been played out in a different world at a very different pace. One of the first things he had to face up to was just how much of Brooklyn was really still inside him. The whole divide between America's east and west coast psyche loomed into sharp relief for him. In simplistic terms, he had for a long time devolved it into two distinct parts. New York represented his rigorous fight for survival. Los Angeles, although he had taken time to settle in when he first arrived, had offered him the chance to become far more introspective in his music. But it was more complex than that.

Diamond said of New York: 'That's a city with a tremendous amount of energy, rawness, life in front of your eyes, ambulances, people dying. In California it's a very pastel kind of setting in comparison.' He could only talk, of course, of the Los Angeles he encountered. Downtown LA was not pastel, rural or peaceful, and was just as down and dirtily desperate as the hardnosed seedy side of New York. But Diamond lived in luxury LA. By now, he knew that his intrinsic make-up had become an amalgam of the locked-in, intense and dramatic elements hewn from his birthplace, and the easy-going tolerance and free openness redolent in the place he had made his home. Those intertwining elements had taken a lot of weaving together; they were working well for him. Now, he was expected to unpick and separate the strands for examination.

It's not something that he had never ever contemplated. He admitted: 'A New Yorker who's been out in LA for twenty years is still a New Yorker and still has these vague thoughts of going back.' He declared that since he had lived in New York as 'a down and out', it was one of his dreams, now that he had money, to go back there and sample the life lived by the privileged set. Now was his chance; moreover, it would be for a good reason. With this mission to soak up the old atmosphere back east, Diamond decamped for New York for a two-week stay in summer 1975. He wanted to melt back into the streets, take photographs, absorb the high-wire bustle of the kaleidoscopic nerve centre of one of the greatest and meanest cities in the world. He didn't go alone. His family went with him, and they took a suite of rooms in a plush hotel on Manhattan's Fifth Avenue, where his two daughters, Marjorie and Elyn, also joined him.

Something about Neil Diamond that became obvious over the years was that he was a natural chameleon. He could look so very different, seemingly without a great deal of effort. Despite being one of the most recognisable stars in the world, for parts of each day in New York he drifted unobtrusively and on his own, back into the shadier parts of the city – places where no man would wish to take his sheltered young children. Fairly swiftly, he found what he'd come looking for from the sights, sounds and smells, which had not changed much in the seven years he had been away.

Even so, the influences he absorbed through every open pore, although valuable, were not what directly sparked his first songwriting inspiration. That came from his vivacious elder daughter. One evening in the living room of the hotel suite, Neil had his family around him and was happily capering on his guitar, singing snatches of lyrics that ran out of steam, making merry with this exciting proposition in front of him, not yet seriously bending his mind to actual songwriting. Marjorie, who had been standing at the wide, gleaming window, looking down at the city sights, suddenly cried to her father: 'What a beautiful noise!' She was not referring to her father's guitar playing, but to the mingled sounds of a Puerto Rican Day parade that were wafting up from street level. To some people, the cacophony coming from the variety of bands playing was distracting; the mix had hit Marjorie in a vastly different way.

Captivated not only by the unusual sentiment, Diamond's intuitive ear picked up a special nuance in the way his offspring had spoken. He joined the girl at the window and, looking down at the view, told her that one day he would write a song called 'Beautiful Noise', as it was such a lovely phrase. But, with the impatience of youth, 'one day' was too far away for Marjorie who, by her bedtime, had extracted a promise from her famous father that he would get started on the idea, pronto. Whatever else Neil Diamond took back to California after the fortnight in New York was up, he had the melody and nearly all of the lyrics to a strong song that would become the title track of this new concept album in the making – all instigated by four words from a nine-year-old. Home in Los Angeles, Diamond played the nearly completed song to Robbie Robertson. 'He liked it right away and we went from there,' recalled Neil.

The pair worked in close collaboration for a year on this album, time in which they indulged in lengthy discussions about what they wanted to project in, and achieve with this work. It was a two-way street that Neil found enormously nourishing, surprisingly so for someone who was, by nature, a lone wolf. In the end, Robertson and Diamond co-composed one song, 'Dry Your Eyes'. In addition to his talents as producer, Robbie also played on almost half the cuts finally selected for the album. Part of the later work was undertaken at Kendun Studios in Burbank where, in company with a couple of sound engineers, they devoted endless hours to experimenting with various sounds. Neil sometimes felt there was too much of an edge to the sound, but they were all determined to find the correct balance that would convey the basic thrust that these songs stemmed from an extremely nervy existence.

When word leaked out on music's grapevine about the professional pairing of Neil Diamond and Robbie Robertson, it raised several eyebrows in the industry. Like Diamond, Robertson understood why people thought that they made an odd union. He told rock journalists that pursuing whether this particular experiment would work musically was what had mattered, and that it had seemed to be sufficiently novel to make it worthwhile.

Diamond confessed that it was not a natural pairing, but he stated that though he and Robertson were such separate entities, coming together in itself gave rise to the possibility of creating an interestingly unique hybrid entity. It is hard, however, not to conclude that they must both have received unwelcome flak for their decision to collaborate. For there was more than a hint of touchy defiance when Robbie Robertson said: 'When I worked with Neil on *Beautiful Noise* a lot of people asked, "Is this a put on? This doesn't fit." And I felt like, "Don't tell me what fits. I'll *show* you what fits!"'

Too independently minded to be influenced by outside elements, the two men knew that what was important was that it worked for them. Their professional relationship extended beyond this album. In Robbie, Neil had found someone who could sometimes help him surmount those panicky periods of writer's block. As ever though, when it came to assessing his own material, Neil had no more unvarnished a critic than himself. Almost from the start, he had the capacity to evaluate his songs objectively, even when he had invested a considerable amount of himself in a song's creation. When going through the process of avidly pulling a song together, he would regularly tear it apart, discarding any parts he felt didn't absolutely work. He measured every word, its place and significance in a three-to-four minute number. Sometimes the melodies would come in for some serious rewriting. It all meant that while he could ruthlessly jettison songs that didn't fit perfectly, what he was left with, he treasured all the more.

As *Beautiful Noise* was coming together, Neil had big plans. The fact that it was a concept album had, from the start, afforded it an extra dimension. Because he had not set out to write a dozen individual numbers, but rather to craft the basis of a story with a running thread, as he watched it develop he began to see the unfolding story as potential film material. During the album's promotion he would state as much, declaring that he viewed a film version as 'another step in the sophistication of the thing'. He also came to consider the story potential fodder for a Broadway musical.

All in all, he was greatly buoyed up by the patent progress on the album. He began consciously to let still more air into his personal life by going out and about to see what other music stars were up to. Throughout the second half of 1975, Neil went to a variety of gigs. He caught up with The Rolling Stones, who were on tour plugging their compilation album *Made In The Shade*. A good 12 years down the career track, Mick Jagger was going through a phase of being reviled by some sections of the US press. But a measure of how potent The Stones' wild reputation remained was shown in December 1975, when a church minister in Tallahassee, Florida, publicly condemned all Stones' records as being flatout sinful. The clergyman was outraged at the findings of a recent poll showing that out of 1,000 unmarried mothers, all but 16 had conceived to the sound of rock music. Seemingly prepared to blame The Stones primarily for this lusty statistic, he invited his flock to make a bonfire of Stones' records.

A concert by The Who was another must-see event for Neil Diamond. Even though he had been shocked by their destructive stage antics when they first toured America back in the mid-sixties, Neil could still appreciate their brand of music. 'When anything is done well, I can really enjoy it,' he explained. Neil's thoughts would linger longest on The Who's frontman, Roger Daltrey, because he had recently made a highly successful transition from rock star to film star. Daltrey had newly won awards for his role as the blind pinball wizard in the Ken Russell-directed, much talked about rock opera, *Tommy*. The Who frontman was due to star in another Ken Russell movie, called *Lisztomania*. Diamond wondered if a trend had started, especially when it was announced that British pop icon David Bowie had signed to make it onto the silver screen the following year in the Nicolas Roeg film *The Man Who Fell to Earth*.

That Neil's persistent inner tug towards the film world had made its presence felt again by the end of 1975 was part of a bigger picture. Finally, after over three years, his sabbatical was about to come to an end. He had, of course, a burgeoning album to be released in the new year, but it was more than that. The time to re-emerge had just about arrived; the prospect was simultaneously frightening and hugely exciting. When he had bowed out at the top, he had been exhausted and in desperate need of taking care of business at home. Now he had itchy feet once more. He admitted: 'I wanted to be in front of an audience again. I wanted to test myself again.' But it could never be as straightforward as that. Neil was in no gung-ho mood to charge bull-like into the spotlight. He wanted to go back on stage, yet the idea of entering the public arena once more somehow scared him.

Where it had counted, he had done a pretty sterling job of cocooning himself in a world of his making, a world under his control, and he liked that, had felt secure in that. It was a lifelong trait. He had carved himself just such a state as a child by creating his imaginary friend. At the end of 1975, he admitted: 'I still live in a fantasy world sometimes, because it's safe. It's a cushion, a protective thing you build, and nothing can hurt me, at least in my own mind.'

When he opted out of the limelight, he had issues of low self-esteem to confront. The fact that, by the end of 1975, he was able to talk publicly about this problem indicates that he was a fair way towards resolving it. He told journalists that whenever he received a standing ovation from audiences, he assumed that people were just being very polite. He owned up: 'There was a contrast in my personality because of a low self-opinion, coupled with tremendous self-confidence. The confidence was in the music because, at the very least, I could always hide in a room and write songs, whereas I never felt I was very much as a human being.' Deep down now, he knew that these past three years had allowed him to gain a new and better perspective. He was also certain that he had figured out how to pace himself in the future to avoid the pressure of work schedules getting to him and, by extension, affecting his family.

As for his relationship with Marcia, as at 1975 he believed that his long lay-off period had preserved their marriage. He called the sabbatical the years that saved his life. And in the new millennium, then seemingly light years away, he would still maintain that the time spent away from the road had given him the valuable opportunity to get to know himself as a grown-up. He insisted: 'It was the most important part of my life in the last thirty years.' Certainly, Diamond acknowledged that the period between October 1972 and the end of 1975 had been a time of enormous growth for him as a husband, father, artiste and human being. He had conscientiously taken care to improve all areas of his life, and his part in his family members' lives. It had been a unique spell, never to be repeated again in that form.

Backing away from the stage when he had been at the top of his game had been viewed in the music industry either as a very risky move indeed, or as an unusually brave decision. It took even more courage to contemplate going back. Proving to oneself that it was achievable once was big enough; proving it twice would be too tall an order for many.

Part of Neil had been able to say in 1972 that, even after a few years' absence, people would undoubtedly still want to come back to see him perform. He reflected on the period immediately following ten blistering gigs at the Greek Theater and the twenty memorable appearances at the Winter Garden Theater, that he had reached the height of what he had had to prove, that he hadn't needed to pack out some gigantic sports stadium to feel that he had earned his superstar stripes. But having now found the pieces that had been missing in his life, did he have the same belief that he could walk back and whistle up the same adulation, from as enthusiastic and as large a congregation as before? When quizzed on the subject of fearing that the fans had forgotten him, Diamond was calmly candid that he could not afford to be controlled by the tides of popularity. He aimed, he maintained, somehow to float above that. He preferred to concentrate on the music and, when the time came, on turning in the best live shows he could; beyond that, it was in the lap of the gods.

A series of live shows had by now been lined up for the new year. Looking ahead to these, he declared: 'Confidence is different from nervousness. I'm confident I'm making the right move at any one time. But until an audience enthuses, I'll worry.' Then again, fear was still a strong motivation for Neil Diamond, for it tended to make him produce his sharpest best. By any stretch of the imagination, for any artiste, coming back after a long lay-off is a daunting business, not least because the music world can change so much in a six-month stretch, let alone a period running into years.

In the mid-cradle of the 1970s, the music scene was in a fairly fragmented state. The land that had given the music world The Rolling Stones, The Beatles and The Kinks was being blighted – albeit temporarily – by a new and abrasive form of expression called punk. Purporting to reflect the cynical seventies, bands like The Sex Pistols, The Clash, The Jam and The Stranglers sprang to prominence, all doing their level best to be as outrageously crude and uncouth as possible, expressing anti-royal sentiments, gallows humour and general apathy towards life.

In America, where disco fever was more than a year away, things were a bit more mellow. The Walker Brothers were singing of no regrets. In July 1976, Brian Wilson played on stage with the rest of The Beach Boys for the first time in seven years. The whiff of nostalgia hung thickly in the air. Perhaps the best exponent of the American mood, at the dawn of 1976, was The Eagles; the rock-pop group were flying high and had newly been joined by guitarist Joe Walsh as a permanent member, just in time for the group to take Australia and New Zealand by storm in the opening two months of the new year. The Antipodes were also where Diamond was destined to face his first baptism of fire after stepping back into the spotlight. But he did not tour Down Under straight from cold. Some half-dozen US dates eased him back into harness first. Yet despite his careful planning, good, old-fashioned nerves still caught him unawares.

CHAPTER 6

All That
Glitters ...

NEWLY TURNED 35, Neil Diamond performed his first live concert for 166 weeks on 30 January 1976, when he travelled north from his Hollywood home to step back into the spotlight with the first of three consecutive gigs at the Community Center Theater in Sacramento. At this big moment, he was so keyed up by a volatile mix of emotions that his adrenalin level was sky-high. At the forefront of his thinking was the sturdy belief that his long lay-off was going to work for, not against him; that because it had given him a new inner strength, it rendered him in a better position to deliver a more interesting show for fans this time around. After over three years of no concerts and no interviews, he said it felt real good to be back. He was outwardly confident that the fans were still out there in large enough numbers to ensure that his comeback was a great success. Yet that phantom fear festering at the fringes still got through to him. How could it not?

Diamond didn't delude himself. He knew that all his glamorous triumphs of the early 1970s would quickly count for nought if he slipped back from that pinnacle now. He also knew that he had no God-given right to expect that he had not been forgotten. He later confessed: 'It was scary, especially in those days when careers were not twenty-year situations.'

One source of comfort was the fact that tickets for all three concerts at the Sacramento Community Center's 2,500-seat theatre had sold out a clear seven weeks in advance of his appearance. On opening night he drove into town determined to hold on to an exhilarating feeling of excitement. By the time he took to the stage, though, that buzz had turned to burning nervous tension. To some onlookers in the audience, he seemed tense as he waded through the first few opening numbers, mistakenly skipping a whole verse of 'Kentucky Woman'. At times, he appeared to have difficulty hitting certain notes. Those with a discerning eye could spot his displeasure.

Yet his loyal fan base was there to support him wholeheartedly. Even from out of state, people had telephoned the theatre to beg for tickets. So those who had bagged themselves a ringside seat to witness Neil Diamond's comeback, up close and personal, were not going to be thrown by a slower than expected start to proceedings. Indeed, the two-hour concert was only a quarter under way when the crowd encouragingly sprang to their feet. They remained standing for the duration, clapping, swaying and singing along. This gave Neil an incalculable lift, and from that point he loosened up. Nothing could hold him back then – not even when a cover from an overhead spotlight came loose and crashed down, missing him by a fraction as he concentrated on reconnecting with his audience.

He began to stride the stage with an air of commanding confidence again, coping with affectionate dignity with the young ladies who scrambled inelegantly on stage to be near him. The man who was once kept quiet between songs because of awkwardness, now peppered his performance with an effortless series of humorous asides and jokes. It was quickly clear that his charisma had only doubled with the passage of time; whenever he strayed from trusty past hits, to try out unfamiliar numbers such as 'Beautiful Noise', the crowd readily accepted it. Renditions of songs like 'Song Sung Blue' and 'Holly Holy' were dynamic, while the sober 'Solitary Man', riddled with mood and nostalgia, gripped the audience anew.

By the time he was finished, the roars of approval rattled the rafters. So it made the star's immediate backstage reaction even more of a surprise to those around him. No one filing out of the theatre that night, into the nippy Californian January air, deliriously happy with the entertainment, could know that the atmosphere behind closed doors inside the venue was considerably hotter. Twenty years on, Neil laid bare just how raw those first-night nerves had actually been when he revealed: 'I was sitting in my dressing room with my agent afterwards and I threw a bottle at him and said, "You son of a bitch! You made me come back and do this again!"' He explained that although everyone else had had a great night, he himself felt that he had just been in the ring for ten bruising rounds with Muhammad Ali. This dramatic explosion was uncharacteristic and short-lived, and he had not struck the agent with the handy missile. But the incident provided a graphic insight into how tortuous an experience the gig had been for Diamond. The anticipatory rush of returning to live appearance had been one thing. Curtain up had clearly been quite something else – a real do-I-still-have-it-or-not moment of truth.

If any showbiz watchers picked up the wrinkles in Neil's performance, the press were of the opinion that Diamond was firmly back on the block. Steve Connell for the *Sacramento Union* wrote: 'Even diamonds become tarnished when shelved, but their aura of brilliance keeps shining. Neil Diamond was rusty on the first night. This was to be expected, and he did eventually drive the packed throng wild with approval. But in opening in Sacramento, Diamond made a wise choice. Had he opened in New York City with a show like the one he put on here on Friday night, the influential critics there would very likely have canned him.'

Diamond has never been renowned for taking particular notice of critics. His generic definition once of a critic was: someone who has never managed to learn to play the guitar. But at the same time he is never unaware of what is being said about him. He could appreciate the valid ambivalence woven into the patchwork of this first write-up on his all-important return to the fray. The *Sacramento Union* critic was frank about flashes during the concert when Neil's trademark baritone voice had lacked the old familiar zing, and the fact that the last ten minutes of the show, by being given over to some of his lesser-known songs, had 'dragged'. By the same token, he pointed out how easily Diamond had stirred up the same deep devotion from his audience, and that the sticking points he highlighted in his review were just areas in need of some polish, and that all too soon the performer would be shining as brightly as ever. 'For Neil Diamond,' Steve Connell ended, '*is* a bona fide star.'

While Diamond was determined to give his all in each of these US dates, they inevitably served as useful warm-up performances, from which valuable lessons could be learned and any glitches ironed out. He paid close attention, therefore, to reactions – his own and others' – to his performances after Sacramento, when he headed to Utah for three one-night stands at the BYU Marriott Center in Provo, the State Spectrum, Logan, and Salt Lake City's Special Events Center; this small stint finished on 7 February. His eyes were then firmly fixed on his upcoming three-and-a-half-week tour of Australia and New Zealand, which was due to commence in a few days' time.

One of the plus points he could be sure worked for him was the new members he had introduced into his backing band; among them were piano player Tom Hensley, guitarist Doug Rhone and King Errisson, a Jamaican-born maestro percussionist with a larger-than-life personality to equal his musical ability.

In returning to the fore in music, Neil Diamond wanted to challenge himself, and this Australia and New Zealand tour would be his first on that continent. It could be argued that it was not the toughest test to face. While he had never yet played live Down Under, in that part of the world he was without doubt still the biggest-selling recording artiste, and so the risk of his concerts not selling out was negligible. Proof of his enormous popularity had already been borne out by the staggering reaction among the music-mad population to the merest rumours of a Neil Diamond tour in early 1976. An Australian radio disc jockey had announced on air that Diamond was coming; that was enough to unleash a tidal wave of fans mailing signed blank cheques to those theatres where it could be reasonably assumed he would be playing. Seats were sought at any price, and punters trusted venue managers to fill in the relevant amounts. This produced the crazy situation that Neil had sold out theatres across Australia at which he had no plans to perform. It was obvious that he could tour Australia and New Zealand many times over and still not satisfy the tens of thousands of fans who yearned to see him in person.

Almost immediately after his final gig in Utah, Diamond and his backing band flew to New Zealand, where the opening night of this much-anticipated tour arrived on 13 February 1976, at Western Springs in Auckland. John Denver had previously played at this open-air rugby field before a crowd of 12,000. Elton John had rustled up 33,000, and the audience for the famous American evangelist Billy Graham went 1,000 more than that. But Neil Diamond shattered all attendance records at Western Springs when 36,000 fans flocked to see his solitary gig there. Many more people turned up ticketless, on spec, and had to be turned away. Two nights later, the Queen Elizabeth II Park in Christchurch was packed to capacity for the second of his two New Zealand gigs. After this, he landed in Australia for what would turn out to be a dozen memorable dates.

The fervour whipped up by his imminent arrival showed in the swamp of media coverage he elicited. A genuine sense of friendly welcome pervaded everything, and his quiet altruism was also busy earning him kudos. His kick-off appearances in Australia were three gigs at the Festival Hall in Brisbane, starting on 18 February. The barrage of ticket requests for these consecutive nightly concerts was such that hordes were ready to pay $15 a head for standing room only places, behind the stage. Yet Diamond had previously stipulated that 1,200 tickets be set aside, to be given away free of charge to disabled people and those from underprivileged groups to come to see the show from comfortable side stalls.

Hard after Brisbane, Diamond's next stop was at Sydney's Hordern Pavilion, again a three-gig stint. By playing this venue in late February, Neil just missed crossing paths with the UK rock band Queen, likewise on its first tour Down Under. The Sidney Myer Music Bowl in Melbourne came next, and marked the last of the three-night slots. Then March arrived with a single date at the WACA Ground in Perth. Two nights later, on 6 March, it was the turn of the people of Adelaide to show up in their droves at West Lakes Football Park, before Diamond returned to Sydney to complete the tour with a gig at the spectacular city's Sports Ground.

Details of this final gig had only been released days before; because of the stampede for tickets, the 40,000 available places sold out in a flash. More than the same number of people also turned up just to stand around outside the venue, making officers from the Sydney Police Department somewhat nervous. However, the crowd remained good-natured, despite being denied access to the sweeping lawns of the outdoor sports arena. This farewell Australian performance was covered by the nation's network TV Channel 9, which beamed the concert live at prime viewing time. An estimated one-third of the population tuned in to watch. A particularly intense rainstorm the day before had left the ground saturated, but the air quality was invigoratingly fresh for the show, which had been dubbed 'Thank You Australia'.

For Neil, it proved to be an extraordinary feeling when the ecstatic crowd responded to him with wild enthusiasm. The symbiosis between himself and his body of fans had never been more pronounced. That particular night public transport stopped operating at 9.00 p.m., long before the gig ended. Having been made aware of that, Diamond had arranged to have a fleet of 27 buses on standby outside the grounds after the gig, to take people back free to the centre of Sydney, from where they could easily disperse.

By any yardstick, this Australia/New Zealand trip would take some beating. Neil should, metaphorically, have been able to float back to America on the proverbial cloud nine. Yet the only indication that the experience had given him long-term confidence came when he told the *Australian Post* before leaving: 'A few years back, I thought I only had a couple of years left until I retired. But now I think I'd like to go on for, say, another thirty years.'

After a brief rest period at home, he was certainly raring to go when he took to the road again on 1 April with a gig at the Pan Am Center in Las Cruces, New Mexico. Showing up the next night in Tucson, Arizona, before playing in Tempe, he hiked north to Seattle, then on to Vancouver in British Columbia, Canada. The road map of gigs stretched far ahead, and in a very short space of time April, May and half of June had gone by. Yet Neil had not let these months come and go in a blur. On the contrary, he was very much alive to what this whole professional re-emergence had brought him.

He knew that his self-imposed exile had enabled him to grow in valuable ways. Better than ever before, he was learning how to handle the reality of being a public personality. He had figured out that having such a broad fan base was a decided plus, rather than a worrying negative. He explained: 'At first, I was taken aback when I realised that my audience ranged from teenagers, right through to grown-ups older than me. It disturbed me because I couldn't really be sure who I was talking to. Who was that person buying the record or the concert ticket? Then I realised that it gave me an enormous latitude.'

He welcomed the fact that his original followers had grown up with him, and that their changing musical tastes still matched the breadth of what he was able to offer them. He felt a prized sense of freedom in what he wrote and in the way he could perform, precisely because he did not have to contemplate honing himself to appeal to a limited stratum of the record-buying public. Basically, he came to the conclusion that he ought simply to focus on reflecting what was important to himself, and what spoke of his own experiences and struggles in life. 'It was just me and them, whoever they were and whoever I was,' he declared.

It was a fair assumption that the myriad aspects of human nature's fundamental frailty contained a huge pool of evocative emotions to draw upon, and that this allowed him to write songs that people could identify with and be moved by. It had also been re-emphasised that, live on stage, he did still touch some deep emotional chord in his audiences. The effect of the act of concert performance on Diamond came into focus when he publicly likened it to the act of making love. He is not alone in this thinking.

Talking about the sensation of delivering the goods to audiences hundreds or thousands strong, former Marillion vocalist Fish says: 'It's an incredible feeling of power and satisfaction. There are so many different emotions involved. Some say it's like sex, others that it's like standing on top of a tall building and leaning over. You can't equate it with anything else, at least nothing that I've found so far. If you want to, you can really turn on the stage stuff. There is a mechanism that you've got to learn how to trigger and how to control, to be a master of it.' Years later, charismatic Bon Jovi frontman Jon Bon Jovi declared with some authority: 'Trying to seduce an audience is the basis of rock and roll.'

On the concert experience being like sex, Neil Diamond proffered: 'There's the interplay during the actual act of lovemaking. There's built-in excitement and intensity, which only increases the feeling of love and warmth and excitement. And the concert performance does reach a climax at some point. So I think it makes a good comparison.'

Yet despite having reached a new level of openness, Diamond would not be Diamond if he didn't also have co-existing, conflicting feelings about being a feted star. He simply was not, 24/7, comfortable with having celebrity, heart-throb status. Although he acknowledged that it was not realistic, he maintained that his ideal dream would be to be an anonymous star – someone whose music was widely appreciated, but who was also able to move about freely without being recognised.

It seemed a strange sentiment from a performer who had

badly needed to resume his place in front of an audience, who had not only come thundering back into the limelight but who had, it had been proved by now, emerged from his cocoon in a startlingly different style from the one he had adopted when he had retired from view. A decade earlier, Diamond had dressed in funereal black to make himself less conspicuous while performing. It had been a major milestone when, over the years, he had gradually shaded out to wearing white. This time around, the name of the game was full-on glamour.

Neil no longer needed to 'hide' on stage. On the contrary, he wanted to glitter, to shimmer, to be the focal point for the person in the seat farthest away from the stage, stuck at the very back of the largest auditorium. And so he had let flamboyance – never present in his off-duty existence – loose on stage, another interesting example of his many contradictions.

After his first comeback appearance in Sacramento, in February, music reviewers had described Diamond as a sleek, rhinestoned figure because of the dazzling shirts he had stunned the crowds by wearing. Under the stage spotlights, these costume shirts had a scintillating effect that Diamond's devotees adored. They became synonymous with the star's image from the mid-1970s onwards, but they were also regularly ridiculed by critics and rock audiences. To this day, Diamond will quietly correct anyone using the word 'sequin'. His startlingly jazzy showbiz shirts are glass-beaded, and a little heavy to wear for nearly two hours in a sweating performance under baking hot, bright lights. Said Neil: 'It's my one chance to really let 'em have it between the eyes.'

In conjunction with this highly distinctive stage style, Diamond's reputation among critics as an excessive nightclub-style performer was established. Whereas earlier reviewers had tended to comment on his introverted depth, some now took to accusing Neil of hamming it up. They also decided his music was veering more towards middle-of-the-road, easy listening stuff. Neil Diamond saw no need to pigeonhole it in any way. The way he saw it, his music was changing because it stood – as it always

would – as a mirror of himself as a writer. And as he was naturally not the same person as before, it was to be expected that he
would be different as a writer. 'I've become wiser and happier,'
he said. 'I like to think I've become better, and the music reflects
that.'

There was no change, however, in the way he viewed his
songwriting. That remained a very intense process, which he has
likened to the conception, growth and birth of a baby. He drew
the analogy that a woman carries a child through all its stages of
development in the womb until the moment labour pains herald
the beginning of the baby's arrival into the world. According to
Neil, labour pain was the sort of experience he went through
when getting to grips with creating a song in his head and bringing it successfully to life on paper. Developing this theme, he
stated: 'Then you hope it's born whole and has all its toes and
fingers.'

In the midst of a past period that had been chock-a-block with
terribly worthy songwriters, he had once stated that rather than
find fault with the ways of the government of the day, or with
society as a whole, he preferred to concentrate all his energies on
writing about inter-personal relationships. He still preferred to.
That approach plays its part in Neil Diamond's enviable longevity
as a lyricist.

Triple Oscar-winning lyricist Sir Tim Rice has maintained
that, time and again, what lies at the root of a long songwriting
career in such a crowded music industry is not allowing oneself
to be buffeted by shifting trends and fads in music. Quality and
structure will out, it appears. Sir Tim feels: 'When writing a
song, it doesn't really matter if you are writing it for the charts or
not. It's getting the context right that is much harder for people.
A lot of people in the pop world can write a decent lyric or a great
tune. But whether they can construct them together around
something that really makes sense is another thing entirely.' He
adds: 'Successful songwriting is a good insurance policy for your
old age.'

Neil Diamond had already proved that he was a powerful

commercial force. Coupled with his new showy stage style, that was about to prove a dynamite combination in the world-famous home of glitz and flashy glamour – Las Vegas – where he had historic concerts lined up at the Aladdin Hotel in July. Immediately prior to that, though, one potentially big, black cloud was ready to rain on his parade. In the past, Neil had admitted to a mild flirtation with marijuana, though he was far better known as an outspoken denouncer of drug taking. It was almost surreal, then, when headlines at the end of June 1976 screamed that the police had carried out a drug bust at the star's Hollywood home. It was an eye-opening experience for the whole family – and it was all sparked off by an anonymous tipster.

Neil Diamond's life-size picture was emblazoned on a huge billboard hoisted high above Hollywood's Sunset Strip, advertising his Las Vegas Aladdin Hotel concerts, when practically on the eve of these five shows some anonymous person rang the Los Angeles police department to claim that Neil Diamond kept a stash of cocaine at his home. Despite the knee-jerk sense of disbelief that first reigned at Los Angeles Police Department, an operation was immediately mounted, comprising 50 officers drawn from the LAPD and the Sheriff's Department. On 30 June 1976, armed with a search warrant, they went calling on the superstar at home with his family in plush Holmby Hills, just outside Beverly Hills.

It was 10.30 p.m. and Neil was checking the preparations for his departure the following day for Nevada. He was concentrating his mind on what would be one of the most important engagements of his career yet, when he was disturbed by the unmistakable noise of a low flying helicopter, coming closer. Then the phone to the estate's electronic security gates rang. He answered personally, to hear the voice of the officer heading the detail tell him that it was the police, and that they had reason to suspect that there was an intruder loose in the grounds.

At first shocked, Neil turned stone-like. The inspector said that he and his men would like to come in and check the place out. Unknown to Neil, a plainclothes detective had already penetrated security and was in the garden. So when he looked out of a window and saw a shadowy presence lurking in the darkness near to the house, he immediately activated the mechanism that opened the gates at the end of the drive. All too quickly, however, the whole complexion of affairs changed. Some, but not all, of the fifty men fanned out and began to comb the grounds, and a plainclothes officer handed Neil the search warrant. His suspicions were aroused now that this was not quite what it seemed, and he requested sight of some appropriate ID. Uniformed cops then suddenly poured into his home. At that point, Diamond faced the inspector, supposedly so concerned with burglars, and told him drily: 'I don't know what you're looking for. But you're not going to find it.'

In today's wall-to-wall media world, the attempted shakedown of one of the world's biggest stars would bring CNN and other satellite systems to capture the sensational drama live, second by unfolding second. As it was, it was still extremely upsetting, especially for Neil's wife, Marcia, and their six-year-old son, Jesse, who had been fast asleep in bed when the startling intrusion began.

As the ear-busting racket from the hovering helicopter, ready with powerful wide-range search beams, drowned almost everything else out, the swarm of coppers went through the ten-roomed house with a fine-toothed comb. After three hours of exhaustive searching, they had to conclude that a stash of cocaine at the Diamonds' home was a figment of the anonymous caller's imagination. They did come up with a small packet containing less than one ounce of marijuana. But the juicy collar they had been told was theirs for the taking had not materialised.

If Neil Diamond and his wife had expected contrition, maybe embarrassment, or even an apology from the police inspector in charge, none was forthcoming. Indeed, the light-hearted way in which those heading the detail accepted defeat turned up an alarm bell that had been set off in Neil's head. The rank and file cops were mostly a little shamefaced, but Neil made their departure from his home easier by cheerfully distributing signed copies of his as yet unreleased new album *Beautiful Noise*. All the time, his mind was racing.

Some very disturbing things had been happening in the period just prior to this drug bust, which Neil had been keeping a lid on. He had been receiving anonymous death threats by telephone. Showbiz-obsessed kooks were one thing, but these threats were seemingly different. Apart from anything else, his private telephone numbers were not exactly in the LA phone book and Neil had begun to wonder if the calls were connected with his imminent engagements in Las Vegas. In his tense state, it felt as if the intimidation behind the threats stemmed from monetary considerations. Now, naturally, it crossed his mind that this malicious tip-off to the police was not an isolated coincidence, but was linked to the recent threatening phone calls.

Neil Diamond certainly would not be the first music star to be set up. In Britain in the late 1960s, Rolling Stone Brian Jones, who had had a valid drug conviction against him in 1967, was nevertheless widely seen as having been fitted up for another, the following year. In any event, for a time Diamond found it hard to shake the suspicion that these intimidatory events *were* tied in to his appointment with a new complex opening in Las Vegas, the gambling capital of the world.

Since the Prohibition period, from 1920 to 1933, when the making, selling and shipping of alcohol was banned in the US, the Mafia had sunk its formidable talons into the live entertainment scene. Behind the glitz and pizzazz of some high-profile showbiz careers had lain the seamy underbelly of organised crime. It was naive not to accept that, decades on, parts of the big-moneyed business end of the music scene were still infiltrated by the mob. Diamond's mind toyed with the sinister possibility that these shadowy elements were trying to prevent him from playing Las Vegas. The reason might be that they were opposed to a threatening shift in the traditional showroom entertainment world there, not every aspect of which was scrupulously on the level.

The new theatre Diamond had been booked to inaugurate

was an actual theatre, as distinct from a showroom. Tickets were sold strictly via above-board box offices, and all areas of the business were transparent. If Diamond's shows proved as successful as anticipated, might it have been the case that certain figures viewed that as a threat? This new theatre set-up catered for several thousand people a night, at upwards of $30 per seat. The majority of Las Vegas showrooms and banquet rooms had capacities of around just 1,500, and put on shows lasting less than one hour.

Artistes, too, were expected to hire Las Vegas-based backing musicians and singers, and were not encouraged to come complete with their own backing band. If the new set-up at the Aladdin took off, it was possible to theorise that other big stars could turn away from the old stomping grounds, costing everyone involved a great deal of money. It was not out of left field, then, to wonder if the Mafia's fingers had been trying to pull strings to prevent this new set-up from getting started in this neck of the entertainment world. Neil had believed his life was in danger once before, years earlier. Now, all over again, he was distinctly uneasy.

Later, he logically tried to play devil's advocate. In all, around 37,000 people came to his five shows, and since the Aladdin's hotel accommodation block could only hold approximately 1,000, then many other hotels would reap sizeable benefits from the overspill of visitors to the Aladdin shows. His fears of possible Mafia involvement in these threats didn't always make complete sense, but that scarcely registered as at 30 June 1976. The whole business of having the police arrive mob-handed to trawl through his home and personal possessions, based purely on an anonymous tip-off, had a marked effect on Neil. Looking back, he admitted that he had been numbed by it all. He declared: 'It made me aware of the vulnerability of the average, law-abiding citizen. I'd never felt so naked.'

As for the immediate legal fallout concerning the less than one ounce of marijuana the cops say they found that night at Neil's Bel Air home, Diamond was not arrested. In mid-1976, though, even such a small quantity of grass was sufficient to come under misdemeanour possession. So, details of the find were turned over to the Los Angeles city attorney's office for consideration on how to proceed. Diamond, meanwhile, headed as planned to Las Vegas. On 2 July 1976 the Los Angeles city attorney's office decided to charge Neil Diamond with misdemeanour possession of marijuana. Diamond instructed lawyers to lodge a not guilty plea when it came to court. The outcome was that Neil was later offered a six-month drug awareness programme course, and the charge was dropped in 1977.

The 2 July 1976, however, when he received word of the charge being laid against him, was the date of his opening night at the Aladdin Theater for the Performing Arts on Las Vegas Boulevard, Las Vegas. Not so long ago, the whole aura surrounding this event had been so very different. For a long time, Neil had resisted offers to give performances in dinner clubs or any situations where playing was against the backdrop of people getting heartily stuck into their food and drink. He hated these kinds of noisy distraction from way back. He recalled: 'When I played small clubs in Greenwich Village, even the sound of ice cubes colliding in a glass became as grating as chalking up a blackboard.'

When the offer came through to inaugurate the brand new, $10 million, 7,000-seater Aladdin Theater – which remains one of the largest theatres of its ilk in America – it was a different story. And the carrot had been substantial. At first, the newspapers in America and Britain reported that Neil Diamond had signed a deal to play three gigs at the Aladdin for a then staggering fee of $500,000, which well outstripped Frank Sinatra's record payment of approximately $300,000 for a week of shows. At that time, it was a salary for three nights that would make Diamond the highest-paid performer in Las Vegas history. In the event, he was paid $650,000 for five sold-out shows between 2 and 5 July 1976.

Prior to recent events, the kind of issues preoccupying the star had been the sound system in the new, untested venue, and his wardrobe for shows that would attract massive media attention. As to the sound system, although the Aladdin Theater had excellent facilities, the US press reported in early June that Neil had forked out $75,000 of his own money to install some extra elements to the sound and lighting set-ups to enhance the show. When it came to his wardrobe for the event, working with a fashion designer, he had specific ideas in mind. He opted for self-coloured shirts and leather trousers. When performing songs from the *Jonathan Livingston Seagull* soundtrack, he envisaged himself all in white; in contrast, all black seemed appropriate for the number, 'Brother Love's Travelling Salvation Show'.

By the time first night arrived, he had much more serious matters than sartorial style on his mind. Apart from his obvious contractual obligations to appear, there is a strong stubborn streak running through Neil Diamond. And *if* his suspicions that he might be the target of intimidation by Mafia elements, or by anyone else, had any foundation, he was determined that they would not prevent him from going ahead with his performances as planned.

His parents, Rose and Kieve Diamond, attended this historic opening night, and were among 7,000 people to gape at their first sight of the sweeping, stylish interior of the air-conditioned Aladdin Theater, which featured an abundance of gleaming glass, all lending light and sparkle to the atmosphere, and which boasted an impressive domed ceiling that provided great acoustics. With fixed, flawless smiles, an army of ushers dressed in silver tunics directed people to their seats, while leggy usherettes working as sexy flower sellers glided among the aisles. As people seated in the scallop-shaped rows pored over their copies of the concert programme hailing Neil Diamond as 'the world's greatest performer', Neil sat backstage, having applied his own stage make-up, drawing on a cigarette and alone with his thoughts. This was no ordinary psyche-up period. He was intent on going out on stage and defying anyone present to divine the strain he had been under, and was still under.

And he did. He turned in a two-hour show that met with near blanket approval. The *Los Angeles Times* decided that this was the night when: 'Diamond crucially moved from singer-songwriter to performer to personality without sacrificing quality in either of the first two areas. That gives him a potent arsenal indeed.'

Neil Diamond's on-stage tendency to sway his body to the beat still stemmed from his own inner response to the music coming out of him, and was not a direct attempt to turn on the ladies. However, in a city not renowned for its subtlety or restraint, his sex appeal was certainly effective enough, judging by the number of overwrought young women who gatecrashed the stage, hell-bent on receiving a hug and a kiss from the handsome star. As Diamond prowled the stage, periodically talking to the audience, he projected a man who was totally focused and in complete, unruffled control. Only *Rolling Stone,* picking up on the night, made brief mention that the star's humour at times had seemed a trifle nervous. If that was the faintest chink showing in Diamond's armour, still no one would have been able to identify the roots of any anxiety. A lavish post-gig party was thrown for Neil that night in a banquet hall within the complex, coincidentally called the Diamond Room, and each performance at the Aladdin Theater thereafter went down as well as the first. Diamond had no complaints about how the theatre people had treated him. But when he left the gaudy, neon-obsessed city after his final engagement, he inwardly vowed that it would be a very long time before he would return to Las Vegas, if ever.

He had a one-month respite before taking to the road in America. During this period his new album, *Beautiful Noise,* was released. Diamond had toyed briefly with calling it *Street Life,* but had quickly reverted to his belief that the track inspired by his daughter, Marjorie, ought to name the work. With this album, Neil had set out to tell the tale of what Tin Pan Alley had been like for all aspiring young songwriters, and of how most of them ended up having their dreams shattered, while only a relative few became long-lasting success stories. He had come up with a batch of songs to encapsulate that.

The self-explanatory tracks, 'Street Life' and 'Jungle Time', portrayed life in tough New York neighbourhoods. 'Stargazer' struck a slightly cynical note, and held a cautionary tone regarding the teasingly transitory nature of fame. The likes of the soul-searching 'Surviving The Life', spoke movingly of the struggles to cope with life's vagaries while striving to find a positive route in the world. 'Lady-Oh' yearned for something or someone perpetually just out of reach. One song, called 'Listen', had been left out of the final selection because it appeared to be better suited to live performance than vinyl. Neil liked the song so much, and had worked so hard on it, that he said it caused him pain to omit it from the album. 'Yet, I was persuaded the decision was right,' he revealed.

That apart, *Beautiful Noise* was an immensely personal album for Neil. A slant on how he felt he had risen to the challenge came in 1976, when with uncharacteristic boldness he announced: 'I consider myself one of the best songwriters in the world today.' He added, 'People don't all know it yet, but they will – maybe five years from now.'

Sporting a view of the dramatic New York City skyline on its front sleeve, *Beautiful Noise* also displayed prominently the production credit for Robbie Robertson; cynics might have wondered if Robertson's involvement played a part in the album receiving unusually warm critical praise. The album's popularity in terms of sales, however, was crystal clear. In Britain it charted at number ten, while in the US it climbed to number four. Farther afield, *Beautiful Noise* excelled, going quadruple gold Down Under and double gold in territories throughout Europe and Africa. It rapidly became West Germany's biggest-selling album of 1976.

'Dry Your Eyes', the song co-composed with Robbie Robertson, was singled out as a favourite by many, although it was a sad song. Diamond described it as being about the sixties' generation inevitably losing the very innocence that had made everything so spontaneous, vital and alive in that mould-breaking decade. He revealed, too, that he had hit a strong emotional peak while writing 'If You Know What I Mean'. This powerful song, which expressed both joy and a disappointment at not quite accomplishing all his targets in life, backed by 'Street Life', was released as a single, reaching number 11 in the States in August. In Britain, this lead-off single tailed off in the mid-thirties as Diamond meanwhile returned to live performance.

Setting off with a gig at the Richfield Coliseum in Cleveland, Ohio, on 6 August, he pitched up next in Illinois for a double-header at Chicago Stadium, paid a flying visit to Landover in Maryland to pack out the Capital Center, only to land in New York City mid-month for three sold-out nights at the Forest Hills Stadium in Queens. It was the first time he had performed in New York since his stint at the Winter Garden Theater on Broadway had ended in October 1972.

Neil Diamond put the same effort and energy into all his performances, but there always seemed to be more of a beady eye on him when he returned to the city of his birth – more at stake somehow. The *New York Times* was quick to weigh in with a critique of the first night's concert that both praised and picked holes with it. The piece lauded Diamond's musical virtues and, broadly speaking, his stage manner between songs. But it questioned the wisdom of his devoting a 20-minute slot near the end of the show to material from *Jonathan Livingston Seagull*. The reviewer called that a miscalculation, going on to say: 'Popularity is in at least some sense its own reward. Mr Diamond unquestionably pleases his fans and perhaps that's enough.' Perspicaciously, he concluded: 'One wonders, though, if it's quite enough for him.'

In a stark change of scenery, after quitting New York City, Diamond played in Denver, Colorado, at the spectacularly craggy natural amphitheatre of Red Rocks, stopping in then on San Diego, before returning to the scene of past glories – the Greek Theater in Los Angeles – where, commencing on 13 September, he was set to give an eight-gig stint, his longest engagement at one venue since coming back to the fore. Any notion that his hometown fans had seen it all before was quashed when in excess of 100,000 people queued in their cars, bumper to bumper, at the Greek Theater and at three ticket agencies in LA, to part with their cash; 37,000 tickets were sold in under two hours, and pandemonium erupted when so many would-be concert goers, having patiently waited for so long, realised they were out of luck. Television cameras were on hand to cover the police operation to calm the atmosphere outside the Greek Theater ticket office.

The Greek Theater being in Diamond's own back yard, as it were, meant his performances there tended to be special almost of their own accord. That is not to say that his mesmeric and powerfully emotive performances were not the product of consci-entious hard endeavour, night after night. At this venue, three hours was the normal duration of each show. This time, the final performance of the eight was videotaped for television. In the audience that night were Los Angeles's mayor, Tom Bradley, Olivia Newton-John before her sky-rocketing fame in *Grease*, Australian singer Helen Reddy, whose biggest chart hit had been 'Angie Baby' the year before, and actor Henry Winkler, a cool cult figure as The Fonz, star of the phenomenally successful US TV comedy series *Happy Days*.

Diamond had three times before considered putting together a television special, but on each occasion he had suddenly pulled the plug, at some considerable financial cost to himself. This time, however, it felt right. Producers Dwight Hemion and Gary Smith handled work on this project, and Neil Diamond's first TV special was aired in the new year.

On 23 September 1976, days after the last Greek Theater concert, Neil Diamond's international public profile was raised yet higher when he was the cover story in *Rolling Stone*. By then, he himself had retreated once again to be with his family during a small hiatus in his US tour. Home at this point was a summer house leased in Malibu. The drug raid incident in June had remained so upsetting that the Diamonds had decided to place their Holmby Hills house on the market. The vivid memories of that whole episode looked like taking time to fade. At the summer house, Neil was able to relax with his family, which included his parents for a while. He was pleased that they had been able to retire these past few years. Diamond was particularly delighted to note how naturally his father had adjusted to taking things easy, after so many years of hard work. As Neil grew older, he seemed to study life in even greater depth. He knew it would benefit him if he too were able to adopt a more laid-back attitude to life. But his ever-present need to drive himself would scarcely permit it.

Just as his US tour reconvened at the end of the first week of October in Fort Worth, Texas, *Beautiful Noise* spawned further single releases on both sides of the Atlantic. 'Don't Think...Feel'/'Home Is A Wounded Heart' featured on the US charts at number 43. In the UK, 'Beautiful Noise'/'Signs' made a better show by getting to number 13. Meanwhile, MCA released a Neil Diamond compilation album called *And The Singer Sings His Songs*, which stood outside the Top 100.

These throwbacks to his recording past were a regular occurrence, but Diamond concentrated on looking forward. He had no problem in turning down lures already coming his way from the Las Vegas entertainment scene, to bring his money-spinning act back to Nevada. Year on year, these approaches would be made to him in vain. Towards the end of 1976, however, the end of an era had come for a friend of Neil's. The Band staged its farewell concert on 25 November at the Winterland Ballroom in San Francisco, and Robbie Robertson invited Diamond, whose tour had recently ended in Honolulu, Hawaii, to be part of an all-star line-up for the event.

The Band had decided to finish with a flourish. In addition to the stellar line-up including Bob Dylan, Eric Clapton, Van Morrison, Neil Young and Muddy Waters, among others, the group had drafted in director Martin Scorsese, better known for feature films – *Alice Doesn't Live Here Anymore, Mean Streets* and *Taxi Driver* – to film the emotional last hurrah. Fittingly, San Francisco's Winterland Ballroom had been the scene of The Band's live debut in February 1969, and they intended making this event, on Thanksgiving Day 1976, a night to remember.

When it was time for Neil to take centre stage he sang 'Dry Your Eyes', the song he and Robbie Robertson had co-written; for the next 16 years that would stand as the only time Diamond performed the song in concert. Dubbed 'The Last Waltz', this farewell concert was released two years later as a film-cum-documentary-cum-concert. *Halliwell's Film Guide* called it: 'Perhaps the best movie so far of a rock concert, that also features many of the most influential performers of the era.'

Just weeks into the new year, on 21 February 1977, Neil Diamond's first TV special, which had been videotaped five months earlier at the Greek Theater, Los Angeles, was aired nationwide on the NBC network. Diamond must have been pleased with it, but he retained very focused views on this medium that brought him into the homes of nearly every American citizen. He called television one of the last frontiers for him to breach, seeing it as the entrée to future possibilities. Yet he said: 'Television is a seductive thing. I can't say, though, that I needed TV, or that TV needed me.'

Maybe still raw from that 1976 minor drug charge, which had yet to go away, it was in the same spirit of bluntness that Diamond used the media attention he was receiving to reiterate his anti-drug stance. Speaking of how he felt some had treated him for his unhip views on the scourge of drugs, he said: 'I was looked down upon by the underground press because I did a documentary musical piece on New York City's drug rehabilitation programme many years before a publication like *Rolling Stone* would do anything on me. But I don't regret it for a moment.'

Judging by his public utterances throughout the first half of this year, Neil Diamond was in something of a maze, mentally. He talked of the scary uncertainty of the future for everyone, but also of his own future line of work, which was no big surprise – fame is a fickle mistress for all stars. On the one hand, he stated that he was happy; on the other he confessed to feeling every day that he was barely managing to get through when it came to achieving and maintaining the right balance of career and personal life.

Just as writing is a highly solitary profession, nothing much had altered personally. Intrinsically, Neil Diamond was still a solitary man who neither sought nor craved a gaggle of people around him at any time. He cared to count a comfortable number of people in Los Angeles as very good friends with whom he would occasionally meet up. But he continued to have no interest in being a member of any social clique. Inside, the man was still the same boy who went to Surprise Lake Camp and stood back from the crowd, impenetrable and watchful.

The year 1977, though, would be a tough one for artistes like Neil Diamond. By now the music press had latched firmly onto the punk movement, to the exclusion of established, showy performers such as Neil Diamond, Queen and Abba, seeing them as the antithesis of punk's philosophy. In 1977, The Sex Pistols' song, 'God Save The Queen', became a UK number one hit, outselling Rod Stewart two to one. It was banned from the airwaves, at least one major retailer refused to stock the single, and many distributors would not touch it with the proverbial bargepole.

Malcolm McLaren, once manager of The New York Dolls, who handled The Sex Pistols, calls the band's contentious single: 'The most English, angst-ridden, toughest, mother-fucking rock song that's ever been written. That was to me, punk rock at its best!' To McLaren, if an artiste's song appealed to parents, it was the absolute pits. Alongside this nihilistic punk music, teenagers were emulating their new anti-heroes by clomping about in heavy Doc Marten boots, sporting short, spiky hairstyles, scruffy slashed denim and leather jackets hung with chains, while their noses were invariably lanced with earring studs or bars.

Punk was so prevalent at every level that the music press had taken to announcing that rock was dead, and that groups such as Led Zeppelin, Genesis and Queen were passé. It went without saying, then, that any ostentatious display was guaranteed to goad the critics. In Britain, Queen, whose 1975 single 'Bohemian

Rhapsody' and its accompanying ground-breaking video had put them firmly on the map, came in for a great deal of flak from critics. Flamboyant frontman Freddie Mercury would appear on stage sheathed in skintight silver lurex bodysuits so heavily sequinned that they would dazzle audiences whenever he shimmied under large banks of spotlights, or poured into black leotards, often with a diamante-studded crotch, and other equally subtle outfits.

The Swedish pop group Abba, frequently swathed in satin, fell foul too. It would take two decades for Abba to begin belatedly to receive their just critical acclaim. U2's lightning rod, Bono, once reflected: 'It was the era of punk rock, and Abba were to be beheaded, and I probably would have held the axe.' It had not in any way spared the talented foursome that one of their best-loved hits, 'Dancing Queen', was riding high at the top of the American charts in April 1977.

Like Queen and Abba, Neil Diamond made an easy target for attack on this front. By now, his fondness for wearing glitzy, glass-beaded shirts on stage was attracting knock after knock from the critics. Some people did point out that since the days, decades earlier, when Jerry Lee Lewis would climb on top of his piano and seemingly play the instrument with his booted heels, over-the-top showmanship was an integral ingredient of entertaining. But it cut no ice with the new wave of reviewers.

Tedious though the carping must have been, Diamond's response to these barbs about his costume shirts was to order yet more. It wasn't just that stubborn streak again. Diamond never particularly set out to antagonise critics; he simply knew their place and their relevance. Just as he had never permitted critical opinion to control what he wrote, now he pointed out that if all the reviewers could pick on was how sparkly his stage shirts were, then he was not doing too badly – a calm, disinterested reaction that probably ruffled critics' feathers even further.

Away from the cosmetics of his sartorial style, it's what Diamond found to drive him on that was worth noting. He maintained that his continued motivation came down to: 'a sense of the demons in me, goals and standards I've set that are well beyond my reach. That's what keeps me excited.' To be forever seeking stimulus could suggest a soul that is never satisfied. However, a dose of gratification came his way in early April 1977 with the release of his second live double album, *Love At The Greek,* which had, like the TV special, been harvested from his most recent performances at the Greek Theater. Produced by Robbie Robertson, it peaked at number eight at home, going five places higher in Britain.

On the tail wind of this success, Diamond took off for Indiana, where his tour resumed on 23 April at the Market Square Arena in Indianapolis. Over the next six weeks he played in Ohio and Kentucky, concentrating then mostly in the southern states of Alabama and Louisiana, before trekking through South and North Carolina and Virginia. All the while, he anticipated the European leg of his tour which, following a fortnight's break, kicked off at the Ahoy in Rotterdam, in the Netherlands, at the end of May. Dates in France and Austria bookended eight concerts, spread over four major cities in Germany throughout early summer, before Diamond headed for London for five nights at the Palladium, commencing on 23 June.

Rock writer Ray Coleman hailed Neil Diamond on the eve of these Palladium dates as: 'A seventies counterpart to the greats such as Cole Porter or Irving Berlin, Diamond has this knack of combining established old-fashioned showbiz qualities with a contemporary feeling that gives the impression of modernity.' Smack at the height of summer 1977, punk rock may have been said to be in and showmanship firmly out. But every ticket for Neil Diamond's five Palladium concerts sold out in a single day.

Just as Diamond had often contemplated the breadth of his appeal, so Britain's *Melody Maker* now puzzled at the pulling power of a man who, in his mid-thirties, drew people aged between 14 and 50 to see him. The music paper dubbed Diamond: 'a curious amalgam of hip middle-of-the-road giant and progressive pop singer-songwriter'. In other words, he didn't fit a category – which would have pleased Neil no end to read.

Although the London Palladium was one of those prestigious venues to play, the venue Neil chose to cap this European tour was of special interest. On 2 July 1977 he staged a one-off appearance at Woburn Abbey, in Bedfordshire. Woburn Abbey was what it sounded – ancient. Down countless decades the family seat of the Dukes of Bedford, the Abbey had begun life as a 12th-century Cistercian monastery. Its luscious grounds extended for 3,000 acres; features included a deer park, picturesque ponds and an impressive maze. Diamond played in the grounds of this, one of England's premier, stately homes, before 55,000 excited fans. The concert was filmed, and excerpts from the event appeared in a second Neil Diamond US television special, aired later in the year.

Quitting Bedfordshire and Britain altogether, Neil went back to his family. He, Marcia and Jesse had left the rented summer house in Malibu by now, and had bought a nearby property, which they were busy turning into a home. Quizzed by foreign press about just how luxurious a lifestyle he lived privately, Diamond revealed that his new abode had nine bathrooms and fifteen telephones, and that there were usually four cars blocking the driveway. 'I need only one of each, but Americans tend to be terribly spoiled,' he quipped.

Presumably not all fifteen phones burst into life at once whenever someone called the Diamond household, for peace and quiet was now the order of the day. Neil knew at this mid-point in the year that it was time to knuckle down again to write songs for a new studio album. The remaining live concert dates for the year were heavily clustered in December, the only exception being two individual gigs in late August. So he had time to let the creative juices flow and to unwind once more with his son and wife, who was now pregnant with their second child.

It must have been a fairly benign time. His young son was developing apace, wallowing in having both his parents' attention, and Marcia was preparing for the new arrival. When Neil sat back and assessed his professional comeback, which had had no absolute guarantee of success, he was entitled to feel secure in the knowledge that he had not slipped at all, that he was still at the top of his game in such an ephemeral business. The fates would not be so kind elsewhere.

In the hot, idyllic summer of 1977, the music world was suddenly rocked to its foundations by the news that Elvis Presley had died. At 2.20 p.m. on 16 August, Elvis had been found on the floor in one of the second-floor bathrooms of Graceland, his palatial mansion in Memphis, Tennessee, by his then girlfriend Ginger Alden, whom rumour had had it Elvis was due to wed later that month. Presley had been rushed to the Baptist Memorial Hospital in Memphis, where he was officially pronounced dead an hour later. The cause of death was cardiac arrhythmia. He was just 42 years old. The universal sense of profound shock around the world was not confined to Presley's massive global fan base, nor even to within music's parameters. When his funeral took place, days later, there was an outpouring of intense public grief such as the world had never seen. Practically everyone was touched to some degree by the tragedy.

Neil Diamond had frequently been described as 'the Jewish Elvis', and he was stunned and saddened by Presley's death. In subsequent years, many would find fault with the direction Elvis's professional path had taken, citing one example as the years of over exposure, playing season upon season at a Las Vegas hotel. But that had not all been down to the East Tupelo-born star – a mistake, as Diamond would point out. Said Neil: 'In order to make a career last in this business, you've got to eliminate as much interference as possible. One of the things I learned from Elvis was to avoid becoming public property. Nothing ... is worth that.'

CHAPTER 7

Challenging Times

NEIL DIAMOND'S FIRM VIEWS on how to body-swerve becoming public property included not allowing himself to be tempted into doing a whole series of TV specials. Seven months after transmission in February 1977, his first television show had newly attracted four Emmy Award nominations, one of which was for The Outstanding Special – Comedy, Variety or Musical Award. On 17 November, NBC-TV aired his second special, called *I'm Glad You're Here With Me Tonight*. But he intended being careful of overexposure.

In late August, he played half a dozen gigs, split between East Troy, Wisconsin, and Clarkston in Michigan. Other than that, he devoted his energies to the new album he had in the works, which would have the same title as his second TV special. As that title suggested, Diamond's new work centred heavily on love and the tangled path of relationships. The first cut was 'Desiree', a number redolent of an innocent young man's initiation into the joys of sex at the hands of an older, experienced woman – a brief, but sweet interlude. Backed by 'Once In A While', the single, released in December, soon halted just inside the UK Top 40 but made number 16 in America, early in the new year.

Just in time for the lucrative Christmas market, *I'm Glad*

You're Here With Me Tonight hit the shelves. Sixteen, this time, would be its highest UK chart ranking, while Americans took the sentiment-laden album sufficiently to their hearts to lift it to number six domestically, perhaps aided by the fact that Diamond was able to promote the album during the remainder of his performance dates, which were played throughout December 1977. Starting at the St Paul Civic Center in Minnesota, Diamond performed ten gigs in seven cities over a ten-day period, culminating with two concerts in Fort Worth, Texas. He took to the stage at the Seattle Center Coliseum in Washington, mid-January 1978. After that, he gave touring a miss until the middle of the year.

In the intervening time, something unexpected occurred. On the album *I'm Glad You're Here With Me Tonight,* the track 'As If' told the poignant tale of a troubled relationship. But it was another song, 'You Don't Bring Me Flowers', about a once precious love affair that had gone stale, that would prove to be astoundingly popular. The origin of this emotive ballad was that Neil had been asked to write a theme song for a US TV show, *All That Glitters.* Although Neil remained largely a solo songwriter he had on occasion collaborated on songs with a handful of people. For 'You Don't Bring Me Flowers', he had teamed up with award-winning lyricists Alan Bergman and Marilyn Bergman. The number had been composed on piano, and Neil liked it so much he decided to put it on his 1977 album.

By the end of the year, the ballad was being singled out for airplay by radio disc jockeys across America, and it had come to the ears of Barbra Streisand, who had once been in the same choir as Neil at Erasmus Hall High School. Throughout the 1970s, Brooklyn-born Barbra Streisand had broadened her stellar singing career by acting. In 1974, she co-starred with Robert Redford in the screen romance *The Way We Were.* Three years later she took the lead in *A Star Is Born,* the film for which Neil had rejected the offer to play the leading man.

In March 1977, the theme to *A Star Is Born,* 'Evergreen', written by Paul Williams and Barbra Streisand, won the

Academy Award for Best Song. At the Oscar ceremony, Neil Diamond presented Streisand with the coveted gold statuette. Although these two stars hailed from the same New York City borough and had attended the same school, their respective careers had rarely overlapped. However, Streisand was so taken with 'You Don't Bring Me Flowers' that she had released her own version.

Gary Guthrie worked for WAKY-AM in Louisville, Kentucky. One day in early 1978, comparing the two versions, he noticed that Neil Diamond's growling baritone made an earthy counterweight to Barbra Streisand's shattering soprano. On impulse, he played the two singles simultaneously on twin turntables, as if it were a duet. Once he had perfected his experiment, he put together a spliced version and played it on air; listener reaction was astonishing. Soon, Neil Diamond and Barbra Streisand each received a tape of this makeshift duet. The intercut renditions gelled so remarkably well that the two stars inevitably decided to record a real duet of the song. Pleased as they were with their endeavours, it's not likely that either realised how well it would do on its release near the end of the year.

In the meantime, Neil's priorities were focused on the home front, for on St Valentine's Day 1978, Marcia gave birth to their second child, again a boy, whom they named Micah Joseph. Diamond was now the proud father of four – two daughters and two sons. By now, he also knew the importance of being around in the very early months of a baby's development, and would not be taking to the road until well into summertime. He reverted, therefore, to balancing domesticity with yet more songwriting for another studio album. Even when he did take to the road again, he did not entirely leave his family behind.

On 27 July, Diamond relaunched his live show in Providence, Rhode Island, then promptly travelled to Canada to play the Forum in Montreal and a concert at Maple Leaf Gardens, Toronto. On his return to the States, after playing in Indiana, he showed up in Cincinnati for a concert at the Riverfront Coliseum in Ohio in early August, where at one point in the proceedings he introduced his son, Jesse, on stage. With a new baby being fussed over at home, it was a unique way of ensuring that Jesse did not feel left out. Years later, Jesse Diamond would join his father professionally on stage. In 1978, it must have been a mind-blowingly exciting experience for the eager eight-year-old.

By 1978, Diamond's stage act had moved with the times. The quality of the sound system had always been vital to him. Now, to make his appearances dazzle even more than by courtesy of the glamour provided by his distinctive stage wear, he was employing high-tech laser lighting. Before Neil made his entrance on stage at the Riverfront Coliseum, with the house lights dimmed, beams of yellow laser light suddenly flurried and dashed all over the stage. Seconds later, orange shafts of pinpoint light crisscrossed with the vibrant yellow, while the backing band burst into life, playing 'The Flight of the Bumblebee'. The furiously fast tune and the darting coloured beams of light conspired to create an exciting, captivating atmosphere.

Skilfully blending his most recently released material with a selection of his most popular hits, Diamond stayed on stage without a break for over two and a half hours. When introducing the 12-year-old favourite, 'I'm A Believer', he told his attentive audience: 'Here's a song I wrote in half an hour. It sold six million copies. The only problem is, I didn't record it!' Finishing the concert with 'I Am...I Said', he had to return for two rapturously received encores before the audience could be persuaded to let him go.

By mid-August, Diamond had packed away his microphone. Within another month, the second of his live 1977 TV specials, *I'm Glad You're Here With Me Tonight*, had secured two Emmy nominations; again, one was for The Outstanding Special – Comedy, Variety or Musical Award.

During his summer concerts, Neil had regularly road-tested numbers that were under consideration for inclusion in his new album, and he had often played a slow, bluesy number called 'Teach Me Tonight', which had been very well received live. It did not, however, make the playlist of *You Don't Bring Me Flowers*, which was released towards the end of the year. By early 1979, the album was number 15 in Britain, while bristling at number four in America. But it was the title track single that would outshine all. Neil Diamond and Barbra Streisand's duet of 'You Don't Bring Me Flowers', backed by an instrumental version of the number, had by early December 1978 soared to the top of the US charts, giving Diamond his first number one single since 'Song Sung Blue' in 1972.

In Britain, the single reached number five. Also in the UK, in December 1978, an MCA Neil Diamond compilation album, titled *20 Golden Greats*, stormed into the number two slot on the charts. Helped by TV promotion, it stayed there for six months and became Neil Diamond's biggest-selling UK album. Against the backdrop of these releases, in mid-December, Diamond set out on a 15-date tour, spread over seven US states in a two-week period, winding up at the Omni in Atlanta, Georgia. By the end of 1978, Neil Diamond was one of the most successful solo artistes in showbiz. He was annually grossing between $9 and $14 million, and had sold 47 million records. He also had an exciting project up his sleeve, details of which he would soon be revealing. On the domestic front, come early 1979, he felt things were pretty much in order.

Marcia was an American Civil Liberties Union volunteer, but she had refused the offer of a job with the organisation when she fell pregnant with Micah. A very focused woman, it was she, according to Diamond, who kept his sanity in one piece. He openly declared that the fruits of his successful career would not have the same meaning if he did not have Marcia at his side. According to his wife, Diamond was finally beginning to mellow in his attitude to life, but Neil confessed that underneath it all he was still a restless guy. He could not be comfortable for too long in any one spot. He admitted: 'I guess I haven't got over being lost, a wandering gypsy.'

For all that, his home base remained Los Angeles, and he liked to settle for stretches into a daily routine. He still conducted his songwriting mainly in the small hours of the morning, taking

advantage of the quiet. One wonders when he took the chance to
sleep, for more often than not he then went out for breakfast at a
Malibu delicatessen, before Marcia drove him to his West
Hollywood office. Part of the business he conducted there was
overseeing the several generous donations he gave to charity.
Neil had never lost his sense of being brought up on the breadline, and he quietly used his wealth to help a range of
underprivileged people. He also continued to support the
Phoenix House drug rehabilitation programme back east, in New
York City. He put money towards a recreational camp that was
being built north of Los Angeles for artistic children whose
parents did not have the resources to help their talented kids
realise their potential. He also ploughed cash into providing
sword fencing scholarships.

For leisure, Neil and Marcia enjoyed trips to the cinema, and
Diamond continued to be an avid bookworm. His prodigious
interest in Broadway composers, past and present, made some
close to him wonder if he would one day write music for a stage
show. He had also developed a penchant for motorcycles, and
occasionally he wondered what it would be like to throw all aside
and take a cross-country bike trip. A decade earlier, he had told
Britain's *NME*: 'I travel a lot while I'm working in the States, but
I'm not ambitious to get to know the places because America
doesn't have the same personal magic about it. It's too big and
lonely.' Now, he saw things differently, but whether he would
ever take the opportunity to go off on a trip of discovery was
another matter.

'You Don't Bring Me Flowers' became a worldwide hit. For
Diamond, Alan Bergman and Marilyn Bergman, the song
secured a Grammy nomination for Best Song of the Year. There
were even rumours that it might form the basis for a movie. *You
Don't Bring Me Flowers* was also performing well. Perhaps Neil
wondered what would have happened if the album had taken the
form he originally envisaged. The work had started life as an
intended double album, to be titled *The American Popular Song*.
It was to have included cover versions of songs such as the Burt

With co-star Lucie Arnaz while filming the *Jazz Singer* in 1980.

On 16 May 2002, 40 years after dropping out from college, Neil returned to perform 'Forever NYU' at the New York University commencement ceremony.

Singing 'America' in the memorable finale of the *Jazz Singer*, 1980.

January 1979, relaxing with his guitar. Composing songs on acoustic guitar often helped Neil to express his feelings and provided inspiration for timeless classics such as 'I Am … I Said'.

Neil Diamond at the 33rd Annual Songwriters Hall of Fame Awards induction ceremony, 13 June 2002, New York City.

June 2004, Neil and fellow Brooklyn-born superstar, Barbra Streisand, join forces on stage to perform for the Kerry Victory 2004 Concert at the Walt Disney Concert Hall, Los Angeles.

Bacharach/Hal David composition, 'Do You Know The Way To San Jose', 'Spanish Harlem', which had been a hit in 1961 for Ben E. King, and Bob Dylan's sensual 1969 number, 'Lay Lady Lay', which had originally been written for inclusion in the John Schlesinger-directed hit film of that year, *Midnight Cowboy*. However, when the duet with Barbra Streisand had worked out so well in the studio, plans had been redrawn, with the project retitled and scaled down to a single album.

The first single of the year to come off *You Don't Bring Me Flowers* was 'Forever In Blue Jeans'. Co-written by Diamond and Richard Bennett, and backed by 'Remember Me', this rocking, up-tempo number claimed Top 20 positions in both America and Britain in spring 1979. Along with the album's title track, it became one of the best-known Neil Diamond songs from this period. 'Say Maybe'/'Diamond Girls' followed, but did not fare as well, sticking at number 55 in the States.

By then, Neil's first batch of live dates had already come and gone. In February, he took to the stage for a one-night stand in Vancouver, British Columbia, Canada, and played six US gigs, split equally between Seattle in Washington State and San Francisco back west. These three Frisco concerts had a decidedly nostalgic flavour, for they were held at the Cow Palace where, over 12 years earlier, Diamond had played his first gig of that size. With fond bluntness, he was able to look back critically on those raw days. He said: 'My first two concerts were on bills at the Cow Palace and the Hollywood Bowl. I didn't know what the fuck to do. So I wore a big cowboy hat and came on very cocky – it was terrible!'

Any fright Neil Diamond had felt in his life to date paled into insignificance as spring 1979 beckoned. By nature, he seems distrustful of life, of success, of any smooth period, and that intrinsic guardedness is always at risk of undermining him. But something happened now that he had never bargained for. With his live performance schedule just gone into abeyance, he had cleared the decks, ready to embark on a brand new challenge, the likes of which he had hankered after for years. His excitement and plans were abruptly derailed and the skids shot from under him, when he received the results of some recent medical tests.

Neil had undergone a medical examination for a persistent back problem that had caused a feeling of numbness in his right leg. During his most recent stage performances, he had been particularly plagued by this strange sensation. When the test results came back, they revealed that he had a tumour that was compressing his spinal cord. As a heavy smoker for many years, one can only imagine the fear the very word must have struck in Neil. The tumour was benign, however, but it had to be removed, and in mid-March 1979 Neil was admitted to Cedars-Sinai Medical Center in Los Angeles, where he underwent a major, nine-hour operation to remove the tumour. The surgery was successful, and then he had the task of recovering and regaining his mobility. For a while, he needed to use a walking stick to get about.

Primarily, Neil needed time and space to heal, and he got that. He also needed to look forward, and it was in June, while he was recovering, that news broke that he would be starring in a remake of *The Jazz Singer*. Originally, Diamond was to have started filming in 1979. But, because of his operation, principal photography had been bumped back to begin early in the new year. *The Jazz Singer*, about a cantor's son with ambitions of making it big in show business, had come from the pen of Samson Raphaelson, initially as a short story called 'The Day Of Atonement'. That short story then became a play, then a film directed by Alan Crosland. Released in 1927, it holds the distinction of being the very first talkie.

The lead role was played by Al Jolson. Lithuanian-born as Asa Yoelson in 1886, the 41-year-old, who blacked up his face for the part, became one of the movie world's first screen legends because of *The Jazz Singer*. The movie drew warm reviews, won an Oscar, and Welford Beaton for *Film Spectator* said of it in 1927: '*The Jazz Singer* definitely establishes the fact that talking pictures are imminent.' In 1953, the first remake emerged. Again a Warner Brothers film, it starred Danny Thomas and Peggy Lee.

Despite having director Michael Curtiz at the helm it was, in contrast to the original, denigrated by film critics as schmaltzy.

Twenty-six years on, a third version was now in the pipeline. Adapted by Stephen H. Foreman, the Herbert Baker screenplay saw the lead character of Jesse Rabinovitch aiming to break away from his life as an assistant cantor of a poorly funded New York synagogue. He wanted a shot at pop stardom out west in California, thereby going against the wishes of his father and his wife, both firmly rooted in the traditional Jewish way of life.

Diamond had watched other stars around him in the music business make a successful transition into acting. Closer than that, his friend Robbie Robertson was about to star in a sexy melodrama called *Carny*, directed by Robert Kaylor and co-starring Jodie Foster. Although Neil had wanted to see if he had 'any acting chops', the right role mattered to him. In addition to the part in *A Star Is Born,* he had received offers over the years to appear in anything from cowboy westerns to futuristic films. Some roles had been easier than others to pass over. When the part in *The Jazz Singer* came along, he did not hesitate to accept. He called it the story of an immigrant, and declared: 'I had to talk for my people.'

Not since he had screen-tested to portray the late comedian Lenny Bruce at the beginning of the decade had he wanted a role quite so much. The filmmakers, EMI, believed that they had pulled off a coup in securing Diamond's services, particularly since Neil, ranked among the world's top five selling stars, would also be writing an original soundtrack for the movie. Plans for this project had been bubbling behind the scenes for some time. Latterly, EMI's new chief executive, Lord Delfont, had on three occasions flown from London to meet Diamond personally at his Los Angeles home to negotiate the final terms of a deal. The story hit the press in June 1979.

Neil Diamond arrived in Britain that summer for the first time since his Woburn Abbey concert two years earlier, and made the announcement alongside Lord Delfont. Diamond told journalists: 'I know exactly how to play the part, because the character is very like myself. He suffered the same generational gap with his father as I did.' To devotees of the famous black and white original film, Diamond explained upfront that none of the classic Al Jolson hits, like 'Mammy' and 'Swannee', would feature. And he warned people that his character, Jesse Rabinovitch, would not be blacking up.

Lord Delfont was very optimistic. EMI's record division had recently been in a downward swing, and he trumpeted *The Jazz Singer* as: 'Part of my campaign to get EMI moving again. We see it as a clean, family story which will appeal to audiences as much today as it did over fifty years ago. And we see Neil Diamond as very big box office indeed.' What also caught the media's avid attention was that Neil Diamond's fee would be a cool $1 million. It went down in movie history as the largest salary ever paid for a debut film-acting role.

If Neil sometimes privately felt frayed at the edges at the prospect of taking on this challenge, he had the staunch support of his wife to help. But, of course, although he was raring to go, part of him had to wrestle with questions as he examined his motivation for doing this film. For many people, the pay cheque alone would be sufficient reason, but Diamond's concerns went deeper. His cogitations clustered around the question of whether it was a good career move to depict his Jewishness so clearly. Diamond was proud of his heritage, but he was obviously well aware that a section of society had prejudices against Jewish people. Talking openly on this issue, he said that while he could understand some of those prejudices, a lot of them he did not; in any event, all prejudice against Jewish people hurt him. Rather than steer clear of a film like *The Jazz Singer*, then, Diamond felt strongly that he had an actual responsibility to do it.

Richard Fleischer would direct the film, while Jerry Leider was set to produce. Casting had opted for Catlin Adams to play Jesse's wife, Rivka Rabinovitch. Although Deborah Raffin was said to have been front-runner to play the love interest, Molly Bell, the part was destined for Lucie Arnaz, the 28-year-old daughter of actor Desi Arnaz and one of America's most famous screen comediennes, Lucille Ball. The other main roles were claimed by Franklyn Ajaye as Jesse's best friend Bubba, Sully Boyar as influential LA booking agent Eddie Gibbs, and Paul Nicholas making a brief appearance as raucous rock star Keith Lennox. EMI's choice of actor for the important role of Jesse's father, Cantor Rabinovitch, caused a big stir when it emerged that it was none other than Sir Laurence Olivier. He was 72 years old when he signed up to play Neil Diamond's screen father, keen to keep his talented son in the family fold.

Working in such illustrious company as Sir Laurence Olivier was months away in summer 1979, but Neil was already gearing himself up for the project. In addition to studying the film script, he endlessly watched the original *Jazz Singer* for research, even though he knew he would be playing the character very differently. He also had to write songs which would complement the film, for a soundtrack that would be released on the Capitol Records label (not Columbia Records) for contractual reasons. At the same time, he had to pull together an album he had been working on for Columbia. With all this in his lap it was as well that he was making good progress healthwise.

His Columbia Records album was called *September Morn*. Written and recorded in 1979, it was released at the turn of the year; by February 1980, it had notched up a number ten hit in America and 14 in Britain. The title track was an evocative love song, co-written by Diamond and lyricist Gilbert Becaud. 'September Morn'/'I'm A Believer' followed its parent album into the US singles chart a month later, stopping at number 17. Gilbert Becaud was among a handful of Neil Diamond's collaborators on the songs for *The Jazz Singer*.

Two soundtrack tracks, 'Adon Olom' and 'Kol Nidre', were traditional Jewish songs, and Diamond worked with Uri Frenkel to come up with appropriate adaptations of these for the film and the album. On three songs, Neil teamed up with three of his band members when it came to putting music to his lyrics. On the slow, tender ballad 'Hello Again', Diamond sought the services of Alan Lindgren. On two faster numbers, 'Amazed and

Confused' and 'Acapulco', he was assisted by Richard Bennett and Doug Rhone respectively. Lyricist Gilbert Becaud's presence, meantime, was felt on no less than five numbers.

Becaud worked with Diamond on the words and music for a moody, atmospheric ballad called 'Summerlove', the jaunty get-up-and-dance number 'On The Robert E Lee', the rocker 'Hey Louise', and one of the finest numbers on the album, 'Songs Of Life' – an introspective and moving insight into a troubled man trying to work himself through some deep-rooted problems. The best known of the Diamond/Becaud collaborations was 'Love On The Rocks' – a sometimes cynical look at a man who is trapped in a relationship and is disillusioned with life.

Of the 14 songs put together, Neil alone wrote the words and music for four: an ultra short song titled 'My Name Is Yussel'; two up-tempo numbers, 'You Baby' and the religious overtoned 'Jerusalem'; and what turned out to be one of his most famous songs ever. 'America' was far more than simply rousing and nakedly patriotic. It was, first and foremost, a deeply personal song. From the outset, Neil made no bones about the fact that the song told the story of his grandparents coming to the land of universal opportunity. He called 'America' his 'gift' to his grand-parents.

He laid no claim to the four-minute, 21-second song (the longest track on the album) being terribly intellectual. Nor did he ever imply that it had come as the product of long-drawn-out, agonising thought. It had come on a wave of sheer emotion. As such, it was the quickest song he had written in a very long time. Once he focused upon it, the lyrics almost fought with them-selves to tumble out of his head. Everything he wanted to say and convey was so close to his heart that it was there on tap. It was purely a matter of getting it down on paper.

In a wider sense, it would also prove to be a source of profound satisfaction to Diamond that 'America' touched a chord with so very many people. He once said that it spoke to 'the immigrant in everyone'. Perhaps that was why so many different groups could empathise with it. Neil could not know it in summer 1979, but 'America' would become an anthem adopted by people in a host of different situations. For example, when a group of hostages was released and returned home from the US embassy in Iran in the early 1980s, 'America' was played by network news channels as they covered the emotional arrival back on US soil of these traumatised people. In 1986, 'America' featured during the Statue of Liberty's centenary celebrations. Two years after that, Democratic presidential nominee Michael Dukakis used it as a stirring campaign song. Not surprisingly, 'America' swiftly became identified as the outstanding song on the soundtrack album.

The chance once more to write original songs for an entire movie had, in itself, meant that there was no way that Neil would have turned down the offer of *The Jazz Singer*. When he listened eventually to the fruits of the work that would be spread over five recording studios, he knew he had put together a pretty special collection, one that was perfectly tailored to progress the film's plotline, but also a set of songs that could have stood on their own.

As the year's end approached, filming crept closer. Before that, Diamond had to honour some tour dates scattered across four US states. Commencing in Texas on 10 December, nine nights later he wrapped up with two gigs at the Salt Palace in Utah's Salt Lake City. With his fitness clearly no longer an issue, and looking lean, Neil Diamond greeted the dawn of the new decade with a mixture of rife anticipation and gnawing anxiety.

Filming for *The Jazz Singer* began mid-January 1980, and wrapped on the last day of April, with locations split between New York City, Los Angeles and the Venice district of Hollywood. The colourful settings of Venice had been the nerve centre of the American film industry since the days of the silent movie. Numerous scenes for *The Jazz Singer* were filmed at a beach-front home, several blocks north of the famous Venice Fishing Pier. Lucie Arnaz was under contract to appear in a Broadway show at this time, so some scenes involving her character had to be relocated and shot in New York.

As the date to start shooting neared, Diamond's sense of responsibility deepened considerably, until he came to feel that, although he was not in control of the project, it nevertheless all rested on his shoulders. Some seasoned actors metaphorically chew the carpet prior to embarking on a lead role that requires them to be on screen for practically every frame. So it is scarcely surprising that, on the verge of making his acting debut, Neil Diamond found his nerves starting to shred. They crowded in on him so badly that, on the night before the first day's filming, Diamond called upon co-star Sir Laurence Olivier at his hotel suite. There could hardly be a bigger gap between the two in experience, and Neil desperately needed some basic advice. Diamond recalled: 'I asked the most rudimentary questions about what I would have to do. For instance, did I have to memorise the entire script all at once? He told me just to memorise each night what I had to do the following day.'

Neil would never have anticipated being able to assist the legendary actor in return. But in *The Jazz Singer*, Olivier was sometimes required to speak Yiddish; Diamond grew up with Yiddish, and took Sir Laurence painstakingly through the proper pronunciation. Olivier wrote these lines of dialogue out phonetically on a small blackboard slate, which he carried around all the time off-camera, practising an authentic delivery. Neil remembered that on set Lord Olivier carried off the expressions: 'perfectly, with all the proper inflections and with two thousand years of history behind him'.

Neil Diamond and Sir Laurence Olivier shared several scenes in the film, particularly in the first half before Jesse Rabinovitch quits New York for California. As someone with a serious interest in acting, Diamond had an invaluable opportunity to study a master at work. Down the decades, Sir Laurence had on countless occasions shown a rare mental dexterity for capturing and conveying the complexities contained within a single character. His grasp of nuance and his timing were impeccable; he could hold the moment like few others.

Director Robert Bierman once described some actors as

being like thoroughbred horses – the really brilliant ones respond to the lightest touch, and the amount of subtle adjustments they can make are limitless. Portraying Cantor Rabinovitch was by no means a complex role for the veteran. But for a novice like Diamond, Olivier was still worth studying. Sir Laurence once famously declared: 'Without acting, I cannot breathe.' And although he was in his sixth decade as an actor, he had clearly lost none of his commitment to his craft.

Diamond noted just how determined Sir Laurence was to be creative and how hard he still strived to improve. He had enormous respect for the English elder statesman, and over the weeks there was a disagreement between them only once; this occurred over a line of dialogue. It is fair to say that Neil sometimes seemed overprotective of how his character was portrayed. He took exception to a line giving the impression that Jesse Rabinovitch was pursuing a career in music for the money, so he argued for a small rewrite. As a man who had worked hard to make ends meet as a young, hungry actor, Lord Olivier failed to see the point of Neil's objection. Diamond dug his heels in and got the dialogue line changed, even if not everyone understood his sensitivity. Other than that, matters took their course.

Years later, Diamond can look back fondly on *The Jazz Singer*. It was a fascinating experience for him. But, at the time, the process of starring in his first film was too steep a learning curve. Indeed, he has graphically described it as having been: 'hell on earth'. Not only was he extremely busy, having to intersperse recording the music with filming the movie, he was also frankly scared. Potentially, he had bitten off far more than he could chew. Every day he felt that he had a huge task on his hands even to ensure that he was not seen to be wanting in the company of the other experienced actors. 'There were times I didn't think I would survive the whole thing,' he admitted in the aftermath.

His nervousness had already been made apparent to Sir Laurence Olivier by dint of that visit for advice the night before filming had commenced. But Diamond's screen lover, actress Lucie Arnaz, also spotted Neil's fear practically from day one on the set. She has unequivocally stated: 'I think Neil was scared to death!' It did not help, either, that he found the whole process mentally draining. He could only reflect with awe that a man almost twice his age was able to work from 8.00 a.m. to 6.00 p.m., go back to his hotel, swim for a while in the pool, and change to go socialising with friends for the evening. While Olivier dined out and relaxed, Diamond was exhausted, flat out emotionally, and in bed with the alarm clock set for dawn so that he could be up to study his lines for the day, before reporting to the film location for make-up.

Some of the strain he felt came from another source; he has confessed that he did not take easily to following someone else's schedule, to obeying the dictates of others. That was new to him. He said frankly: 'I was not accustomed to being told when to show up and when to go home, and at first I didn't like that at all.' Odd breaks in the shooting schedule, or functions away from the realms of movie making, must have given him welcome alleviation from the pressure.

The first such distraction happened on 27 February 1980, when Neil took time out to appear with Barbra Streisand at the 22nd annual Grammy Awards show to perform their duet, 'You Don't Bring Me Flowers'. The song was nominated in two categories that night: Song of the Year; and Best Pop Vocal – Duo, Duet or Chorus. The next break came in the following month, when there was a brief hiatus in filming. At the recent Grammy Awards ceremony, The Eagles' number 'Heartache Tonight' had walked off with the award for Best Rock Vocal Performance by a Duo or Group. Neil relaxed a while one evening by taking in a mammoth concert by the California-based supergroup. Days later, he was back at work with the rest of the cast, crew and Brooklyn-born, 64-year-old director Richard Fleischer.

Perpetually nervous of his acting duties, Neil must surely have been consoled that, because of his character's ambitions, he had the chance to perform music during the film – a craft that he *was* familiar with. *The Jazz Singer* contained two concert scenes, one midway through the movie, and another at the very end.

These were shot at the Pantages Theater in Hollywood in early April 1980. Before an audience of 2,700 movie extras and Neil Diamond fans, he performed 'Summerlove', 'Hey Louise', and the film's finale scene, which depicts him as a glittering star on stage singing 'America'.

Sir Laurence Olivier's presence was required for the finale concert crowd scene. When the 72-year-old showed up at the theatre, Neil surprised him by calling him up on stage and introducing the crowd to this revered veteran of the screen and stage. Olivier received a resounding, five-minute standing ovation.

Other performance shots showed Diamond, in character, performing in clubs. But some memorable scenes depicted the assistant cantor dutifully leading the singing in the synagogue, particularly on Yom Kippur, the Day of Atonement, when Jesse sings 'Kol Nidre' in place of his ailing father, from whom he has been estranged for some time. These close-up scenes were filmed at Breed Street Temple in Boyle Heights, Los Angeles, towards the end of April and were, therefore, among the final takes for the film.

Olivier had been in America for this shoot without his wife. Lady Olivier was the highly accomplished actress Joan Plowright who, in spring 1980, was busy working in theatre in Britain. Sir Laurence died in 1989. Joan Plowright, made a dame in the 2004 Queen's honours list, clearly remembers that while her and her husband's work schedules meant that they did not have daily conversations during this time, Sir Laurence very much enjoyed working with Neil Diamond. Two of their children, Joan recalls, visited the film set at one point and were given 'Neil Diamond' jackets, which they proudly displayed when they returned home.

By the time *The Jazz Singer* wrapped on schedule and within budget, Diamond had had a second single released from *September Morn*. 'The Good Lord Loves You'/'Jazz Time' creaked to a halt at number 67 in America. But it was not at the forefront of Neil's mind. Along with his nine-piece backing band, he had played at *The Jazz Singer*'s wrap party on 1 May, and was naturally concentrating on how the film would do. A 26-minute clip was shown at that year's Cannes Film Festival, where it received encouraging responses. Neil attended the annual glitzy event in France, and afterwards he and Marcia stayed in Venice as guests of Lord and Lady Olivier. All eyes for Diamond and EMI were trained on the end of the year, when the film was slated for cinema release.

The Jazz Singer's world premiere took place on 17 December 1980 at the Plitt Theater in California's Century City, followed two days later by its New York City premiere, held at the Ziegfield Theater. Diamond had been prepared to enter into the round of TV interviews and appearances to promote the movie and its accompanying soundtrack. And he quickly turned up on the popular network programme *Good Morning America*. But no amount of personal appearances could persuade enough film critics to like the film, or any of the performances in it.

Diamond later observed that any person who was in or remotely associated with the film was savaged by reviewers, including Lord Olivier. Lucie Arnaz confirmed that the critics 'crucified' Neil Diamond. It was her contention, having worked for months alongside Diamond, that he could have developed into a fine actor had the critics been kinder to him on his first outing. Five years later, Queen's Freddie Mercury confessed to Sir Laurence Olivier his sensitivity about harsh criticism, to which Olivier replied with a curt: 'Fuck the critics!' Had Neil expressed any similarly anxious sentiments to his co-star about reaction to *The Jazz Singer*, the great thespian would doubtless have given him the same advice.

Criticism of any kind *is* something Diamond finds difficult. He has admitted that: 'it hurts and often depresses me'. The lift he needed came courtesy of knowing that the man and woman in the street were more independently minded. *The Jazz Singer* may not have come anywhere near breaking box-office records, but it is nevertheless a movie which means a great deal to many. The other lift, of course, stemmed from the soundtrack album, whose fortunes were very different.

The single, 'Love On The Rocks'/'Acapulco', released in December 1980, made the British Top 20 and was a number two hit in America. 'Hello Again'/'Amazed and Confused' was a slow burner in the UK, but at home it pleased Diamond by rising to number six, come February 1981. In summer, 'America'/'Songs of Life', by claiming a number eight position, gave Neil three US Top Ten singles chart placings from the three spin-off singles released from *The Jazz Singer* album. In early 1981, the album itself slotted in at number three on both sides of the Atlantic. It would be two decades before Diamond appeared in a movie again, but he could wallow in the success of this soundtrack. It sold over six million copies, and was nominated for a Grammy Award in the category for Original Score – Motion Picture or a TV Special. In Britain, it had a two-year chart tenure. At the end of 1981, it won the top soundtrack album trophy in *Billboard's* The Year in Music Awards. *Rolling Stone* later asked: 'Who else but this Jewish Elvis could go multi-platinum with an album that featured a version of "Kol Nidre"?'

Two days after Neil Diamond turned 40, in January 1981, *Time* magazine ran a feature on him titled 'Bandmaster of the Mainstream'. By summertime there was nothing ordinary about the new record deal Diamond struck. Although the runaway success soundtrack had to be released on the Capitol label, Neil was delighted to sign once again to Columbia Records for a handsome $30 million. He duly turned his attention to writing and recording material for his next album.

By midway through the year, Neil had come to the end of another rollercoaster period which he felt had not only given him much, but had also taken a lot out of him. Like life, his moods still had a propensity to swing between delightful elation and deep despair. It was enormously essential that Marcia had been prepared to learn to live with these peaks and troughs. It is not something that Neil ever appears to have taken for granted. He has publicly admitted that he was not always the easiest man to live with. Indeed, he wondered how it was that his family put up with him at times. On balance, however, family life was good.

His two daughters were lively, pretty teenagers. Son Micah was still an inquisitive toddler at three; 11-year-old Jesse was developing into a good-looking adolescent, whose interest in music must have quietly pleased his father.

Speaking admiringly of Marcia, Neil was unusually frank about his 12-year marriage when he also admitted: 'We've had our difficulties, but we've got a strong marriage.' In today's celebrity-obsessed media, some stars seem to feel the need to advertise the rock-solid, happy state of their marriage; at which point the cynics watch and wait to see how long it will be before the relationship begins to fall apart. Sometimes it does disintegrate and sometimes it doesn't. In the Diamonds' case, they almost reached their silver anniversary before their marriage foundered for good.

In the meantime, love and affection permeated the bedrock of the songs for Neil's new album, *On The Way To The Sky*, which was released towards the end of the year. By early December it nudged just inside the UK Top 40, but performed considerably better in the States, where it made number 17. Once again, Diamond had collaborated with members of his backing band on some of the tracks. Gilbert Becaud co-wrote the words and music to 'Rainy Day Song', and another lyricist and friend, Carole Bayer Sager, co-composed the title track.

The fact that Diamond had taken to involving members of his backing band when it came to creating music for certain songs was no particular surprise, given that he viewed this tight-knit unit as a second family, wherein loyalty and trust were almost as important as the individual, professional talents. That loyalty and trust went both ways – Neil has talked of these friends as having been 'in the trenches' with him. The only female band member was backing vocalist Linda Press, who had married bass player Reinie Press. A measure of how family-oriented the set-up was came when the couple had a daughter, who spent a lot of her growing up on the road, cocooned in a safe, controlled travelling environment specifically created by Neil Diamond. The band members appreciate that Neil, as they have put it, 'insulates' them from the sometimes mad-hatter element of being a band on the road. To the band and entourage, this special environment is known as Diamondville.

For a fortnight in mid-December 1981, Neil boarded the luxury tour bus to play a dozen dates from Tempe, Arizona, through Texas and Washington, to San Francisco, arriving back in California five days before Christmas, just as *On The Way To The Sky* was ready to spawn the first of three cuts. The ballad-heavy album contained a track called 'Fear Of The Marketplace', that extolled the virtues of going out on a limb in life. When 'Yesterday's Songs', a love song urging the benefits of leaving the past behind, backed by 'Guitar Heaven', was released, there were no fears of it underperforming in the US singles chart – by January 1982 it reached number 11.

Three months later, 'On The Way To The Sky'/'Save Me' managed just number 27. But a new generation was taking over in the music industry, in television, radio and the music press. The hip music TV channel *MTV* was also on the horizon. All of this meant a tighter squeeze on established older artistes getting essential exposure. Although Diamond started feeling the pinch on that score, it was counterbalanced by the fact that in live performance his pulling power grew stronger and stronger. His colossal fan base just kept evolving and became even more loyally rooted in support.

Diamond reciprocated that devotion by putting as much of himself as he could into his concerts. He once said that of the myriad facets a performer projects on stage, only one was himself as he really is. Whatever package he presented, his audiences were up for it. Neil spent most of the first half of 1982 on the road. Setting off in Detroit, Michigan, he kept up a steady pace through sixteen states, playing multiple gigs in certain venues – such as three nights in March at the Brendan Byrne Arena in East Rutherford, New Jersey, and five nights at the Chicago Stadium in Illinois, late May–early June. Two concerts days later at the Civic Arena in Pittsburg, Pennsylvania, called a halt to his roadwork for a while, just in time for the release of another compilation album, *12 Greatest Hits Volume II*.

Released on Columbia Records, this album was a hybrid of Columbia's past Neil Diamond hits and the three biggest hitters from Capitol Records' soundtrack of *The Jazz Singer*. Its chart performance was tepid – 32 in Britain, sixteen places higher than the best it achieved in America. The final cut from *On The Way To The Sky* followed in July – 'Be Mine Tonight'/'Right By You' – which peaked at number 35. Whether or not Diamond was on the lookout for fresh songwriting inspiration, it came anyway from an unexpected source during his break from live performance.

In summer 1982, the blockbuster movie drawing people to the cinema like iron filings to a magnet was *E.T. The Extra-Terrestrial,* starring Dee Wallace, Henry Thomas and Drew Barrymore. Written by Melissa Matheson and directed by Steven Spielberg for Universal Films, it was the must-see movie for the family around the world. As cinemagoers anyway, the Diamonds hotfooted it off to join the throng. Even so young, Micah was probably entranced by the magic of the unashamedly feel-good film. Pauline Kael of the *New Yorker* called *E.T.*: 'The most moving science fiction movie ever made.' Steven Spielberg declared: '*E.T.* is the closest film to my own sensibilities, my own fantasies, my own heart.' The movie's sentiments of acceptance, love and selfless assistance made a big impression on Neil Diamond.

He came away that night not only inspired to write a song – he wanted it to be specific to the film. For that privilege, it is reported that he subsequently paid several thousand dollars to use the subject of *E.T.* specifically in a song called 'Heartlight'. All about friendship and love, it was written by Diamond and two of his friends, Carole Bayer Sager and Burt Bacharach. From that beginning, Diamond put together an entire album of the same title. Both single and album were scheduled for release at the end of the year. In the meantime, refreshed after his touring break and invigorated by the 'Heartlight' experience, Neil stepped back on stage in early September in Indiana. Playing mainly

American dates, he did raid into Canada to perform in Montreal and Toronto. Taking a clear eight weeks off, he showed up next in Florida in late November, then he headed to Alabama, Louisiana, Texas and other southern states. By now 'Heartlight'/'You Don't Know Me' had been released, and lodged quickly at number five in the US chart. *Heartlight* came hard on the single's heels, and also jumped straight into the US Top Ten, making number nine in the album chart. In the UK, both new single and album got no higher than the forties. But Diamond was focused on energising the increasing crowds flocking to his shows, the playlists for which now incorporated his new material.

It was his older material, however, that made a particularly big impression on 2 December 1982, when Diamond took to the stage at the Tarrant County Convention Center at Fort Worth in Texas. Before a 14,000-strong crowd, Diamond played his usual breakless set. His playbook of 35 numbers for the night was bookended by 'America', long since acknowledged as the most requested song played on US radio. In between he performed, near chronologically, his hits from 1966's 'Solitary Man' onwards. By half the way through, parts of the audience were up dancing in the aisles.

When it came to 'You Don't Bring Me Flowers', backing vocalist Linda Press stood in as best she could for the beltingly powerful Barbra Streisand on the duet. When the night came bang up to date with the live rendition of 'Heartlight', thousands in the darkened auditorium lit up matches or lighters and held them high, adding to the sense of community and spirituality. Three thunderous encores were needed to satiate the crowd. Reviewer Roger Kaye of the *Fort Worth Star Telegram* next day singled out a number from 1976 as the clear concert highlight. He wrote: 'There was one moment above all others when Neil Diamond demonstrated why he has taken a step above super-stardom status, into a pop music class of his own. That came when he delivered an emotionally charged rendition of "If You Know What I Mean" that was positively chilling. The sheer intensity of Diamond's singing matched anything that Springsteen, The Stones, or anybody else, can offer.'

With that sort of endorsement ringing in his ears, two nights later, two gigs at the Kemper Arena in Kansas City, Missouri, once again brought the curtain down on live performance for some months. Two more cuts from *Heartlight* arrived in the opening months of 1983. The Neil Diamond–David Foster number, 'I'm Alive', backed by 'Lost Among The Stars', ran out of steam in the mid-thirties in America. 'Front Page Story', a three-way collaboration between Diamond, Burt Bacharach and Carole Bayer Sager, teamed up with 'I'm Guilty', faded thirty places lower, at 65.

These lukewarm to stone-cold reactions to the singles could still be legitimately offset by studying the contrasting statistics when it came to Neil Diamond's concert ticket sales. The year 1983 would see him pass yet new milestones. The professional rewards he would reap as he approached his 20th year as a charting recording artiste, however, could not cushion the personal blow that would befall him.

CHAPTER 8

Plaudits and Pain

THE GREAT WESTERN FORUM, which occupies an entire block on the south-east corner of Manchester Boulevard and Prairie Avenue in Inglewood, California, was once primarily the home of the Los Angeles Lakers basketball team. Today it is an arena which recording stars are thrilled to be able to fill for consecutive performances. For most, a two-night engagement there is classed as an exciting, pinnacle event. Initially, in spring 1983, Neil Diamond had ambitiously envisaged pulling off four shows at The Forum. In March, when the tickets went on sale for these June gigs, they sold out within two hours, necessitating the addition of another three concerts. Finally, for all seven shows, a total of 130,000 tickets was snapped up, setting an all-time record for this imposing stadium.

As an indicator that Diamond was beginning something of a roll, it was spot on. When he resumed touring on 21 April with the first of five sold-out concerts at Detroit's Joe Louis Arena, the stint grossed just short of $1.4 million. Thereafter, he swept through Missouri, Illinois, Colorado and Arizona, before arriving in Inglewood on 13 June to commence the seven dates at The Forum. These constituted his first Los Angeles engagements since his 1976 Greek Theater shows and so, for Diamond, it felt akin to a homecoming.

After Inglewood, Diamond lay low for a chunk of the year, before resuming live appearances in October and December. Touring also occupied part of the first half of 1984. In spring, a special highlight occurred for Neil at a ceremony held in New York City by the National Academy of Popular Music, when he was inducted into the Songwriters Hall of Fame. This recognition could only have encouraged Diamond. Between engagement obligations, as he had done in the previous summer months, he knuckled down to writing and recording material for his next album. By mid-June, his attention turned once again to the road. After appearing at the Convention Hall in Atlantic City, New Jersey, Diamond flew to London for six nights at Earls Court, prelude to a UK and European trip that culminated in the Netherlands in late July.

Accustomed to garnering great memories on the road, after performing at Croke Park in Dublin, he played four concerts at the National Exhibition Centre in England's Birmingham. One of these concerts was a benefit gig for the Prince's Trust; on the night, Neil was thrilled to be presented to Prince Charles and Princess Diana, who made it clear that she was a fervent fan of his music.

After a series of nights, each memorable for their individual impact, Neil arrived back in the States for the American leg of his tour in August, just as his new album, *Primitive*, entered the charts. In Britain, where he had lately enjoyed good visibility, it reached number seven; in the US, it managed a more modest 35. That was a much better domestic performance than the lowly 62 notched up for the first spin-off single from *Primitive* – 'Turn Around'/'Brooklyn On A Saturday Night'. 'Turn Around' was Diamond's last single to chart at all for some time.

As his chart positions waned, Diamond worked still harder in live performance to sustain his place as a major draw in music. By the tail end of 1984, he made his stage presence felt in several US cities from Salt Lake City, Utah, to Indianapolis in Indiana, where he bowed out of the limelight in late December with a double-header at the Market Square Arena. He returned with a vengeance in March 1985, with five nights at San Francisco's Cow Palace. But any perceived pressure he may have felt to keep proving his popularity was catapulted into perspective when tragedy struck.

Having played in Washington and Oregon, Neil had travelled to Canada for dates in Vancouver, Edmonton and Calgary, when, as he faced audiences at the Northlands Coliseum in Edmonton, Alberta, on 23 and 24 March, he received news that his father had died. Kieve Diamond was only 67. Neil had just stepped off stage, both exhilarated and drained from the performance, when his wife telephoned with the devastating news. He immediately postponed his shows in Calgary, and went directly home to mourn the loss of a much-loved parent.

It must have been tough on him to return to Canada to fulfil the two Calgary concerts when they were rescheduled for early April. But when he showed up for the gigs at the Saddledome, he had one great comfort – his teenage son, Jesse, joined him on stage. Although never less than a consummate professional, inwardly Neil needed shoring up. He got that simply from being able to look sideways and see his vibrant young musician son, ready with an encouraging smile. It's what played a major part in helping Neil to get past his heartache just long enough for two concerts to please his public. After Alberta, though, he retrenched for months to allow time for the grieving process.

Bereavement and other traumatic events frequently signal a time for making a reappraisal in life. Perhaps the death of Neil's father in some way shaped his shifting priorities throughout the mid-stretch of 1985, for he entered a phase of being less absorbed than usual with songwriting. Despite the negative critical reaction to *The Jazz Singer* almost five years earlier, Neil hankered after acting in another movie. He had a plethora of half-formed ideas in this respect. Plus, for nearly a decade now, there had been rumours of a film project stemming from his celebrated concept album, *Beautiful Noise*. At any rate, he was interested in expanding himself, sure that he had the ability to explore other avenues.

Movies are notoriously difficult to get off the ground. Often projects which begin with great momentum and surging enthusiasm become mired in delays and snags, or simply run aground due to internal studio politics. So it was not a complete surprise that, after some months, any ideas Neil had nurtured in this direction had to be shuffled onto the back burner. His is a dynamic nature, not conducive to freewheeling for too long, and he'd had a dozen concert dates fixed up for a fortnight in December.

Before that, though, in November 1985, Neil and his wife were invited to a glittering reception at the White House, hosted by Republican President Ronald Reagan and Nancy Reagan. The lavish dinner was in honour of the visiting Prince Charles and Princess Diana. Neil headed to the black tie event on the understanding that he was there purely as a guest and would not be called upon to perform. But, as he and Marcia joined the well-heeled crush, a string quartet was playing 'Song Sung Blue'.

It could have been coincidence, except that Diamond was immediately targeted by Nancy Reagan's secretary, who shanghaied him over to the First Lady's side. The President's wife asked Diamond straight away if he would sing for Princess Diana. Neil said he would be honoured, but he had not rehearsed with the orchestra. That turned out not to be a problem. Dragooned, ever so civilly, to the conductor of the smart Marine Corps band, Diamond discovered that the band's repertoire contained over twenty of his compositions, every one of them orchestrated in his key.

Shown a list of these songs, Neil picked two very different ballads, 'September Morn' and 'You Don't Bring Me Flowers', and gave renditions of both to the assembled crowd that night, a unique, impromptu performance which he still treasures. The skilled musicians played his music to perfection, and Diamond called the experience 'mind-blowing'.

Ironically this was a time – not too far into her marriage – when Princess Diana, for whom he was principally performing at the First Lady's request, was very much perceived publicly as a fabled fairy princess. Subsequent events have shown that the unhappy, disillusioned sentiments projected in 'You Don't Bring Me Flowers', would seem to have been more apt, considering what was going on behind the façade of her outwardly dazzling life. Whatever the case, as an admirer of Neil Diamond's music, the tall, blonde English rose asked the tall, dark-haired Brooklyn superstar to dance. Together they made a sleek, stylish couple as they twirled and dipped gracefully on the dance floor before the avid gaze of hundreds of pairs of eyes.

By the time Diamond had carried out his dozen December concert dates, travelling anti-clockwise from Iowa, through Missouri, Ohio and Michigan to end up north in Minnesota, he had regained his equilibrium and now wanted to push his music career back to the fore. Nothing was transpiring on the film front. But more to the point, he had for some time been working on new songs – albeit in a series of collaborations with other lyricists. Productivity on that score was set to increase, with studio work becoming a priority.

In January 1986, Diamond took part in an NBC-TV special called *The Martin Luther King Birthday Party*, marking a new national US holiday in honour of the murdered civil rights leader, at which Neil performed 'America'. But Diamond did not want to live in the past. He needed a hit album in his home country again. By and large, the results of his latest songwriting sessions pleased him, although some songs were not destined to make it on to his next album. One number which had been around for longer than others was titled 'The Story of My Life', in which Neil expresses the blanket importance of a loved one in someone's existence. He was firmly attached to the song's title, and selected the song for his upcoming album. But he seemed to feel a slight, lingering dissatisfaction with the lyrics, always believing that he might have nailed his meaning better.

May 1986 chalked up 20 years since Neil Diamond had scored his first chart hit in his own right with 'Solitary Man'. This same month, his newly released album, appropriately titled *Headed For The Future*, reached the Top 20 in the US charts, while making number 36 in Britain. The various songwriting and production credits showed just who his cohorts had been in this album's creation, an abundance of talent that included Burt Bacharach, Carole Bayer Sager, David Foster and Maurice White.

To coincide with the album's launch, Diamond's third US TV special was aired throughout America. The exposure had little impact on the chart performance of the first single from the album, 'Headed For The Future'/'Angel', which faltered at 53 by the end of June. But three pinnacle moments were coming – one hard on the heels of the other.

Back in early April, in Pennsylvania, he had taken to the road again, playing at a string of major arenas countrywide. In July, he returned east for eight performances at Madison Square Garden on Seventh Avenue in Manhattan. There, Diamond was given the coveted Gold Ticket Award for playing to over 100,000 fans at this famous New York City venue. Moreover, six months later, *Pollstar* announced that Neil Diamond was responsible for the biggest single concert gross – over $2.9 million – for his eight-gig run at the Garden.

In July 1986, Diamond also took part in the weekend-long national celebrations to mark the 100th anniversary and re-opening of the newly face-lifted Statue of Liberty. Standing 302 feet high, dominating the entrance to New York harbour, this striking landmark and symbol of freedom was the work of sculptor Frédéric Auguste Bartholdi. Ten years in the making, the statue had been a gift of friendship from France to the people of America.

These centenary celebrations were attended by President and Mrs Ronald Reagan and President and Mme François Mitterand of France. At one point in the proceedings, as Diamond performed, a great crowd of people joined in and sang 'America' in front of the Statue of Liberty, which Diamond found to be a profoundly moving experience, despite it being one of the coldest days that year in New York City.

In mid-August, Diamond staged a 14-gig spectacular run at the Greek Theater in Los Angeles, during which he dazzled the audiences nightly with ever more elaborate laser light displays. Shortly after the hectic tour halted, in late September, in Arizona, his third TV special was nominated for six Emmy Awards. Industry watchers had read the signs, so it came as no shock when, in December, *Billboard's Amusement Business* named Neil Diamond as the Top Solo Performer of the Year.

On 25 January 1987, Diamond came to a massive global television audience when he sang the American national anthem at the Super Bowl XXI, when the New York Giants took on the Denver Broncos at the Rose Bowl in Pasadena, California. He must have been told before stepping on to the rostrum that time was of the essence, for he holds the unusual distinction of giving the fastest ever rendition of the national anthem – in one minute flat – by a major star at a major sporting event.

Touring America and Canada dominated much of 1987, a period punctuated by performing on Independence Day at a Vietnam Veterans concert in Washington, D.C., alongside appearances by singer Linda Ronstadt and actor Gregory Peck. His third live double album, *Hot August Night II*, consisting of stage performances culled from his most recent Greek Theater gigs, was released in November. This album's highest domestic and British chart positions, 59 and 74 respectively, indicated a low appetite among his normally hungry fan base. Yet a boxed set collectors limited edition of this album was put together and made available.

In 1988, a feature interview in the March edition of *Rolling Stone* was the only thing to keep Neil Diamond's profile flame flickering until the end of the year, when the HBO cable channel in America aired yet another Neil Diamond television special on 6 December. Two days later, he launched a three-month American/Canadian tour at Fort Worth's Tarrant County Convention Center in Texas. The tour ended in late February 1989, with three gigs at the Nassau Coliseum in Uniondale, New York. By then, his first new album in two years, titled *The Best Years Of Our Lives*, had been released.

Columbia Records had anticipated a lot of interest in this

work. However, although it bettered *Hot August Night II* chart-wise, it did not match *Headed For The Future*. By February 1989, the low-to-mid forties was as high as the album reached on both sides of the Atlantic. When the title track, 'The Best Years Of Our Lives', backed by 'Carmelita's Eyes', failed to chart at all, Diamond focused fiercely on his live performances in Canada and the US. Because of the enormous effort he had consistently put into his shows over the years, it was becoming difficult to outdo himself live. But Neil managed it by giving ten concerts at the Forum in Inglewood around the end of June, which grossed just a fraction under $3.5 million. A month later, he stepped off the circuit after triple gigs in Landover, Maryland. He welcomed two months away from public view, spending them at home with his family. Yet one eye was always on the remainder of the dates, which lay ahead in the last quarter of the year.

Come July 1989, it was 26 years since his one-off single deal with Columbia Records for 'Clown Town', which had failed to claw in even 20 bucks. And in those early days of being starved, financially, physically and creatively, lay the reason why Diamond, long since wealthy and successful, continued to push himself. Just as he could never shake loose the memory of having had to struggle, it was also still deeply ingrained in Neil to write every day – even if the volume did not amount to very much. Diamond revealed around now: 'I try to start an idea, or create a piece of music, every day. Even if it's only a tiny bit of melody, or a line of lyric, I feel I've accomplished something. It makes me feel productive.'

Throughout August and September, while he experimented with lyrical ideas, he was also kept busy gearing himself up for a pending European onslaught that would start in style in Ireland on 13 October 1989 with ten performances at the Royal Dublin Society Hall. Diamond arrived in Dublin ahead of this record-breaking RDS stint to meet the media, who came to the Westbury Hotel for a press conference. Neil rarely gave these conferences – indeed, this would be the only one this trip. Beyond that, he was prepared to meet a handful of journalists on a more personal basis. One of those was Peter Robertson, who had been on Diamond's trail for nine months, hoping to secure an interview for Britain's popular glossy magazine, *Hello!*.

Peter Robertson recalls the long wait to be shown into the hotel suite where Neil had agreed to a face-to-face half-hour session. By this time, the American was perhaps somewhat wearied, for Robertson, a very able interviewer, quickly found the star not uncooperative, but certainly a little tough going. At the end of the session Peter produced his personal copy of *Hot August Night*, in the hope that Diamond would autograph it for him.

Says Peter Robertson: 'I did wonder about taking the album along. But I just felt that I might never again get the chance to meet Neil Diamond and it was such a great album of his. So, as I was packing away my notes from the interview, I produced *Hot August Night* and asked. He took it and wrote on it and handed it back to me.'

Peter freely admits to having been in a tense state, which probably explains what happened next. Says Peter: 'I accepted my album back and read what he had written. To me it read: "Thank you for such a pointless interview." Well, that was it! I had been after an interview with this guy for nine whole months, I'd come to Dublin, had had to sit about waiting for *ages* to see him and I had been allocated just a half an hour. It all boiled up in me and I exploded: "Pointless interview! *Pointless!!*" Neil Diamond very calmly took back my album and redirected me to what he had scrawled. He had actually written: "Thank you for such a painless interview." God! I wanted to crawl away into a hole. I was so embarrassed!'

Apart from the few single interviews he granted, Neil faced a gaggle of assembled representatives from various newspapers, magazines and radio stations from around Europe. He arrived after noon to find the reception room at the Westbury Hotel crammed to overflowing. Perching alone behind a desk, he faced his inquisitors. Surprisingly for such a private man, he made it clear early on that no question was off limits. Indeed, this Dublin press conference has to go down as one of the most open, en masse, that he had ever given. Career questions were coped with, with expected ease, but the journalists were eager to catch even a glimpse into the normally guarded private world of Neil Diamond.

He did not have a reputation for infidelity. On the contrary, in a business that was notorious for divorces and for the endgame of failed relationships being luridly splashed over newspaper pages, his long-standing marriage was among the rare success stories. When asked head-on how he and Marcia managed such unusual marital harmony, Diamond was disarmingly frank that it had not always been plain sailing.

Touching on the fact that his first marriage had foundered because he had been on the road travelling such a lot, he explained that that experience had taught him some crucial lessons and had made him want to avoid the same precipice a second time. He went on to tell the listening, scribbling pack: 'I committed myself to a good solid relationship with my wife and kids. And although it's been very difficult because of the work I do and the fact that we are always in the public eye, we have been able to get through it.'

In sixteen months' time Neil Diamond would turn 50. But he had been, and continued to be, considered a sex symbol in music. When asked if that aspect had ever caused problems between himself and his wife, once again he was remarkably candid. He told his audience: 'There are some strains. It's diffi-cult for Marcia. She used to become extremely jealous when reading some of the cards and flowers that were sent to my dress-ing room before shows. She's got to be a strong woman and has to feel secure in our relationship. I always try to make her feel secure in that.' Again, Diamond stressed that he and his wife had got through it.

He opened up yet further when he offered an insight into what it was like for him as a feted performer out on the concert circuit, coming back to the domestic fold. He maintained that, just as it should be, he would go from being treated as really special by his fans, to being treated as no more special than he ought to be as another family member. He knew that it is not about how thunderously he had just brought the house down at some prestigious venue, nor even that he had set another new box-office record. As he saw it, once off stage and back in the bosom of his family, his wife and children had every right to be most concerned that he be there for them. Love and sensitivity, he believed, were among the linchpins to a successful marriage and home life.

While Marcia, Jesse and Micah were back home in America, days after this press conference Diamond set about his job at hand. After the ten RDS shows he headed to the Hallenstadion in Zurich, Switzerland, for a single gig. One-night stands also prevailed through Munich, Berlin, Dortmund and Frankfurt in Germany, before two nights at Rotterdam's Ahoy saw Diamond subsequently taking himself to Britain for 13 concerts, split between five appearances at the NEC in Birmingham and the rest at London's Wembley Arena to end November 1989.

Sold out wherever he went, he had not lost his touch in connecting with people. Tactfully, too, he remembered in Birmingham to give UB40 a name check – in 1983, the Birmingham band had secured their first UK number one hit with a reggae version of Diamond's song, 'Red Red Wine'. Favourably reviewing Diamond's opening night in this English city, the *Daily Mail* called Neil: 'A man who could probably make a curry restaurant menu sound dramatic.' When Diamond left London for home in late November 1989, it would be two years before he hit the road again.

In January 1990, he was honoured with the Award of Merit at the annual American Music Awards ceremony, held at the Shrine Auditorium in Los Angeles. Almost exactly one year later, on 24 January 1991, he reached the personal milestone of his 50th birthday. By now Neil had benefited from the rest he had taken. But, in his fourth decade as a singer-songwriter, he was glad to find the inspiration to put together a fresh song collection. Primarily love songs, several of the numbers were co-written by Diamond and various members of his backing band, including Tom Hensley, Alan Lindgren, Doug Rhone, Vince Charles and King Errisson. Diamond was also joined in his work by a handful of record producers, among whom was Peter Asher.

In the 1960s, along with Gordon Waller, London-born Peter Asher had formed the duo Peter and Gordon. Peter's sister, actress Jane Asher, was dating Paul McCartney. In 1964, when the Beatle provided Peter and Gordon with the song 'A World Without Love', it gave the duo their transatlantic number one debut single. Later, when the Peter and Gordon partnership had dissolved, Asher went into music management and record producing, for which he earned awards and high acclaim. Throughout the 1970s and 1980s he had worked with many artistes, including James Taylor and, most notably, Linda Ronstadt, whom Asher had spotted performing in her fledgling days in one of Neil Diamond's old haunts – the Bitter End club in Manhattan, New York City. Asher's home by now was in Malibu, California, and in the 1990s a mutual professional respect had drawn him and Diamond together.

Diamond had also enlisted production assistance from Val Garay, Humberto Gatica, Don Was and Albert Hammond. The product of all this industry culminated in an album titled *Lovescape,* which made the Top 30 in Britain by early October 1991, but ground to a halt at number 44 at home.

At this point in Neil Diamond's career, it was difficult to find a straight professional comparison by which to gauge his continuing success. On the one hand, by the 1990s, to remain relevant and active in music, and to be able to offset lower chart positions by packing out the best-known auditoriums worldwide, were achievements that had proved beyond the capabilities of some of Diamond's contemporaries, who had dwindled into early retirement to live off their royalties and memories. On the other hand, there was Paul Simon, whose South American influenced album, *The Rhythm Of The Saints*, released at the end of 1990, had hit number four in the US charts. In August 1991, Simon had drawn a mind-boggling 750,000 people to a one-off solo gig on the Great Lawn in New York's Central Park.

As ever, though, where Diamond slotted in was something for others to ponder. He personally concentrated on ploughing his own furrow, best done on the road. And so, to back *Lovescape*, he embarked on his busiest world tour for years, dubbed the Love in the Round tour. Never having lost his distaste for performing in situations where an entire section of the crowd had a view of his back, this time he would be singing on a specially designed 360-degree stage, which would be assembled in the centre of every single venue he visited.

With a pet venue – the Tarrant County Convention Center in Fort Worth, Texas – as his launch pad, Neil began his new tour in America on 17 December 1991. Again, as was nearly traditional, it included several consecutive nights at the Forum in Inglewood, California. Performing to a total audience of 142,570, on 23 March 1992 (his last night there), Neil Diamond became the first inductee on the Great Western Forum's new Wall of Fame. During his Forum engagements, Diamond donated $25,000 to the Magic Johnson Aids Foundation. Then, after a two-week break, he headed for the Antipodes.

On 8 April, Diamond began a 23-date tour of Australia, which constituted his first visit to this country in 16 years. Kicking off at the Entertainment Centre in Adelaide, he also played in Brisbane and ended with seven concerts at the National Tennis Centre in Melbourne. But the longest run was ten gigs at Sydney's Entertainment Centre – almost the centrepiece of his stay. With May left blank to recharge his batteries, Diamond then hit Croke Park in Dublin at the end of June, before venturing into the north of England to pack out triple nights at the Sheffield Arena. July saw a return to Birmingham's NEC, and an eight-gig run at the Wembley Arena in London.

Well used to adulation, Diamond was also taking some unexpected scalps this trip. When *Daily Express* journalist Frances Hubbard went to one of his Birmingham concerts, she arrived as a sceptic, poised to be cynical about a performer who refused to believe that his flashy Las Vegas-style showmanship might not be considered cool any more. In the end, she wrote in her concert review: 'After three decades on the tour circuit Neil Diamond knows every gesture ever designed to woo an audience. I tried to resist his patter. Neil Diamond is naff, I told myself. Alas, like a binge-eater caught with her hand in the biscuit tin, I couldn't say no.'

Frances Hubbard had dubbed Diamond the smoothest voice on vinyl. *Lovescape*, the album being promoted on this Love in the Round tour, was his last US album issued on that format. In July 1992, just as the Wembley Arena gigs came to a close, Neil's latest release, *The Greatest Hits 1966–1992*, came out as a double CD and topped the UK chart, where it reigned for three weeks. Oddly, the same collection, released at the end of the year in America, dropped anchor at a desperately disappointing number 90. But it had become part of the story of Neil Diamond's life that poor US chart showing did not correlate with his popularity live.

The second US leg of this tour began in early August in Maryland. After stopping in Pennsylvania, Diamond landed mid-month at Madison Square Garden, New York. By this time, those clocking up statistics had a new bone to chew on. *Billboard's Amusement Business* revealed that Neil Diamond was the top concert draw in the United States for the first six months of 1992. By the year's end he stood officially as the second highest grossing act of 1992 in America. By then, he had been seen in performance by more than 1.5 million people, with box-office receipt money running beyond the $40 million mark. That would beat even the likes of Bruce Springsteen, whose box-office take stood at $30 million for 1992. All this amid a hard-biting recession in the US economy.

Buoyant in the extreme, Diamond barrelled his way around his home nation and Canada, where the tour came to a halt on 27 October at the Northlands Coliseum, the venue in Edmonton, Alberta, at which seven years earlier he had received the news about his father's death. Almost a month later, Neil notched up his last UK single chart placing for several years with his version of 'Morning Has Broken'. The popular children's hymn, written by Eleanor Farjeon, had entered the Top Ten UK singles chart 20 years before when recorded by British-born performer Cat Stevens. Neil Diamond's rendition peaked at number 36. One week later, on 28 November 1992, HBO-TV in America aired *Neil Diamond's Christmas Special* just as *The Christmas Album*, a blend of Diamond's renditions of popular Yuletide pop songs and traditional carols, claimed number eight in the US, but only number 50 in the UK. Diamond also featured in the *Christmas In Washington* television special, broadcast coast to coast in mid-December.

The dawn of the new year saw a new record deal coming Neil Diamond's way when he signed a lucrative, long-term contract with Columbia Records' parent company, Sony Music Entertainment. With his recording future sorted for beyond the remainder of the decade, Diamond fired up the Love in the Round tour again with a third hectic US leg, setting out on 16 February 1993 in North Carolina at the Charlotte Coliseum, and ending on 19 June at the Carrier Dome in Syracuse, New York.

At this stage in his 27-year recording career, Diamond had sold in excess of 92 million albums. With a new deal under his belt, now that he had stepped off the tour circuit, he had to train his energies on coming up with his next album. The kind of worldwide tour that Diamond had just completed usually stimulates lyricists to come up with new inspiration. However, instead of opting for creating original material, Diamond selected an album's worth of numbers that had been penned by other songwriters. His first criterion on this mission was that he really had to like the song. Next, he was determined to sing his own interpretation of the number. He did not want to try to copy the original artiste's version. Even setting such parameters, he came up with far too many potential songs. In time, he whittled the pile down, first to 50 then, with difficulty, down to the final 16 selections. Each of these hand-picked numbers came from the

1950s and 1960s; all had been written by celebrated songwriters or songwriting teams originally closely associated with the Brill Building songwriting system.

Peter Asher came on board as producer, which Diamond much appreciated. He declared: 'It took a lot of nerve for Peter to accept the assignment, because we were following in the footsteps of a lot of classic records.' With Asher at the helm, Diamond threw himself into interpreting songs by, among others, Burt Bacharach, Hal David, Barry Mann, Cynthia Weil, Jeff Barry, Ellie Greenwich, Jerry Leiber, Mike Stoller, Carole King and Gerry Goffin.

Drawing from the annals of popular music, Neil recorded such tracks as: 'You've Lost That Lovin' Feelin', one of the most enduring pop classics ever written, recorded by The Righteous Brothers in 1964; the UK 1964 number one Manfred Mann hit, 'Do Wah Diddy Diddy'; the Ike and Tina Turner 1966 raucous belter, 'River Deep, Mountain High'; and the more melodic, 'Save The Last Dance For Me', which had been recorded by several artistes, including The Drifters.

Prior to the album's release, Diamond finally gave in to a long-standing urge, and took off in September on a cross-country motorcycle trip with friends, jokingly tagging themselves The Mild Ones. On his return, Neil plunged into a promotional blitz to plug the new album, now titled *Up On The Roof – Songs From The Brill Building*. By early October 1993, this album of cover versions peaked in both the US and the UK charts at number 28. It received mixed reviews, which did and did not bother Diamond.

Over the years, Neil had not changed his stance. If it came his way, critical approval was nice. But basically, he still considered that he was his own harshest critic, which meant that if his work pleased him, then it didn't really matter a whole lot what some journalist had to say about it. Between the end of October and the middle of the following June, Neil reverted to playing concerts. When the echoes of the last cheers had died away on the final night at The Forum in Inglewood, it would be more than two years before Diamond returned to the tour circuit. By now, music commentators were remarking that, as at 1993, it had been some considerable time since Diamond, usually a prolific lyricist, had written his own material for an album. Even his two albums released in 1994 were a live collection, called *Live In America*, and a second festive creation, *The Christmas Album Volume II*, neither of which set the heather on fire, chartwise. So why, many wondered, the dearth of lyrical creativity?

By his own admission, Neil normally had to write at least a line of lyric every day. Or so he had felt, up until the end of the 1980s. Now he admitted: 'Basically, I've not written anything in the last two to three years.' It was not a disinclination to write, he stressed, pointing out that he intended to set aside the first quarter of 1994 specifically for songwriting. In hindsight, though, after years of writing and of exhaustive live performance, it seems that Neil had hit a creative block. Nothing new was known to be flowing from his pen, despite this intended concentrated session.

If Diamond was suffering from a temporary writer's block he received an unexpected shot in the arm in 1994, when the Oscar-winning Hollywood movie *Pulp Fiction*, starring John Travolta, Samuel L. Jackson and Uma Thurman, was released. Hailed as a clever, witty and violent celebration of junk culture, *Pulp Fiction* was directed by Quentin Tarantino. The hit film soundtrack featured a very early song of Neil Diamond's – 'Girl, You'll Be A Woman Soon', recorded by the American band Urge Overkill.

Nash Kato, the lead singer of this alternative rock group, had for some time considered himself 'a diamondhead'. With friends, he had gone to one of Neil's concerts in the early 1990s and been blown away. Kato revealed: 'Neil was unbelievable. I expected a little bit of has-been to have crept in, a little bit of rust. Not the case!' Quentin Tarantino had heard Urge Overkill's unique rendition of the 1967 Top Ten Diamond hit, and considered it ideal for a moment in the movie. On the strength of the movie's success, extensive airplay was given to 'Girl, You'll Be A Woman Soon'; hence there was a resurgence of interest in Neil Diamond's back catalogue. This spiralled beyond his loyal fan base, attracting a welcome new generation of fans. By then, however, all professional issues were completely overshadowed for Neil, who was facing yet another major personal crisis – one that he had never wanted to happen.

At the end of the 1980s, he had talked publicly of how impor- tant a foundation in life his family was, and of how vital his marriage was to him. He had not hidden the fact that there had been strains to cope with along the way. But as he and Marcia approached what would have been their 25th wedding anniversary in 1994, despite all efforts, those strains by now had proved to be too much. Diamond appears to lay the cause of the disintegration of his second marriage once again at the feet of his demanding career, his devotion to his craft. With dignified regret, he has talked openly of the irrefutable fact that being as involved with and as passionate about music as he was, important aspects of his life had taken – or seemed to take – second place. In such a climate, sooner or later something usually has to give.

On those occasions when he has been prepared to talk about the break-up of such a long and precious union, he has spoken purely in terms of the price of his fame with regards to his private life. With innate honesty, he told Q magazine in 1996: 'I've been willing to pay the price, to the detriment of my chil- dren and my ex-wives.' In October 1994, Marcia filed for divorce in the Superior Court in Los Angeles, citing irreconcilable differ- ences, and the couple separated. It was a development that took showbiz watchers by surprise, since the Diamonds' marriage was among the very few assumed to be fireproof.

Having been together for so very long, and having two chil- dren, it must have been an enormous wrench for both Neil and Marcia to split up. If they made attempts to repair the damage between them, these clearly did not succeed. In due course, in March 1995, their divorce came through. Exact details of divorce settlements are always a private matter, but paper talk in the Diamonds' case put it as having been very pricey indeed. One newspaper report reckoned that Neil had parted with a stagger- ing £75 million, without contesting his wife's claim.

Whether or not this figure is accurate, when news of Neil Diamond's second divorce hit the media, it was generally perceived that he had arrived at one of the most generous – or most costly, whichever way it was looked at – divorce settlements in the world; certainly in the showbusiness world, as at the mid-1990s. The cost to the couple in personal terms, of course, could never be quantified. Having been through the trauma of divorce once already, and having to part from his children, Diamond had truly never envisaged it happening to him a second time. Despite the fact that he can blame his dedication to his career, he was no less gutted to lose someone who had been integral to his life for so long. He had been floored before in his personal life, and he knew his way back up. But he couldn't kid himself – it was not going to be easy.

CHAPTER 9

Finding the Future

DIAMOND DEEMED IT running away when, four months after separating from Marcia, he left Los Angeles and headed east to Nashville, Tennessee, where he rented a place to stay. In an emotionally fragile state, he needed to remove himself from the geography of his hurt, maybe even from a raw sense of failure. His choice of new locale was significant. For practically all his life, music was the rock to which he had clung through good, bad, or indifferent times. In 1995, as he faced going through the rigours of divorce once more, it was no different; it was vital to find friendship and understanding.

Nashville, the renowned home of country music, suited Diamond's mood. To those with no taste for country music, the genre seems to thrive on misery, heartache and perennial depression. The country music community, however, has a reputation for offering warm companionship; it was a sympathetic environment that appealed to Neil. He also knew Nashville as a songwriters' community, where there was guaranteed to be a lot of interaction between lyricists and musicians – reason enough to go there – and he was not coming in cold. Bob Gaudio, who had produced *The Jazz Singer* album, already lived in Nashville; a long-standing personal friend of Neil's, country singer Waylon

Jennings, had for years tried to persuade him to record there. Diamond felt it was the perfect solution. He said: 'Everything fell into place at that time, so I went to Nashville and just jumped in with two feet.'

Remaining in Nashville for roughly a year, he immersed himself in work on a new album – a kind of catharsis for him. Neil Diamond's sidestep into country would baffle a few, yet one clue had come near the tail end of the previous year, when he took part in the television show *Opryland's Country Christmas*. Plus, on *The Christmas Album Volume II*, he had dueted on the carol 'Away In A Manger', with country doyenne Tammy Wynette. As though answering his bemused peers, Diamond made it patently clear how much he had needed to take this turn, when he talked of country music as the healthier alternative to throwing oneself off a tall building. That is not to suggest that he personally had felt suicidal, even at his lowest ebb, but he did say: 'I had to throw myself into something to keep myself sane, and to express some of the feelings I was dealing with.'

The country music market was much more lucrative than Neil Diamond knew at that point. His motivation, though, lay purely in finding the right vehicle to make sense, in song, of his inner turmoil. It was never going to happen in an instant of arriving in the Tennessee heartland, but that was okay; he just enjoyed being among old friends, and relatively easily made new ones.

Absorbing as his odyssey to assuage his personal pain was, it was not to the absolute exclusion of all else. His marriage to Marcia was over, and it was now down to lawyers to cut the divorce deal. But, as had happened when he parted from Jaye in the late 1960s, it was of paramount importance to Neil that he continue to maintain his close bond with his children. Family was vital to him. In March 1995, the same month as he and Marcia were formally divorced, a new arrival brought some welcome sunshine into Neil's world when his daughter Marjorie and her husband had their first child – a son, whom they named Alexander.

Neil was very proud of his first grandson. Two months later, he was proud in a different way, to receive an honorary Doctor of Fine Arts degree from New York University, the institution from which he himself never graduated all those years earlier. It still gave him pleasure to perform for the students at the graduation ceremony that year.

By spring 1995, he knew that his creative juices had revived and were flowing fast, a fact in which he wallowed. 'I knew that when I needed music, it would come,' he later declared. He felt invigorated, prone to and provoked by the very same impulses and strength of determination as he had felt at the outset of his career long ago. Certainly, he was not subject to the desperately lean circumstances of that early-to-mid-1960s period. But that factor did not lessen a jot his return to adopting a gimlet-eyed approach to his work.

Interestingly, when talking of this mid-1990s stretch, Diamond pointed out that in place of the initial hunger which had motivated him three decades earlier, there was an acute new sense of personal pride to be upheld; while different, it still provided a powerful propulsion. Another kickback to the past was how much the Everly Brothers had lately been on Diamond's mind. He said that he yearned to have two sets of vocal cords; the next best thing was to embroil himself in a succession of song-writing partnerships.

He worked closely with over a dozen collaborators, among whom were Beth Nielsen Chapman, Bill LaBounty, Harlan Howard, Tom Shapiro, Hal Ketchum, Dennis Morgan, Gretchen Peters, Gary Burr, Stewart Harris, Raul Malo and Bob DiPiero. All these people shared his drive and strong work ethic. Although he started from scratch on this first collection of new material in five years, everyone was keen to work every day, which meant productivity was high. Neil was able to get at least one song off the ground as a result of each writing session. He was in no doubt that he would never have achieved such an output had he decided to write and record in Los Angeles.

Each of his co-songwriters was very sharp in their own right.

Diamond later stated that, in a new environment with new collaborators, his ethos had been to keep an open mind and see what transpired. In truth, what emerged was probably more predictable than ever, if one took into account his personal circumstances. He later described the songs he came up with as straightforward and honest. There were a number of very clear references to his defunct marriage. His battered feelings, his passions and his regrets were all stitched into the fabric of the work he put together. As a result of this personal investment and self-analysis, he was creating his most interesting material in years.

'Win The World', on which Diamond worked with Susan Longacre, and 'If I Lost My Way', pulled together with Gary Burr, both deal directly with the break-up of his marriage to Marcia, as does 'Open Wide These Prison Doors', which Neil co-composed with Stewart Harris.

Renowned lyricists have confided that while no one could welcome the pain of a disintegrating marriage, in the aftermath, the break-up and divorce experience very often provides the most evocative material with which to grapple creatively. When reviewing the work, collectively titled *Tennessee Moon*, *Rolling Stone* said that 'Open Wide These Prison Doors' was Neil Diamond's most inspired number since 'I Am . . . I Said'. Giving the album a five-star rating, the magazine singled out this track as the true rock gem among the lot of them, and called the song, 'The new anthem for angry divorced men everywhere. Starting with beautiful, shimmering acoustic guitar and then building into an emotional frenzy, Diamond sings about the toll of divorce like even Bob Dylan on *Blood On The Tracks* couldn't.'

Neil's recent traumatic experiences, and his search to find a new future, impinged on many of the defining songs on this album, as can be determined by titles such as 'Can Anybody Hear Me', 'Shame', 'Deep Inside Of You, 'One Good Love' and 'Reminisce For A While'. In differing ways, each song had its merits.

Diamond sometimes worked on more than one song with

certain lyricists. With Tom Shapiro he co-wrote 'A Matter of Love' and 'Marry Me'; Gary Burr contributed to 'If I Lost My Way', while he and Bob DiPiero both collaborated on 'Gold Don't Rust'. On a song called 'No Limit', Diamond revived a former partnership with Richard Bennett who, by mid-1995, had left Neil's backing band. 'Everybody' was the poignant product of two Diamonds glancing ideas off one another – Neil and his son, Jesse.

Neil has never laid claim to being an obscure lyricist, though his work never lacked thought. This album, however, contained one of his most nakedly blunt and uncomplicated songs. Written with Gretchen Peters, and called 'Talking Optimist Blues', the number was laden from beginning to end with a catalogue of blatant human anxieties over health, feeling old, fading looks and ruined relationships. Punctuating these dreary sentiments, in several places there was an almost manic burst of determination to tell oneself that all will be fine again one day – an indication of Neil's oscillating emotions as he struggled to work through this personal crisis.

Recording took place in Nashville. For Diamond, one particular moment stood out when he came to lay down 'Blue Highway', a song co-written with Harlan Howard about swapping the big city bustle for a simpler life in the country. In line with seeking a complete departure with this album's contents, its musical style more than anything signalled substantial change. Gone were lavish string sections and an orchestral feel. In their place, the emphasis was heavily on guitar, dizzy fiddle work and steel percussion.

It was working with veteran guitarist Chet Atkins on 'Blue Highway' that gave Diamond a buzz. It took him back almost 40 years to when, as a teenager just getting down to songwriting, he had prowled the New York music shops, gazing at the various Chet Atkins guitar models he could not possibly afford to buy. In those days, he had to make do with drooling over the glossy pages of Gretsch guitar brochures, but he had often fantasised about someday being able to own a Chet Atkins guitar. Working in a recording studio with Chet Atkins himself in 1995, Diamond was still dreaming – this time of emulating the man. 'I even begged him to teach me a few licks,' admitted Neil. He was immensely thrilled when the guitar maestro made him a gift of a Chet Atkins guitar, signed personally.

All this aside, it was the material that mattered most. The title track, 'Tennessee Moon', co-composed with Dennis Morgan, was an example of how direct Neil had aimed to be this trip. Once he had added a reprised version of his existing country-tinged 1967 hit 'Kentucky Woman', plus 'Like You Do', written by Sandy Knox and Steve Rosen, Diamond had an 18-track album just about ready. He was determined to view this batch of songs as nothing elaborate, just heartfelt. But that did not mean that recording work would be fast. They looked like missing the 1995 Christmas market, but Neil was prepared to bide his time.

An indication that he was in a more settled frame of mind, and was starting to come out the other side of all the soul-searching, showed towards the end of the year, when he returned for a spell to his work base in Los Angeles. The comfortable modern complex situated in West Hollywood, housing a recording studio, offices and accommodation, gave Diamond a sense of the familiar. Unlike his leased property in Nashville, here the interior walls vanished behind a selection of his framed gold and platinum disc awards. And it was here that he made a homely base for himself.

Besides taking care of business, he could visit his children. He enjoyed the company of two beautiful, much pampered dogs, while also caring for the needs of a little cat which, though slowly recovering from terrible injuries received in a road accident, would never be the same again. When the mood took Neil, he could go out for a spin on either of his two gleaming, powerful motorbikes. But no matter how determined he was to freewheel mentally for a little longer, his thoughts would soon stray towards the release of *Tennessee Moon*.

Come February 1996, he had to tape *Neil Diamond...Under A Tennessee Moon*, a television concert special to preview the imminent release of this country-oriented album. For that, he had to return east, where the show was recorded at the Ryman Auditorium in Nashville. It was broadcast at 10.00 p.m. on 24 February 1996, on the ABC-TV network. By then, Diamond had already undertaken promotional work by appearing on *The Late Show With David Letterman,* and *Tennessee Moon* had been released.

As Diamond had made clear, he had no prior notion of the sales figures involved for a hit country music album. Indeed, he had confessed that for all he knew, *Tennessee Moon* might be destined to rank among his poorest-selling works. That would not be the case. In Britain, *Tennessee Moon* reached number 12 in its first week in the album chart; a month later, in March, it almost matched that in the States by getting to number 14. In Australia, the album quickly went platinum. In the American country music chart, *Tennessee Moon* claimed the number three slot and went gold within the first six months of its shelf life; the bonus was that it exposed Neil Diamond to a whole new market. Younger record buyers also came into close contact with the veteran star when, on 7 March, he gave a live six-song mini concert inside the Virgin Megastore on Sunset Boulevard in Hollywood. It was the giant music chain's first ever live, in-store performance.

With this new-territory release, Neil Diamond had bounced himself back into the spotlight. On the cover of *Tennessee Moon,* wearing denim jeans and a dark jacket, with hands in pockets and an acoustic guitar slung casually across his back, a smiling Neil Diamond looked relaxed and serene. But one has to question if internally he had been 100 per cent ready to face the world again. In answer to a question put to him by Britain's *Q* magazine as to whether he was now content with life, Diamond replied with disconcerting bluntness that he would only be happy when he was dead. A year on from his divorce becoming final was perhaps still too soon to be asking him his take on life.

He continued to reflect without bitterness on the extraordinary personal price he felt fame had extorted from him. He knew that he had chosen consciously to live that professional life, yet deep down, he did not fully blame himself for it. Intrinsically, he believed that he had never had much choice about pursuing his career so avidly. Music was an overcrowded and difficult profession even to enter, and an even more demanding one in which to maintain staying power. It was an-all-or-nothing situation which, by its very nature, meant that anything outside that musical existence was bound to come second. He had come from a solid, traditional family set-up, but he had lost two wives, both sacrificed to his work. He held on tightly to the fact that he had not also lost any of the four children to come from those relationships. The continuing love and respect of Marjorie, Elyn, Jesse and Micah meant the world to him.

In a wider sense, he was philosophical about other aspects. By having recorded and released a country-flavoured album, so different from his normal fare, he attracted music media attention, as usual. Yet part of Neil Diamond seems to feel that he is forever under-appreciated. He could only be fully aware of his own enormous success and his high rating on the totem pole, but it is hard to escape the impression that a small part of him feels that he has a certain invisible quality among music's hierarchy. For instance, on the subject of why, as at 1996, he had not been inducted into Rock and Roll's Hall of Fame, he stated bluntly: 'They won't have me until I'm long dead.' Curiously, he contended that had he died in the early 1970s, he would have been given the honour long ago.

When opening up about the pressures that his professional life had brought to bear on his personal life he had largely meant the effect that his touring had had – the frequent, long absences from home. He knew only too well that in fulfilling his obligations to promote his albums, and in satisfying the fans' thirst for live performance, he had had to neglect his home life, and that it was a lure he had all too often found irresistible.

It was probably not easy to look at it in such a light, but now, as a divorced man, he was mentally freer than he had been in a very long time to succumb to the seductive attraction of the road.

At any rate, in spring 1996 he welcomed the chance to pull on the glass-beaded shirts and get back on stage once more. He was also able now to exert great control over just how packed a tour schedule he would follow. With the majority of the labour involved in going on the road handled by an army of others, he was prepared to try to make touring better for himself. He already loved it as a creative outlet, a sounding-board from which to learn, and an opportunity to press the flesh with his fans. Now he actively yearned for it to become fun.

The one element of which he could be sure at the end of March 1996, when he was set to go back on the road for the first time in 27 months, was of selling out in Australia. Not only was it still acknowledged that Neil Diamond had more fans per capita in Australia than anywhere in the world but, on the eve of this tour, a New Zealand newspaper also revealed that one in three Australian households owned a copy of *Hot August Night*. With *Tennessee Moon* set for platinum status Down Under, Neil eagerly arrived in Sydney to play, on 29 March, the first of seven dates at the Entertainment Centre. Playing multiple nights next in Brisbane and Melbourne, in mid-April he arrived in Western Australia for two gigs at the Burswood Dome in Perth. After that, two dates at the Ericsson Stadium in Auckland, New Zealand, terminated this leg. By mid-May, Diamond was in Britain.

Sixteen dates were scattered around England, with a trip over to Ireland for a single engagement at Croke Park, Dublin. During the promotional duties intertwined with live performance, Neil guested on Britain's ITV show, *Tonight With Richard and Judy*, on the same programme as fellow American O.J. Simpson – the former US football star who had been at the centre of one of America's most sensational murder trials.

Diamond returned to the States to spend virtually the whole of the second half of 1996 on tour there. Starting on 20 June at the Fleet Center in Boston, Massachusetts, he played almost 80 concerts spread over 32 states, breaking house records and setting new ones almost everywhere he went, until calling a halt at the end of December with three appearances at the Grand

Garden Arena of the MGM Hotel in Las Vegas. These were Neil's first Las Vegas concerts in over 20 years. Two decades on, the climate was vastly different; a new generation had taken over and times had changed dramatically.

Way back in summer 1976, tickets for the inaugural performances at the Aladdin Theater for the Performing Arts had been priced at $30 each. Tickets this time for the triple engagement at the 14,500-seater Grand Garden Arena ranged between $50 and $200 each. By any yardstick, this return to the Las Vegas live entertainment scene could be classed as an unequivocal success, and it would not be so long again before Neil returned to the energetic gambling capital.

During the period he had spent pounding the beat around America, he had had two records released. In August, a Sony/MCA jointly produced album of greatest hits called *The Ultimate Collection* had, with the assistance of a TV advertising campaign, lodged at number five in the UK album chart. The release in America towards the end of the year peaked at number 122. The other package was very interesting. It was a 71-track retrospective work titled *In My Lifetime*. For this, Neil had written and recorded the new title song. The CD set also included 37 hit singles, 16 previously unissued early demos of tracks such as 'Blue Destiny', 'A Million Miles Away', 'Clown Town' and 'A Good Kind of Lonely', alternative versions of some of his classic hits, three acetates cut in the late 1950s, a discography and a full colour 72-page booklet containing some rare photographs. As a musical résumé of the works of Neil Diamond to date, it was as comprehensive as it could get. By early 1997, *The Greatest Hits 1966–1992* had gone double platinum, and *In My Lifetime* was already gold.

The latter product would have to sustain the record company's appetite for any new Neil Diamond release for more than two years. Diamond's sights had been set not on recording, but on returning to the road. These tentative touring plans were scuppered that summer, however, when his health became an issue once again. In mid-August 1997, Neil re-entered Cedars-

Sinai Medical Center in Los Angeles to undergo surgery, this time to remove polyps from his large intestine. He was still recovering from this procedure when he injured his back helping a friend to lift a motorbike.

When Diamond did get around to considering a new studio album, he was in experimental mood, choosing for it not to be based on his own original songs. Once again, he seemed to have dipped into a place where he preferred to look outward rather than inward for inspiration. It did not mean that he was anything less than fully committed to the project, however; by early 1998 it was under way. As someone with a lingering fancy to be an actor, and with two huge-selling original film soundtrack albums to his credit, he had decided to hook into the movie world for the basis of this new work.

Not wanting to do things by halves, Diamond straight away approached the legendary film composer and conductor Elmer Bernstein, saying that he wanted to record classic movie songs in the full, rich, orchestral style, and asking for his assistance. Diamond was so fired up about this project that had Bernstein had any reservations, they quickly evaporated. Neil knew that it was something he could pull off with the necessary conviction and heart because, even as a child, he had loved to sing snatches of the tunes which had permanently imprinted themselves on the world's collective consciousness.

His one concern centred on his ambitious plan to sing the songs he selected with the accompaniment of a full orchestra. He was long accustomed to the polished perfection of his own well-rehearsed backing band, but a formal orchestra backing was a whole other deal. When Diamond raised this potential pitfall with Elmer Bernstein, the veteran assured Neil that if he concentrated solely on the vocals, he and the orchestra he conducted would follow him flawlessly. Neil promptly set about sifting through hundreds of songs, making what would turn out to be 20 final selections. By a process of tough elimination, he had eventually come up with a collection that embraced some of his all-time personal favourites, and covered a 67-year span.

From 1930, he opted for the Irving Berlin song, 'Puttin' On The Ritz', from the musical melodrama of the same name. And from 1997, Neil decided on 'My Heart Will Go On', the Oscar-winning song penned by James Horner and Will Jennings, and made famous by the blockbuster disaster movie *Titanic*, directed by James Cameron. Other Oscar-winning classics included: the Sammy Fain and Paul Francis Webster number, 'Secret Love', a hit for Doris Day from the 1953 musical *Calamity Jane*; the Elton John and Sir Tim Rice song, 'Can You Feel The Love Tonight', from Disney's 1994 animated drama *The Lion King*; and from the 1961 movie *Breakfast At Tiffany's*, 'Moon River', written by Johnny Mercer and Henry Mancini.

Two Cole Porter compositions made the final selection – the 1937, 'In The Still of The Night', from *Rosalie,* and 'True Love', which two decades later had famously featured in *High Society*. Starring alongside Grace Kelly and Bing Crosby in *High Society* was Frank Sinatra. And Diamond especially included what he termed a Suite Sinatra in this intended double CD playlist. Suite Sinatra consisted of two songs: Cole Porter's 'I've Got You Under My Skin', from the 1930s black and white flick *Born To Dance*; and the Johnny Mercer and Harold Arlen co-composition 'One For My Baby', from the 1940s musical *Sky's The Limit*. Neil Diamond termed this section: 'a combination mood piece', and meant his own renditions to be a sincere tribute to the legendary New Jersey-born crooner.

Diamond's other personal highlights showed a varied taste. He went for 'When You Wish Upon A Star', written by Ned Washington and Leigh Harline, used in the 1940 classic cartoon feature *Pinocchio*. Later he said: 'I'm very glad I chose it, but I don't think anybody can top Jiminy Cricket's version in the film.' *Pinocchio* was a throwback to Diamond's childhood days. As a young man aching to find success in 1964, he had been impressed by a comedy drama called *Love With The Proper Stranger*, set in New York's Italian east side, and starring Natalie Wood and Steve McQueen. Said Diamond: 'It's a movie I just loved, so when I found out that the theme had been written by

Elmer Bernstein (and Johnny Mercer) I immediately put it on the list.'

The majority of these songs, although classic, were hardly complex. But another personal favourite of his was: 'Windmills Of Your Mind'. This had been showcased in another memorable Steve McQueen movie, the 1968 *The Thomas Crown Affair*. The song's music had been scored by Michel Legrand, and the lyrics written by Alan Bergman and Marilyn Bergman, songwriters with whom Neil had worked previously. Of this Oscar-winning number, Neil said: 'There's a certain insanity in the performance of the song. It's the kind of thing you have to perform very carefully by finding your own perspective in it.'

Because he had spanned so many decades with these songs, it was almost inevitable that Diamond would finally be attracted to one of the most fabled of all movie classics – 'As Time Goes By' – written by Herman Hupfeld, and featured in the 1942 weepy *Casablanca*. Almost organically, this song became the central theme of Diamond's major project. He saw it as so symbolic, in fact, that he decided to bookend the album with it, and to use the song title as the album's subtitle.

Faced with performing and recording such a starry collection of quality, timeless numbers, in order to capture the glory days of old Hollywood, Neil chose to carry out the task at 20th Century Fox's Newman Scoring Stage. The album, *The Movie Album – As Time Goes By*, was helmed by *The Jazz Singer*'s soundtrack producer, Bob Gaudio. Neil also drafted in Alan Lindgren to act as music coordinator. But Diamond sang all the numbers live, before an 80-piece orchestra, conducted by Elmer Bernstein.

The Movie Album – As Time Goes By was released in autumn 1998, and by late October made it to number 31 in the US album chart. In Britain, it died out at number 68. By the end of 1998, Neil Diamond had sold over 110 million records worldwide, and had a fan base that would eagerly support his endeavours, whichever direction he took. By December, *The Movie Album – As Time Goes By* had given Diamond his 35th gold album award. But the critics remained resolutely split in their view of him.

A reviewer for the *Boston Globe* remarked: 'As they say in the trade, Neil Diamond could sing the phone book and still get a positive reaction, but it is his creative restlessness that keeps his fans happy, year after year.' And the *Boston Sunday Herald* critic decided: 'Diamond keeps his vocals admirably sedate. In the end, though, he doesn't offer anything new. He is content to journey romantically into well-covered territory.' But it was the *People* review in November 1998 that picked particular holes in the work.

The review read: 'There's nothing in pop music as scary as the feeling that Neil Diamond is revving himself up for a big finish to a song, and he does plenty of revving on this two-disc set of famous movie songs. Diamond still has to cope with his less than elegant Brooklyn diction, and his humourless approach makes him sound zombie-like. Hardcore Diamond fans will love this album. The same can't be said of hardcore fans of great film music.'

If the critics found fault, it would not stop *The Movie Album – As Time Goes By* from receiving a Grammy Award nomination in the category for Best Traditional Pop Vocal Performance. By the time the critics were having their say about the album, Diamond had embarked on a new world tour. Having launched this trip on 23 October in Texas, he quickly travelled northeast, playing a handful of states before arriving in New York State for two dates in Buffalo and Albany, then heading into Canada. Diamond's date at the Pepsi Arena in Albany, on 13 November, was his first return to that region for five years. Just as the crowd were clearly pleased to welcome him back, so Neil enthused in return.

He opened this show by singing 'Beautiful Noise', performing the gig from the special rotating stage erected in the middle of the arena. There were the usual rafter-rattling roars of approval and a reluctance to let him go at the end. But even on the road, Neil could not escape from critics harping on about his renditions of classic movie songs. Michael Lisi for Albany's *Daily Gazette* certainly made sure to highlight the fact that Neil received an ecstatic reception from his fans packed into the Pepsi

Arena, describing how the star 'routinely brought his legions of Diamondheads to the brink of tears'. Yet the sting came when Lisi ended: 'If there was one true downer to the show, it was when Diamond began to sing motion picture theme songs from his new record. Diamond can do a lot of things, but he can't sing Sinatra. His version of "I've Got You Under My Skin" wasn't pretty. And that goes double for his reading of Elvis Presley's hit, "Can't Help Falling In Love".'

After Canadian dates in the middle of November, Diamond spent much of December filling US auditoriums, ending up on New Year's Eve 1998 again at the Grand Garden Arena at the MGM Hotel in Las Vegas. Touring resumed in February, when he travelled to Ireland, Scotland, England, and through Europe, and on to Australia in mid-May. Leaving New Zealand after four gigs at the Westpac Events Centre in Christchurch in mid-June 1999, he returned to the States and commenced a busy home leg at the end of July, at the Centennial Garden in Bakersfield, California.

By now, touring had become more than a well-oiled operation. Diamond had said that he wanted to enjoy road life more, and he did so now to a great extent because he had created around him, like never before, a travelling troupe which made up his own mini world. It was a kind of family environment, but one in which most aspects could be controlled so as to avoid things going wrong. With the best will in the world, however, not every aspect of life can be controlled. In July, while rehearsals were under way for the US leg, Neil's drummer, Ron Tutt, suffered health problems and had to take time off. In addition to personal concern for his friend, in professional terms it also meant bringing in a replacement musician for the upcoming tour dates.

In July 1999, Diamond was happy to feel singled out when the world-famous guitar makers, Gibson, released a custom-made Epiphone Neil Diamond Signature SQ-180 limited edition acoustic guitar. Strumming his way through the summer months, Diamond pulled up again after two concerts at the E Center at Salt Lake City in Utah at the end of August. After an almost three-month break, he then reconvened with his band

and kept going on the road to the year's end in America. The 31 December 1999 was a unique date, with the historic dawn of a new millennium just hours away. As all kinds of commemorative celebrations were planned, several artistes geared up to turn in extra special performances on this particular New Year's Eve. Neil Diamond's engagement was at the Pepsi Center in Denver, Colorado, where he made certain to give a spectacular show, which was televised by ABC-TV during their worldwide broadcast of the live countdown to the year 2000.

It was a pertinent time for Neil Diamond to take a long look at life. Not far away from his 60th birthday, he had woven quite a colourful tapestry already, rising from a boy brought up on the breadline, to become a multi-millionaire, carving a lone and sometimes stubborn path from backroom boy songwriter uncomfortable with personal attention, to striding countless concert stages as one of the most recognisable, showy performers in the world. The two dead weights on the other side of these scales were his two traumatic divorces and two health scares, setbacks which, in different ways, he had had to fight to survive. Two things, however, remained absolutely true as he stood on the threshold of a new millenium. Professionally, in terms of live performance, he reigned as the top-selling solo concert artiste of the 1990s. Personally, he had four children and one grandson, all of whom it gave him great pleasure to dote upon.

By early May 2000, Neil had a second grandson, when Jesse and his actress wife, Sheryl Lee, welcomed the arrival into the world of Elijah Diamond. Then the following month, although still not inducted into the Rock and Roll Hall of Fame, Neil was honoured at a ceremony in New York City with the Sammy Cahn Lifetime Achievement Award from the Songwriters Hall of Fame. It was especially sweet, since this made him one of a select few lyricists to be twice acknowledged by this organisation. Ironically, as he was being recognised for his lyrical abilities and worldwide, long-standing success, Neil still remained in something of a dry patch as regards writing original material.

Come summer 2000, however, he was mildly distracted by

an invitation to take on a small cameo acting role, playing himself in performance in a new film about to be shot in Vancouver in Canada, which centred around a Neil Diamond tribute band. As an artiste of his style and stature, with one of the most distinctive voices in the world, it was inevitable that Diamond would have impersonators, something towards which he has a slightly ambivalent attitude. He has said: 'I love it because, in a sense, impersonators keep the music alive and, in a way, it's flattering.' Conversely, he also considers it a shade weird, and believes it wise to maintain a light sense of humour about it.

The movie, called *Saving Silverman*, was a comedy written by Hank Nelken and Greg De Paul. With a budget of approximately $22 million, and resting in the hands of director Dennis Dugan, it starred Jason Biggs, Steve Zahn, Jack Black and Amanda Peet. In early July he went to the film's location for a week's shoot. It was the first time in 20 years that he had been on a film set, and this time there were none of the pressures that had come with playing the lead role in *The Jazz Singer*.

Saving Silverman's world premiere took place on 7 February 2001 at the Mann Village Theater in Westwood, Los Angeles. Diamond attended both the premiere and the party held afterwards at the House of Blues in Hollywood, at which he was roped into performing a couple of his best-loved hits. On general release outside America under the title *Evil Woman*, the comedy largely suffered at the hands of the film critics. By summer, Reuters referred to *Saving Silverman* as: 'a critically reviled movie, partly redeemed by Neil Diamond's cameo'. *Halliwell's Film Guide* termed it: 'tired and trivial'. Worse condemnation came from Britain's *Guardian* newspaper which said: 'It manages to be nasty, cynical and dull at the same time.' The *Washington Post* critic could scarcely have been more scathing, by declaring that *Saving Silverman*: 'really stinks'. According to one report, the film failed to take in box-office receipts to match its budget. But from Diamond's detached standpoint, the experience had been productive.

For the film he had been required to sing, and he had duly performed 'Holly Holy'. However, he had also been asked to write a new number specially. That song, 'I Believe In Happy Endings', proved to be what resolved the creative block he had been suffering for a long time. Diamond later admitted that the obligation had not only unclogged the valves, it had served to show him that he still had what it took to go on, musically. Another indication that he was recovering some self-confidence came at the beginning of 2001 when, having just turned 60, he told *Vanity Fair*: 'I think I've always been cool – people are just starting to realise it now.'

Come May, another new light entered Neil's world when his eldest, Marjorie, gave birth to another baby boy named Benjamin, just before Neil's youngest, 23-year-old Micah, graduated from Colorado University in Boulder. Diamond had the double delight of seeing Micah receive his degree, and of performing 'The Star Spangled Banner' at the graduation ceremony.

A sombre note was struck in June when Vince Charles, a friend who was also a musician in Neil's backing band, passed away. But in a professional sense Diamond was by now reinvigorated. Writing that new song for *Saving Silverman* had released in him the verve to work on a new album of original songs, and the project had been under way for many months. Astonishingly, it was the first album for which the songs and music had been written solely by Neil Diamond since 1974's *Serenade*. Produced in Los Angeles by Peter Asher and Alan Lindgren, it was a project to which Diamond had been deeply devoted.

The songs he drew out of himself constituted one of his most personal collections yet, and were reflective of all the emotive happenings in his life up to that point. Just how deep some of his writing had gone was indicated when Diamond referred to stretches of the year spent on this work as a: 'day by day battle'. Certainly, the opening track, 'I Haven't Played This Song In Years', reeks of regret over lost love, and has been described as one of Diamond's darkest ever songs. The album, *Three Chord*

Opera, released in July 2001, included 'I Believe In Happy Endings', from *Saving Silverman*, and an upbeat song called 'At The Movies'. The pace quickened with 'Baby Let's Drive'. On a very personal note there was 'Elijah's Song', and religious over-tones hallmarked 'Leave A Little Room For God'.

Tapping into the gospel world was nothing new to Diamond. But he still proved guarded if asked just how much he consciously allowed religion to infiltrate his creative processes. He was, however, direct about the fact that he definitely found a mysterious and inexplicable element in writing. He maintained that lyricists do not truly know all the time where the inspiration, the words, come from. From his own viewpoint, he was frank that while it is always nice to think of himself as being so creative, deep down he is secretly aware that help of a valuable but indefinable kind sometimes comes from an unknown source.

On *Three Chord Opera* there was a number called 'My Special Someone'. And by this time, there was a new woman in Neil Diamond's private life. She was Rachel Farley, a marketing exec-utive, several years his junior, whom he had met in the latter half of the 1990s in Australia. Happy to hail her to journalists as a very special person, Neil studiously fielded any questions in 2001 about whether they might marry. After two divorces, he had re-defined his way of dealing with his personal life – indeed, with life in general – as he began to anticipate a return to touring.

Then again, no one's life could ever be exactly the same after the terrorist atrocities which were committed against America in a three-pronged series of barbaric acts on 11 September 2001. Two and a half weeks after that mind-numbing tragedy, Diamond's first concert tour of the new millennium started at the Value City Arena in Columbus, Ohio. Naturally, it gave him some unease about whether it was right to go ahead with the tour, which had been planned long before that momentous day. The mood in America was understandably like a tinderbox, with unimaginable sorrow and grief for the thousands of people who had been murdered, mixing with an equally understandable collective, volatile rage. Even though Diamond included in each gig a special tribute to the victims of this terrorist outrage, he remained sensitive to the situation. Though determined not to offend, he really could not gauge what the reaction would be. Would people feel guilty about going out and having a good time for a few hours? He said: 'I was afraid people might be inhibited, but as it turned out people were able to get away from the blanket news of this event and to somehow begin to get on with their lives.'

While remaining watchful of this aspect, Diamond set out to entertain fans across two dozen US states. Along the way, a compilation two-CD album, *The Essential Neil Diamond*, was released. On the road, he maintained his track record of pulling off the top grossing concerts virtually everywhere he played, finally arriving at the Grand Garden Arena at the MGM Hotel in Las Vegas for, yet again, two end-of-year concerts.

During the brief break he took in January 2002, Neil and Kansas-born singer Melissa Etheridge recorded a duet of 'America', which was to be used as promotion for that year's Winter Olympic Games to be held in Salt Lake City, Utah.

While these games got under way, Diamond resumed his roadwork. Kicking off at the Civic Center in Pensacola, Florida, on 10 February, he wound up the American dates mid-March at the Atlantic City Boardwalk Hall in New Jersey. It was early July before he resurfaced in concert for two nights at Lansdowne Road in Dublin. Coming from all parts of Ireland, over 65,000 fans flocked to see an in-form Diamond take to the stage for the two shows. On opening night, Neil was greeted at the outset with a standing ovation. When both the Irish and American flags unfurled together to form a patriotic backdrop, the crowd noisily joined in with the words to 'America'.

That same sort of fervent response was elicited across the water when Diamond hit Glasgow in Scotland, where he gave three concerts at the city's SECC. His performance had a positive effect on Jeremy Novick, writing for the *Daily Express*, who also pointed out his surprise at the veteran American's effect on the female contingent in the audience. He said of Neil Diamond: 'A great songwriter, owner of a rich voice and a consummate professional? Yes, these things I knew. But the 61-year-old as Johnny Testosterone? Mr Sex-On-Legs? This, I didn't know. My mistake.' Applauding the evening as high energy, top entertainment, Novick remarked that he had found it hard to absorb Diamond's display of showmanship without thinking that some of today's young pop stars should be tethered to a chair and made to watch Neil Diamond at work.

The compliments kept coming when, after performing in Manchester, Newcastle, Birmingham, Nottingham and Sheffield, towards the end of July Diamond began a sold-out triple engagement at London's Earls Court. A concert preview in the *Evening Standard* contained the praise: 'Few performers earn such a consistently euphoric audience response as Neil Diamond, who is capable of working a crowd up into a frenzy simply by walking over to their side of the stage.'

The welcoming warmth Diamond found in Britain helped him not only to enjoy the performances, but also to open up on a personal level. When he did, in the face of such success and glowing write-ups, what came through most poignantly was that he was a man still searching for sustained personal happiness. In the past he had, he confessed, dipped out on contentment in life, but hoped that he was now on the brink of a permanent change on that score. At the same time, his occasional propensity to be dramatically blunt remained very much in evidence when he credited the ability to make music as being a means to 'fend off death'. He made no bones, either, of the fact that what had kept him going through thick and thin for decades was music.

Taking August off, back in America Diamond then completed his touring obligations between September and December by commencing in New Orleans and ending in Denver. His 2001–2002 tour had been such a global triumph that it had grossed $80 million. Said Neil at the end of it: 'I don't know if I could do it again, but I felt it was necessary.'

With Neil planning to rest up from roadwork for an

appreciable while, his fans awaited the possibility of a compilation album popping out of the woodwork here and there. But there was a different buzz at the end of July 2003, when *Billboard* magazine revealed that a new box set was due for release in the autumn, which would comprehensively highlight the live performance side of Neil Diamond's long, illustrious career. Sure enough, in October, *Stages – Neil Diamond Performances 1970–2002* was released.

The definitive five CDs plus one DVD collection comprised 83 rare live recordings (all but one previously unreleased), which racked up to over five hours of live performance, spread over the five compact discs. There was a 52-page colour booklet, featuring rare photographs, and liner notes written by Neil. Finally, there was the bonus DVD, which was nearly two hours long. This impressive retrospective set was not in any sense indicative of farewell. Moving inexorably further into his sixties, Neil had no intention of retiring. Tentative ideas were percolating for another new album. And by the dawn of 2004, he was also being potentially linked to working with two very different music outfits.

In January, the glam rock-style band The Darkness, most members of which hail from Lowestoft in Suffolk, were said to be amenable to co-composing a song with Neil Diamond. This arose from an interview The Darkness gave while promoting their debut album, *Permission To Land*, when vocalist Justin Hawkins mentioned that he rated the Brooklyn superstar's lyrical abilities. Diamond is said to have read this, and approached the British band with the idea of collaborating on a song.

Then, in March, it emerged that The Bellamy Brothers, one of America's longest standing and most revered country music duos, wanted Neil to be among a select number of artistes to join with them in re-cutting a selection of the duo's greatest hits for a new album. Showing his political colours, in the summer Neil shared a stage with Barbra Streisand to perform on 24 June at a victory concert for the Democratic presidential candidate John Kerry at the Walt Disney Concert Hall in Los Angeles.

And as 2004 progressed, news was awaited as to whether

Neil Diamond would take to the road again to provide another fix for his fiercely loyal and insatiable global fan base.

Looking way back to Neil Diamond's beginnings, it could be said that there was no hint that the skinny, intense lad who found it hard to communicate with others, and who briefly used his fists to express himself, would grow up to develop into one of the most widely recognised popular music entertainers in the world. One of the top twenty most successful artistes in America ever, he has to date sold in the region of 120 million albums world-wide. While he considers the likes of Paul Simon to be a more intellectual lyricist, there is no doubt that his own songs have enriched the lives of many. Diamond's eternal appeal crosses over a wide age range. No matter which direction he takes, for millions Diamond is a bright dazzling star that will never fade.

As for Neil Diamond himself, his is an intriguingly complex personality. Instinctively impenetrable, he can still be excruciatingly frank. Finding the balance between the personal and professional in life has been fraught and costly for him, as his abiding love of songwriting has been hard to compete with. He recently confessed: 'To me, work is the most fascinating thing, and so long as I can still come up with something that I find worthwhile, it gives me a little hope.' In typical style, he added: 'Hope for what exactly? I don't know.'

Index